larkin about in IRELAND

To my dearest Jeanette,

"May you be in heaven an hour before the devil knows you're dead."

I hope you enjoy "Larkin About..."

Cheers!

23 July 2003

Happy Birthday Jeanette
with much love always
from Karen xxx

PS Hope it's a good read!!

A Hodder Book

Published in Australia and New Zealand in 2002
by Hodder Headline Australia Pty Limited
(A member of the Hodder Headline Group)
Level 22, 201 Kent Street, Sydney NSW 2000
Website: www.hha.com.au

Reprinted 2003

Copyright © John Larkin 2002

This book is copyright. Apart from any fair dealing for
the purposes of private study, research, criticism or
review permitted under the *Copyright Act 1968*,
no part may be stored or reproduced by any process
without prior written permission. Enquiries should
be made to the publisher.

National Library of Australia
Cataloguing-in-Publication data

Larkin, John, 1963- .
 Larkin about in Ireland : an Irish writer's pilgrimage to a
 homeland he has never lived in.

 ISBN 0 7336 1398 5.

 1. Larkin, John, 1963- - Journeys - Ireland. 2. Ireland -
 Description and travel. 3. Ireland - Social life and
 customs. I. Title.

914.1504824

Cover images by Getty Images
Cover design by Ellie Exarchos
Author photograph by Mark Macleod
Text design and typesetting by Bookhouse, Sydney
Printed in Australia by Griffin Press, Adelaide

larkin about in
IRELAND

An Irish writer's pilgrimage to a homeland he has never lived in

JOHN LARKIN

HODDER

For my father, Brendan Larkin, with
thanks for his gift to me: Ireland.
&
In memory of my aunt, Sister Margaret Larkin
1936–2001

Prologue

The Dancing Nuns of Tullamore

My father left Ireland for England some time in the mid fifties. Though from what I can gather *fled* is probably the more appropriate verb. If maids are any indication of prosperity, it appears that the Larkins were doing rather nicely. So it's hard for me to imagine what led Dad from his upper middle class rural life in County Offaly to working class South Yorkshire, but imagine is all I can do, because he is simply the quietest person I have ever met and rarely talks about himself.

I've heard that, as a barman, he staged one too many lock-ins at the Bridgehouse Hotel in Tullamore, and that he was charged, found guilty and appeared in the local paper for riding his bike without the appropriate lighting. Even in a town as small as Tullamore, though, where gossip spreads like Nutella over a carpet, it's doubtful that these two incidents would have been enough to send him into exile. But whatever skeletons remain in Dad's closet have long since turned to dust and are best left undisturbed.

He's only told us a couple of stories from his childhood: the obligatory ones about ghosts and about dead hunchbacks strapped to tables during wakes—with the straps eventually severed by a couple of small boys hidden beneath the table, much to the amazement of those present. There's also the one about him receiving a ball every Christmas. One Christmas morning, he woke to find a jumper where the ball would normally have been and, realising that this was his gift, spent the morning beating it against the foot of his bed in a fit of unfathomable rage. From what I know of Grandad Larkin, it amazes me that he didn't storm into Dad's room and smite him dead.

I was born in England and my first trip "home" to Ireland came when I was three. My parents had started to talk more and more about Australia, and had obviously decided that it was time for me and my older sister, Trish, to discover our roots and our grandparents while we were still able.

Trish was an extremely violent child, given to inserting objects of varying length and sharpness into my spine. She had a strange phobia about buttons and margarine and would take revenge on me whenever she encountered either. So, having spent much of my life up to that point as a sort of human pincushion, I was looking forward to getting as far away (or getting Trish as far away) from the cutlery drawer and Mum's sewing kit as our limited budget would allow.

We flew from Manchester to Dublin in the halcyon summer of 1966. The England football team had just won the World Cup, and although the country hadn't witnessed such an outpouring of national pride since it had kicked Hitler's hairy little one-balled arse, the entire event passed me by. I suppose at three years old I was only interested in the fact that I was going on a plane. And of course with an Irish father, who must have been in agony over each of England's four goals, we were kept well clear of the street parties that followed their win.

The fact that we actually flew to Ireland still has me perplexed. Dad generally crossed the heaving Irish Sea by ship. This didn't have so much to do with a deep and unyielding love of the ocean (he once nearly drowned in the shallow end of our neighbours' pool when Death had a go at him with a cramp and a blocked snorkel). Rather, it was due to an abject dread of all things airborne. He thought that if people were meant to fly, they would have been born with boarding passes in their hands. But Mum had obviously convinced him that the plane was the way to go.

Dad and Trish sat on one side of the plane, while Mum and I were just across the aisle. Trish and I were thrilled to have been given the window seats. I suppose it was because our pious parents believed that anything worth seeing from 30 000 feet was not down but up. And until they were given their own harps, music sheets, wings and operating manuals, they were in no hurry to witness anything at that altitude.

The plane tore along the runway with Dad gripping the armrest so tightly he became embroidered in its floral pattern. Midway through the flight, just after he had downed his fourth Guinness so that he was now on a flight of an entirely different sort, I looked out the window and was amazed to see the clouds below us. I asked Mum what had happened, but because she'd had a bit of a go at the in-flight service trolley herself, she could only tell me that the clouds weren't below us: *we* were above *them*. No matter which way I looked at it, this appeared to be exactly the same thing. So I decided to let her get back to clinking her little bottles. I suppose she had enough on her plate already without having to explain about spherical earths, gravity and meteorological patterns to a toddler. This was not only the first time that she had flown, it was to be her first meeting with Dad's parents and she suffered from that dreadful condition of being English. I can see now why she insisted on flying—she wanted to be off the planet.

As we thumped down at Dublin Airport, Dad almost ripped the armrests from their sockets. I think he'd said a couple of decades of the rosary on our descent, slurred no doubt by the amount of Guinness flowing through his devout veins.

Larkin about in IRELAND

We hit the airport bar to recover from the flight and eventually repaired to our hire-car, which had doors and window frames made entirely of polished wood. I think it was a member of the Morris family. Because it was an estate car, and neither seatbelts nor the concept of child safety had yet arrived in Ireland (not to mention random breath-testing), Trish and I were allowed to lie down in the back, provided that we behaved, while Mum sat up front with Dad and worked on her Irish accent. Her father was himself Irish, so redemption was possible.

Trish and I were a dead loss linguistically. As was the South Yorkshire practice, we pronounced "shut up" as "shurrup" and "give over (stop doing that)" as "ge-ore". Mum and Dad must have secretly hoped that in front of our more austere grandparents we would retreat into our respective shells and speak only when spoken to. I had absolutely no problem with this. Trish, though, was bound to be trouble, and I'm sure they'd considered leaving her at home. Not long after we'd left Dublin's city limits Mum had five cigarettes on the go, Dad was well into his second century of the rosary, and both of them exchanged furtive glances as they joined in a communal prayer that Trish would be struck mute for the duration of our stay.

They needn't have worried. Trish was a lot smarter than they gave her credit for. She knew how to play the demure English-rose of a granddaughter whose mouth wouldn't melt margarine. She was so transformed that

I felt humbled by her presence, which made a pleasant change from being injured by it.

I remember much of that trip to Ireland but very little about my grandparents, except that Grandad Larkin held court like Caligula. Even Mum appeared meek around him and I'd never witnessed that before, nor have I since.

Everyone in Tullamore, from relatives to passing drunks, some of whom also doubled as relatives, seemed absolutely delighted to see me, though I couldn't understand why. I'd only managed to make it to age three by blending into the shadows and trying *not* to exist wherever possible—especially within sight of the cutlery drawer and Mum's sewing kit. Now people were paying me so much attention that even *I* was forced to acknowledge my existence. Fortunately Trish was given the same treatment, which saved a beating or two when night fell and we went to bed.

Just about every uncle and alleged uncle we met had the endearing habit of giving us money. Old men have always derived some sort of strange satisfaction from pulling coins from behind children's ears. But when these uncles of ours ran out of coins and notes, they started to issue cheques, which made them a lot more appealing than just any demented old goat with an earlobe and copper fixation.

And everywhere we went someone insisted on dragging out an accordion. Either there was one obsessed

Larkin about in IRELAND

accordion player wandering from house to house in a frenzy of national pride while we were there, or the Tullamore accordion maker was working seven days a week to keep up with demand. Whatever the case, it didn't matter. We thought it was brilliant.

Mum and Dad owned only one record, which they played until it was smooth. It was by The Dubliners, a collection of talented musicians who wore white woollen jumpers that they'd obviously acquired directly from the sheep. We had grown up with The Dubliners (I knew all about the seven drunken nights—*she was having an affair, you pickled pillock*) and Trish and I were delighted that we could sing along like proper Irish kids.

These little details of our stay are my first real memories, which is no doubt the reason they appear so vivid. I remember how green everything looked. How friendly everyone was. The laughter flowing thick and fast, along with the music and the alcohol. The pace was slower but the "craic" was indeed mighty. Ireland was England with its hair let down. (And it had plenty of hair to let down—usually sprouting unchecked from the ears, noses and hats of the old men we passed in the street).

I remember a dairy farm, long walks in the country with a dog that would emit an excited yelp and promptly disappear into the undergrowth in pursuit of what I assumed was a rabbit, but my uncle assured us was a leprechaun. I remember conversations being interrupted whenever we passed a church. Everyone would suddenly appear solemn and thoughtful and begin making energetic signs of the cross and muttering about the Blessed Virgin and Jesus himself. But as soon as we were out of sight of the priest's periscope, the dialogue would resume as if nothing had happened: "I tell yer, yer man's a total gobshite." "Get away with yer, yer bollocks." And I remember Trish dancing for the nuns.

My aunt Margaret Larkin was a nun, which I suppose explains why we ended up in a convent.

After tea and cake, one of the nuns pulled out a guitar and (I can still hardly believe it myself and I was there) a set of bongo drums and wondered whether Trish would like to dance for them. Obviously starved for entertainment, the nuns gathered around Trish and proceeded to clap and whoop in an alarming manner. Never one to hold back, Trish put on the sort of energetic performance that at this distance reminds me of a lunatic using semaphore to explain the theory of relativity to someone on a distant hill. Although she had no formal training, she leapt, twirled and pirouetted as if she had, or knew someone who had. I suppose her dance included elements of the twist, the stomp, the birdie song, Shirley Bassey, and the Macarena, with a bit of Irish dancing thrown in—though I'm pretty sure that you're not supposed to use your arms that much in Irish dancing. The nuns, who either had no access to hallucinogenic drugs or were already on them, worked themselves into a frenzy. A couple of the younger ones threw caution to the wind, their wimples to the floor and joined Trish in her gyrations. The strange *twang* that followed hot on the heels of the nuns kicking up theirs, was not the sound of guitar strings snapping (though the noise is so similar that the difference isn't marked), but that of hamstrings tearing as the nuns' legs went higher and into positions that no bride of Christ had ever found it necessary to adopt before.

If there was any fallout from this ecclesiastical moshpit, it was kept from my sensitive young ears. Though years later, long after we'd emigrated to Australia, I did hear that Sister Bernadette Flanagan, the one who did a jig on her wimple, was reassigned from the convent in Tullamore to a small village on the fringes of the Serengeti.

I suppose I could be exaggerating slightly, but there are certain things that a three-year-old boy should never have to witness: his father dressing up as Santa Claus, his parents making love (this counts double if the father is dressed up as Santa Claus), and nuns doing the cancan. I've been wary of the Catholic Church and men in red suits ever since.

Following the incident with the dancing nuns, we left Tullamore—possibly under cover of darkness—and Ireland quickly faded from memory, as the excitement of the future, in the shape of Australia, appeared before us.

Ireland was now part of my past; the ubiquitous old

country. It was like a kindly old aunt you could always drop in on for a cup of tea and some freshly baked scones, but on whom you seldom called or thought much.

But when I hit my mid-thirties this feeling changed and I can't quite explain it. I began to hear the distant echoes of this mystical land calling me back from across the seas. Perhaps I'd been reading too much Oscar Wilde, Roddy Doyle, and Frank McCourt. Maybe I'd been overdosing on Enya, U2, or the Pogues. Or perhaps I relished the thought that writers do not pay tax in Ireland, and that portraits of past masters are hung everywhere, including, oddly enough, in public toilets. On a couple of occasions I've even had to be wrestled to the ground and forcibly restrained from buying a white woollen jumper, a tin whistle and a pipe. As middle age beckons and I seriously start to consider trading in my earring for a cardigan, I can feel a sort of primordial summons back to a homeland I have never lived in.

I want to stand on the banks of the Liffey reading *Finnegan's Wake* and pretending that I get it. I long to sing *Wild Rover* in a pub until somebody pays me to stop. I ache to go to a hurling match and watch grown men set about each other with heavily wielded sticks and not get arrested for it. And I positively yearn to have spontaneous conversations with old men in tweed

Larkin about in IRELAND

coats whose days invariably end in an animated fall off a bar stool.

In short, I want to go home. Maybe it's a salmon thing.

PART 1
GETTING THERE'S HALF THE FUN

One
Poe's Woes

Almost a year after the Emerald Isle began to exert this strange pull on me, I found myself sitting in Sydney Airport, stirring an outrageously expensive cup of coffee and trying to figure out what on earth I was doing.

For the past couple of years my wife Jacqui and I had talked about moving overseas; if not permanently, then certainly for a year or two.

Ever since we were married, we have lived in the quiet, leafy suburbs of north-western Sydney. An area that is often, and not without good reason, referred to as the Bible Belt. It is tidy, safe, leafy, very leafy, and everyone seems genuinely happy with their lot; especially the rake salesmen—they seem monumentally pleased with themselves.

Despite the predictable McDonald's bag or cup on every street corner, the demographic is mostly hot roller and dayglo tracksuit. Given the ailing condition of many of our fellow residents, and the fact that they're mostly house-bound, the area is not surprisingly patrolled by

Mormon doorknockers and cable tv salesmen, each group peddling its own brand of salvation.

The last cable tv salesman I opened the door to started by telling me how lucky we were that cable was coming to the street and if we signed up now we'd get this, that and the other. I came straight to the point and told him that I didn't want cable, would not be getting cable, and what's more, that the producers and hosts of those brain-dead reality tv shows that were popular at the time—*The World's Stupidest Police Car Crashes, The World's Dumbest People, When Pets Get Pissed Off IV, Someone's Stuck a Video Camera in your Bedroom and is Watching you Shag IX*—would be first against the wall when the revolution came. Unperturbed by my argument, or by the fact that I was frothing slightly, he carried on with his pitch, which implied that anyone who didn't sign up for this particular subscription and at *that* price was essentially a moron. I informed him, through grinding teeth, that I didn't want my daughter to grow up with the Sony babysitter, but with books.

'Books!' he shrieked, practically hyperventilating, as if I'd just told the one about the gynaecologist who painted his hallway through his letterbox to a bunch of nuns. 'No one reads books no more!' He actually said "no more".

'Interesting theory,' I replied, the steam starting to curl out of my ears and nostrils too, 'and rather disheartening since the person you are trying to sell your subscription to is a **WRITER**!'

Amazingly, this didn't throw him, and he agreed to go away only after I threatened to turn the hose and the dogs on him.

I almost felt sorry for the guy after he'd fled. Almost. I mean, all evening the only person he'd probably tried his "no one reads books no more" theory on was me.

The more time I spend on this planet, the more I'm convinced that coincidence is one of the governing principles of the universe. Last year I was invited to speak at a seminar on *Boys and Books* at the State Library of New South Wales. During my talk I read out some rather depressing statistics on the number of Australians who visit a bookshop in any given year—it's somewhere in the region of twelve per cent. Despite this we still rank third, behind Ireland and Iceland, in the number of books consumed per capita. I then made a little throwaway quip about how it wasn't really fair to include Iceland in the survey because, let's face it, there wasn't much to do there except watch the mud bubble or rearrange your Bjork CDs, so naturally people tended to read as a diversion. Afterwards, a woman came up to me and said that while she'd enjoyed my talk immensely she was a bit upset because she came from Iceland and was still rather fond of the place.

Needless to say I spent the rest of the afternoon

standing on the roof of the State Library, shaking my fist at the sky and yelling, 'Cut it out!'

By the way, I've since discovered a sure fire method of turning cable salesmen away at the door. Keep a *Bible* handy.

'Have you considered cable tv?'

'No,' and here you lick your index finger and start leafing through, 'but have you considered Luke 13...'

It's not a technique that works quite so well on the Mormons.

But despite the marauding packs of cable guys with their enlightened views on the written word, north-western Sydney remains a comfortable area to live in. That which comforts, however, may also sedate. And Jacqui and I remember this in case we suddenly find ourselves applying for lawn bowls memberships, buying dayglo tracksuits or getting up at four in the morning to take the whippets for their walk.

We've talked about letting our house, preferably to somebody with a gardening fetish, and setting up residence in a London mews, or taking rooms in Cambridge, a lighthouse in Ireland, pottering about in a barn somewhere in the Lake District, renting Dylan Thomas's old boatshed in Wales, a cottage in Dorset, an apartment in Paris, or refurbishing an old farmhouse in Tuscany while making our own olive oil, wine, and listening to the complete works of Mario Lanza on our homemade stereo. In effect living for a while somewhere else. Somewhere exotic. Or at the very least somewhere that doesn't have half a dozen garden centres and multi-level shopping malls within a five-kilometre radius.

It's often said that there's a novel in every life and maybe every writer dreams of writing his or her great one. I'm yet to find mine. But it's unlikely that I will come across it while I pootle around my local garden centre or multi-level shopping mall.

Edgar Allan Poe is credited with saying that you have to suffer to write. And he certainly knew what he was on about. Shortly after he was born, Poe found himself orphaned. Both his parents died tragically young and in quick succession. After a relatively quiet childhood, things began to crank up a bit in his late adolescence. While away at university his fiancée, Sarah Royster, ran off and married another man. Poe subsequently found himself deep in debt, had an argument with his adopted family, left them, and then suffered a brain lesion, which left him prone to bouts of severe oddness. After recovering from this (or possibly not) he married his thirteen-year-old cousin, Virginia Clemm. Later he was fired from his job as editor of the *Southern Literary Messenger* for extreme intoxication. Then, perhaps as final proof of the author's troubled state of mind, he moved to New York where Virginia, though not yet twenty-five, promptly died of tuberculosis. A couple of years later, having recovered from the premature loss of his wife, Poe renewed his engagement to his recently widowed childhood sweetheart, Sarah Shelton nee Royster, and perhaps finally found the happiness that had long been denied him. Or at least he might have—had he not himself dropped dead the following month. He was forty.

Although it is not widely known and is still hotly debated among the type of people who debate these sorts of things, Poe is often credited with coining the expression, "Give me a break!" When death came calling, one suspects it was greeted by the author with a sense of relief. Certainly the subject and a heightened sense of the macabre had a tremendous impact on his work.

Despite his undoubted suffering, or maybe because of it, Edgar Allan Poe remains one of the most significant and influential writers of his age. Perhaps he was right. Maybe writers do need to suffer and endure extreme hardship in order to create. I find it hard to imagine that Joyce conceived the idea for *Ulysses* while he was trying to decide which potting mix was best suited to his geraniums. Or that Emily Bronte would ever have written *Wuthering Heights* if she had been forced to endure the constant interruptions of door-knockers and telesales callers. Heathcliff would not have cut anything like his dashing and ultimately tragic figure had her inspiration been an aluminium siding salesman.

And while elements of Dostoevsky's *Crime and Punishment* (chiefly the section where Raskolnikov decapitates the old money lender with an axe) probably germinated in the author's mind as he stood behind a dayglo tracksuit in the express lane who was trying to find her cheque book to pay for a single tin of cat food—*my* local shopping mall lacks the inner city squalor of nineteenth century St Petersburg.

My trip to Ireland, then, was to be partly a spiritual homecoming, but also some sort of escape from the safety of suburbia. And although I was content to forgo the worst suffering and hardships associated with creative endeavour, I was certainly looking forward to being inspired by the land of poets and priests, scholars and wailing banshees, lock-ins and people who still believe that the accordion is an option.

Two

Killing Skippy

I was six when my family emigrated to Sydney. So despite being born in England with deep Irish roots, I feel entitled to consider myself Australian.

Just prior to my leaving Sydney for Ireland, however, two incidents occurred in quick succession that led me to question this belief and left me wondering where it is, if it's not here, that I do in fact belong.

Both incidents took place out in the country, and made me acutely aware that I could no more function in ninety-five per cent of Australia than an aardvark could on the internet.

The first was in rural New South Wales. I had been invited to spend Book Week visiting schools in and around the town of Temora, particularly the outlying areas. I'd just flown in from Sydney completely exhausted. I had a deadline looming large on the horizon for a book that I'd only just started, so sleep was a luxury. (As I type these words, which are themselves in danger of running late, I am reminded of one of my favourite quotes by the late, great Douglas Adams, "I love deadlines. I love the incredible *whoosh* sound they make as they go by.")

I'd actually started to doze as soon as I boarded the plane, but the flight attendant woke me so that I didn't miss her floorshow. She felt that it was imperative I be cognisant of the aircraft's safety features and I was relieved to learn, as always, that should my aircraft suddenly plummet into Mt Kosciusko at ten thousand kilometres an hour, I had a lifejacket, a pillow and a raft to cope with the resulting inferno. They also give you a plastic whistle (and it's here you realise that they're deadly serious) "to attract attention".

So let me get this straight. You've just leapt out of a burning aircraft wearing a bright yellow lifejacket, which is itself probably on fire. Attracting attention is not a real problem for you right now.

My chaperone, Irene, collected me from Wagga Wagga airport at sparrow's fart and we were soon hurtling through the Kosciusko National Park at a speed not much below that of the aircraft I'd just left. In fact our relative velocity, combined with a heavy ground mist, led to me regret that I'd abandoned my lifejacket, pillow and whistle so prematurely. Eventually, however, much to the relief of my knuckles, which had been turning white on the dashboard, we shot out of the mist like Superman from a boiling volcano that Lois Lane had fallen into while filing a story on the dangers of climbing active volcanoes in stilettos.

Well, it was stunning. The morning literally chimed. The scenery gave me an almost overwhelming urge to leap out of the car, twirl about the fields and break into song like Julie Andrews' Maria Von Trapp. And I would have too, had the car not at that moment reached terminal velocity and my apron not been back home in the kitchen drawer.

I wound down the window and was hit by a blast of wind that drove me back into my seat. The air was so crisp, clean and cool that I immediately developed one of those ice-cream headaches. My hair leapt about my head as if I were in a Bee Gees film clip. Meanwhile my lungs, unused to that much fresh air in one sitting, began coughing some back up. I felt like a man who, never having touched a cigarette in his life, suddenly in his seventieth year commences a sixty-a-day habit, largely to annoy his wife. My lungs just couldn't handle it. I wound the window back up and inhaled the filtered air of the car's heater instead.

As we careered alongside the Blowering Dam we came across a "Kangaroos Next 55km" sign. Irene immediately released the accelerator a fraction so that we were just on the subsonic-boom side of the speed of sound. Her caution was not without good reason. A kangaroo's way of dealing with a fully laden Kenworth bearing down on it at a hundred plus kays in the middle of the night is to stare into its headlights in the hope that it goes away. Or during the day, despite having endless wide-open country on either side of it, the kangaroo will lurch off down the road in an attempt to outrun the thing. The roads of rural Australia are littered with thousands of flyblown corpses that suggest both tactics require further thought. Eventually you would expect natural selection to start favouring those kangaroos that leap to the side when they encounter a truck or, better still, the ones that stay up in the hills. You would think that with all their dead brothers and sisters on the roadside the kangaroos might eventually get around to thinking, *Hang on a minute: there's got to be some sort of connection here.* Or perhaps while standing on the road contemplating that connection, they too are mown down from behind and become part of a vicious cycle.

With the early morning sun beaming in through the windscreen, I soon found my head lolling about on my shoulders like one of those plastic nodding dogs that people have started to put in their rear windows again for no obvious reason.

I slipped into an exciting dream, with me lurching about the deck of a ferry on my pilgrimage to Ireland, when my eyes leapt open and I found the car lurching about the road in an equally excited manner. The kangaroo that had, only moments before, been standing to one side to contemplate the road, the corpses and whether there was any possible connection, now bounded along in front of us, undoubtedly convinced that there was.

I glanced around for a lifejacket or a plastic whistle.

Fortunately (though it might like to argue with me on this point) we connected with the kangaroo at the top of its leap. So rather than squelch it beneath the screeching tyres, we whipped its legs out from under it and it went clunking over the roof in a startled manner after thudding heavily into the windscreen.

We crumbled to a stop on the gravel beside the road.

Irene mumbled something about the car belonging to the library and undid her seatbelt. 'I hope everything's okay,' she added nervously, throwing open the door. 'We'd better take a look.'

I climbed out my side and raced off back down the road to check. The kangaroo just lay there like...it's impossible to say what it was like because nothing lies on the road with a greater sense of finality than a kangaroo that has just come second in a game of chicken with two tonnes of screaming metal.

I knelt down beside it. Things didn't look good.

And then I had one of those rare moments of clarity that you occasionally get just before you fall asleep or have had one too many glasses of wine.

We'd killed Skippy.

I felt completely wretched.

Although as a child I preferred the penetrating social realism of *Tales of the Riverbank*—nothing quite captured the growing discontent of decaying urban London than, say, a hamster in a plastic boat—I was no stranger to the charms of the bush kangaroo. In fact if, as a youngster, I hadn't been dragged out to Terrey Hills to see where the series was filmed, I suspect that *Skippy* might have replaced *Tales of the Riverbank* as my favourite show.

It was one of those disgustingly hot Sundays that I associate with Sydney in the seventies. My parents and some of their friends once fried an egg on the road outside our house in order to send the photo home to disbelieving relatives in England and Ireland. God knows what possessed them to believe that the idea of cooking breakfast in the street would make the place seem more attractive, but there they were, grinning like a bunch of day trippers from the bewildered society with a spatula covered in tar.

Still, it didn't matter how high the mercury soared, every Sunday, without fail, we would be packed into the back of the Holden, our skin immediately fixing itself to the vinyl seat so that only surgery could remove it, and we were carted off to the beach, the bush, or the mountains to work on our third-degree sunburn. Inside the car was always nightmarishly hot (air-conditioning being regarded as a luxury by Australian carmakers in the seventies), the air heavy and poisoned (it was compulsory for both parents to be on a sixty-a-day habit), and the roads choked. What's more, you had to be on a constant lookout for all the English and Irish gits frying eggs in the middle of the road.

When we arrived at Skippy's compound, there was the bush kangaroo herself in a cage no larger than an upturned supermarket trolley. Any cruel little shit could have poked the poor thing with a stick through the bars of its cage. I poked the poor thing just to see if it could be done. This upset me and I suspect that Skippy wasn't feeling all that pleased about it either. A man in a hat and a badge took us on a tour of the compound. I was further shocked to learn that there wasn't just one Skippy but seventeen of them. Well, one Skippy and sixteen stunt Skippys—there's actually a shot where you can see it leap out of Jerry's helicopter wearing a crash helmet and a small, wallaby-size parachute. Needless to say, this experience totally ruined the series for me. If Skippy had been real, she would have picked the lock on that cage, kicked the crap out of whoever it was who'd jammed her in there in the first place, jumped into one of the cars, crossed the ignition wires, put the stick-shift into drive and torn off. Then, pausing only to perform delicate brain surgery on some dangerously ill kid in the barbecue area, she would have hijacked the helicopter and commenced a low bombing raid over the house of whoever it was who'd written that episode about the lake full of killer sharks.

And now we'd killed her.

Actually, to be brutally honest, I was relieved the

thing was dead. If it had only been injured I knew that I was supposed to hit it with something hard to put it out of its misery. And I would have been hard pressed to find a rock big enough to distance myself from having to finish the job. I thought about the contents of my overnight bag. I supposed, if worse came to worst, I could have suffocated it to death with my anti-perspirant.

As I knelt there, preparing to bestow the marsupial equivalent of last rites, I had another of those strange moments. I pulled out my mobile phone and offered it to the kangaroo, 'Here, Skip. Sonny's in trouble. He's on *Who Wants to be a Millionaire* and you're the nominated friend. He wants to know which physicist is generally regarded as the father of quantum theory.'

To my utter amazement the kangaroo casually sat up on its elbow, like somebody ordering a Cointreau from a deck chair, and said, 'Max Planck.'

Actually, it did stumble gingerly to its feet and, with a shake of its head, perhaps attempting to get its mind back on line, hopped languidly away.

I ran excitedly back up the road towards the car.

Despite her initial concern for the kangaroo, Irene had stayed by the car, perhaps too traumatised by the realisation of what she'd done to venture down the road and join me.

'It's all right,' I gasped, not being as fit as I once was.

Irene was bent over the car hood and examining the grille. 'Sorry?'

'The kangaroo. It's all right. It regained consciousness and just, well, hopped away.' I chose to leave out our brief exchange on the subject of German physicists in case it confused or alarmed her.

'The kangaroo?' she hissed.

'Yeah. You said that you hoped everything was okay. Well, it is. It's fine...'

Irene stood up and bestowed on me a look that I suppose she reserves for all terminally stupid and softened city folk. 'I wasn't talking about the stuffing roo. I was referring to the car.'

We drove the rest of the way in silence.

Shortly after almost killing Skippy, I found myself on a tour of Victoria with fellow authors James Moloney and Peter McFarlane, the legendary Agnes Nieuwenhuizen from the Australian Centre for Youth Literature, actor/director Jenny Lovell, and a troupe of aspiring young actors from Monash University who were to be performing excerpts from our books on the tour.

After driving in the Partridge Family bus for about three hours, we finally arrived in the township of Sheep Shit, Victoria:a remote and listless hamlet where men were men, sheep were sheep, and a large Confederate flag took up the entire wall of the town's music store, perhaps in support of the restoration of slavery to regional Victoria.

To be honest, the town itself was quite pretty, but my memory is coloured by what was to follow. Not having a map of the town, we pulled up outside one of the pubs to ask for directions to our hotel. Jenny Lovell, our director and driver, decided that in the interest of not conforming to stereotype, *I* would be the one to go inside and seek help.

I stepped from the bus and immediately heard a single strum on a banjo, and the distant, high-pitched whine of a mouth organ.

Actually I did no such thing. But a car did pull up alongside us, covered from bonnet to boot in stickers proclaiming the owner's enlightened view on cats. As far as he was concerned the only good cat was a dead one. If your cat was missing then you should probably check under his wheels. He liked cats—they made a nice rug for his dog. And so on. The man stepped from his car with cowboy boots stretching up to his scrotum and the tail of his mullet swaying gently in the afternoon breeze. He nodded me a curt hello that encompassed everything from "G'day" to "You'd better not own a friggin cat", and disappeared into the pub.

At least my encounter with Cat Man gave the afternoon a sense of symmetry. I mean here I was trying not to conform to stereotype, while he was doing all he possibly could to uphold it.

I glanced back at the Partridge Family and gulped. Jenny flicked her hand to indicate that I should either carry on and ask for directions, or run like buggery. The rest of them had their noses pressed to the window of the mini-bus and were busy reading Cat Man's stickers.

I said a silent rosary and stepped cautiously through the pub doors.

Sitting around the bar were about half a dozen guys who had all bought their clothes at the local Blokes "R" Us outlet. Cat Man had removed his hat to reveal that on top at least he had about as much hair as a bowling ball with mange. A bald mullet. Not a good look. Somebody was going to have to pay for that, and he'd obviously decided that he would be damned if it wasn't the cats.

I wouldn't say that the honky-tonk piano exactly stopped when I entered the bar (there wasn't one playing), but the effect was much the same. Every single eye in the place turned on me in a manner suggesting that pretty soon someone would be notifying my next of kin. I began to regret wearing my Oscar Wilde "I have nothing to declare except my genius" t-shirt. Their eyes were burning into my chest. I'd never felt so self-conscious in my entire life. The "genius" proclamation was bad enough—it was if I was rubbing the dumb hicks' noses in it—Oscar's sexual orientation (had it been known), not to mention the fact that he was fond of cats, was surely enough to have seen me lynched. And as for the cargo pants and "Bite Me!" baseball cap, well I would beat myself up later on over those.

I stepped up to the bar and ordered a glass of Pimms.

Then asked the barman for directions to Darlot Street.

The rest of the bar snorted.

Now before you go thinking *what's so funny about that*? I should point out that the rest of the Partridge Family and I had decided that Darlot was of French origin and therefore had a silent "t"—as in "Bardot" (the Brigitte kind). So what they heard was, 'Excuse me. Could you tell me the way to Darlo Street?'

Okay it still isn't all that funny; but I suppose in places like Sheep Shit, you set your humour threshold a bit lower. So when some complete nancy from the city wanders into your bar proclaiming his genius and wearing cargo pants and a baseball cap with an invitation to bite him—well—it's show time. There weren't any guns trained on me at this point, or any that I was aware of, but I still felt unnervingly like a duck that had just come into season.

The man sitting closest to me who was either called Bubba, or good mates with somebody called Bubba said, 'You mean Darlo*T* Street. T. T. T.'

For a minute I thought he had a hairball stuck in his throat, but then I realised he was just removing the urine. Mine.

The rest of the bar snorted.

Okay, I admit it. I'm not the most macho of characters (something that was made abundantly clear to me that day in the pub and then later on while I was traipsing through the mud on an Irish dairy farm—an incident we'll come to later). I will never own a gun, or a ute, or a dog called Tyson. No one will ever ask me to pack down in a scrum, operate a crane, erect a retaining wall, recondition an engine, or appear in drag on *The Footy Show*. And I will never be able to function inside hardware stores. I think I'm missing the all-important "bloke" gene.

Whenever I'm forced to visit my local hardware store through some sort of domestic happenstance involving a mistimed hammer blow or a wildly misdirected nine-inch nail, I usually take whatever it is that I've broken—tap, ceiling fan, ceiling, vanity unit, cistern, leg—and wander around, looking for a replacement. No matter how simple my transaction, however, I invariably end up being sneered at by the sort of man whose uniform consists of a dustcoat and a pipe. All right so I'm a spectacularly bad handyman. I actually blew up a toilet once while I was changing a washer, and a friend christened me Frank Spencer after a spice-rack installation had gone horribly wrong, the details of which, though amusing, are far too painful to recount. Let's just say that spice-racks, structural walls, high-voltage power cables, and buckets of water, are a potentially

Larkin about in IRELAND

lethal combination. And my method these days for fixing a leak in our roof is as follows:

- Climb up into ceiling.
- Scream at pitch only dog can hear when stumble over skeletal remains of possum.
- Locate leak via beam of sunlight like Indiana Jones in the Well of the Souls from *Raiders of the Lost Ark*—make mental note to return staff of Ra to old Egyptian bloke down road.
- Put finger through hole to ascertain size of leak and hope insane magpie doesn't mistake for worm.
- Go outside and climb up on roof.
- Fail to locate leak from outside roof owing to fact that finger no longer sticking through from other side.
- Get really angry with self.
- Call out to wife to have her stick finger through hole.
- Assume wife's reply metaphorical.
- Sulk.
- Write poem about how much able to see from roof.
- Place bucket under leak next time it rains.
- Wander round in daze for rest of year wondering where all buckets have gone.

I grew up in Sydney in the seventies in what I call the *Cleo* generation. It was compulsory for teenage boys to spend our days off school or the holidays leafing through our mothers' and sisters' magazines. If you were lucky you would come across a breast, or better still a buttock, which made the often day-long trawl well worth the effort. Occasionally you found a matching pair.

23

Sometimes they were even on the same page, which was better still. And then there were the articles encouraging us to get in touch with our feminine side, which we did, provided the door was locked and the phone off the hook. While this led to some fairly enlightened teenagers for whom equality—racial, sexual, or social—was not fought for but assumed, it did leave some of us with confused notions of masculinity. So that a boy coming across (so to speak) a glistening model advertising baby oil or Dunhill Extra Mild found himself oscillating between respecting her right to do so as an individual and yelling out 'whaaaaa, haaaaaay!'.

The guy who was now sneering at me with the last "T" from Darlot still hanging aggressively in the air, had no such ambivalence. He was a bloke, I was a screaming nancy from the city who couldn't even get a bit of pro*nounce*iation right, and what's more I probably read women's magazines.

Well I was damned if I was going to be summed up and dismissed like that just because I didn't have my roo shooter's licence number tattooed on my left bollock. It was time to fight back, like the guy in that Kenny Rogers song who goes ballistic in the bar because of something that somebody does to someone or other. This moment was for the *Cleo* generation. For any guy my age who had ever walked into a country pub and asked for a glass of chardonnay only to find his dismembered corpse being dragged along behind a tow bar. For all those men out there who have wandered into a hotel in outback Queensland and asked for a Malibu and ice or a skim-milk decaf hazelnut latte, only to find themselves staring down the barrel of a dozen semi-automatics that have been stockpiled by members of the gun lobby who believe that the Port Arthur massacre was part of a Canberra-based homosexual conspiracy to disarm them.

(The very desire to own a machine gun should be enough reason to ban you from ever doing so.)

I knew Sydney. I knew how it functioned. I knew what to do if my car broke down—stand on the side of the road and shake my fist at the sky. I knew where the good restaurants, pubs, and bookshops were located. The areas to avoid after dark. What to do to get on prime time tv—lie in bed all day after collecting unemployment benefits. I knew which FM frequencies didn't have boy bands on their play-list. And which daytime tv to avoid—all of it.

And here I was, still in my own country but I clearly didn't belong. Nor was I particularly welcome.

'Actually you're quite wrong,' I said after a time. 'It's pronounced "Darlo". The "t" *is* silent.'

The air turned menacing. The barman started to clear away his best glassware.

'Oh yah reckon, do yah?'

It's at times like this that you need Rudyard Kipling: "*If you can keep your head, while all about you are losing theirs.*" Actually, what you really need is a couple of mates armed with pool cues. However, in their absence I had to settle for Kipling. I did wonder briefly how handy James Moloney and Peter McFarlane would be if the shit went down. Perhaps Peter could read them some of his poetry and James could quote the statistical likelihood of their being readers. One of the actors, Ben Mitchell, looked like a handy guy to have around if you found yourself in a barroom brawl on an author tour; but as he was down the street buying Chupa Chups, I realised that it was up to me and Kipling.

'And how would *you* know?' growled Bubba. 'You don't live here.'

'Well I'm an associate professor of structural linguistics at Sydney University,' I replied while sipping casually on my Pimms. '"Darlot" originates from the French *"Parlot"*, meaning "street in difficult-to-find location", which,' and I suddenly realised that I was at the in-for-a-penny-in-for-a-pound stage now, 'which itself derives from the Latin "to leave the house without one's toga".'

The muscles in Bubba's massive forearms rearranged themselves like waves at sea. 'Well, excuuuuuuse me, Professor.'

'You're excused.'

The bar snorted again.

I left the pub with directions from the barman and

with my head held high—though I'd half expected it to be on the end of a pool cue.

I jumped into the mini-bus, told Jenny that our hotel was just around the corner and asked her if she could hurry.

'Oh and by the way,' I said as I locked the door. 'It's pronounced "Darlo*t*".'

Three

Getting There's Half the Fun

So the idea of getting away from all that for a while was appealing.

Okay, I admit it. I love travelling. And not just being there either. I love the getting there. The bit in between. The journey. With the possible exception of surly immigration officials and my luggage jetting off on a holiday of its own, I love everything about it.

It's undeniably exciting to wake up in the morning and know that by the end of the day you will be in another city/country/hemisphere/jail.

I love the thrill of last-minute packing, the trip to the airport, and the drive home ten minutes later because I've forgotten my passport. I love making the flight attendants attend me during the flight. I even love (and put the rubber room on standby) airline food and the intricacies that go with it: most of all, driving my elbow at the windpipe of the guy sitting next to me as I make a futile attempt to remove my cutlery from its plastic packaging.

Although the jet age has made travel more accessible, it has deprived it of so much romance—the mile-high club notwithstanding. Whereas once you left home for a better life on the other side of the world, almost never to return, these days you can pop back a couple of weeks later because you've forgotten your favourite pair of socks.

I imagine myself running tearfully along beside one of those hissing steam trains, waving goodbye to my wife because she'd left something in the jalopy and had sent me back to get it. I can picture myself on board the *Titanic*, helping the women and children safely off before stepping back and casually asking for a brandy. (Though I worry that I would probably be more like that weaselly Billy Zane character and use every means possible to con my snivelling, worthless hide onto the last lifeboat.)

Note to budding screenwriters:

Q: How do you make the audience want the heroine to ditch her fiancé for the penniless artist?

A: You make the fiancé the most despicable, heartless, slimy, duplicitous cad ever to appear on celluloid.

'Shall we make his hair greasy?'

'Oh yeah, no question. Let's slick it right up. But that's only the beginning.'

'He's got to be stinking rich.'

'Goes without saying. No one likes it when someone's *that* wealthy, particularly if they're smug and arrogant with it, and especially if it's Daddy's money to begin with. Besides anything else it will sit nicely with the pitiful heroine who, despite an outward veneer of wealth, is actually quite poor.'

'Well in that case let's have him slapping her around a bit too.'

'Like your thinking. A couple of heavy backhanders ought to do it. I can hear audiences booing already.'

'Then we'll have him frame the poor artist by making it appear as though he's stolen a diamond the size of a kidney stone.'

'Yeah, but we're not quite there yet. I still feel some sympathy for him. Don't forget, ultimately, he loses the girl.'

'Well then let's have him ordering her food for her, telling her that she can't smoke, dissing Picasso, and then bribing his way onto a lifeboat, first with cash and then with some poor orphaned kid that he finds behind a garbage bin.'

'Or in it.'

'I know. I know. Finally, as a sort of last act of defiance, when some poor wretches try to scramble their way into his lifeboat, let's have him beating them over the head with an oar.'

'Now *that*, gentlemen, is a bastard.'

'I smell an Oscar.'

I can imagine myself as Noel Coward, travelling the world in a cravat and smoking jacket and holing up in a hotel in Shanghai to pen *Private Lives*. I think I could have made an okay Noel Coward, though probably not as good a fist as Noel Coward actually made of it.

But the truth is, of course, that romantic as travel was in the early to mid part of the twentieth century, it *was* only for the super elite. The likes of me would have been down in cattle class doing time-share on an upturned bucket.

•

I sat in the Slipstream Café near my departure lounge, drinking coffee and reflecting on all of this, my place in the world and just where that might be.

A little earlier I'd passed through Customs relatively unscathed, which was a new experience. For whatever reason, Customs officers generally take an instant dislike to me and mark me down as someone who is either on drugs or at least ought to be. In 1991 while waiting to board a flight from Sydney to Hawaii on our honeymoon, I was hauled out of the queue by two United States officials (still in my own country, I should point out) who proceeded to ask me penetrating and deeply personal questions presumably on the grounds that my jumper posed a serious threat to democracy.

A couple of years later, as we were heading off to Europe, one of our own Customs officers congratulated my wife on her Australian accent, saying that it was almost as good as his. It failed to register on his double digit IQ when Jacqui told him that she was an ABC (Australian Born Chinese) and her family had been for three generations. Although my gears were grinding at his ignorance, I didn't want to push it too far. When all was said and done I came to the conclusion that it was probably best not to get involved in a heated debate with someone who has, as part of his job description, the option of ordering a rectal probe.

This time I'd handed over my passport to a Customs officer with the sort of ill-advised two-tone beard that made it look like he was trying to French kiss a reluctant goat.

Now for reasons that I won't bore you with (though they are in fact fascinating—or so they seem after a couple of pints) I happen to carry a British EC passport. The goat-kisser examined it and, having found nothing on his screen to indicate that I should be held down, preferably with his knee on my throat, he handed it back.

'When are you pommies gunna learn how to play cricket and give us a half decent game?'

I pocketed my passport and looked him deep in the beard. 'Just as soon as you get your bowlers to stop harassing our nurses on their mobile phones.'

•

After what seemed like forever, my flight was eventually called. I was looking forward to getting the hell out of there if only because the coffee shop insisted on playing Latin American music at a volume that made me wish they were playing it someplace else, preferably Latin America. Why do cafés have to do this? They're places to sit and contemplate, or, if you're a writer without a study, or a startup company lacking an office, they're places to work or hold meetings. I must admit that I don't care much for Latin American music at the best of times. It strikes me as the sort of din musicians would come up with if they were unable to find any other instruments.

I could study the vagaries of music until the end of time, but it would simply never occur to me to put together a guitar, a flute, a set of bongo drums, a couple of dried gourds and a washboard. Then there's the memory of all those dreadful paisley patterned dresses, flared pants and platform-shoed conga lines that snaked their way through suburban houses in the seventies at cheese cube and cabanossi parties. And is it me (I'm starting to sound like Richie Cunningham's father here) or does the music of Ricky Martin bear striking similarities to Barry Manilow's? Think about it: "Go, go, go, ole, ole, olo. Her name was Lola, she was a show girl."

Next to the Slipstream Café was one of those complex climbing gyms that adults should not even contemplate scaling. Having one so near the departure gates at a major international airport is, to my mind, simply asking for trouble. It's quite possible, and I've seen it happen, for a child to disappear into these things for days at a time. And, even then, only agree to come out after being sedated by a tranquilliser dart fired from a high-powered rifle. 'Ladies and gentlemen, this is your captain speaking. We apologise for the slight delay. We're just waiting for the last of our provisions to be loaded and the few remaining toddlers to be bagged, tagged and hauled out of the climbing gym.'

With the last reminder from my wife, 'Don't lose your mobile phone', still echoing in my mind, I boarded the aircraft and promptly lost my phone.

Not realising this yet, however, I took my seat by the window and proceeded to get myself sorted: books, music, pillows, in-flight magazines, whistle. At one point I actually found myself rubbing my hands together and making strange *yippee* noises. I don't get out much.

As a result of reading *The Hitch Hiker's Guide to the Galaxy* in a Paris café when I was backpacking around Europe in the mid-eighties, I had decided to hang up my soccer boots, pick up a pen, and try to make a living as a comedy writer. This was partly because of the fire that was lit in me that day, but mostly because chasing a bag of air around a field while you're dressed like a public servant in summer was an incredibly silly way to make a living. On top of that, your career is generally over by your early thirties and I didn't want to spend the rest of my life being an ex-professional anything.

Later on, before I was replaced by a laughably simple bit of software, I worked as a computer programmer. I wasn't a particularly good computer programmer, as many of my former colleagues will be only too willing to attest. I once inadvertently corrected the Mir space station's orbit and sent it alarmingly close to Washington DC and the world to the brink of nuclear obliteration. Quite an accomplishment, considering the fact that I was working on an in-house subscription billing system for a legal publishing company at the time.

I spent the greater part of my twenties, and a good deal of my thirties, programming during the day, studying in the evening, and then burning the midnight oil while I worked on my young adult novels and downed industrial strength cups of coffee. The following morning would see me back in the office, staring intently at my computer screen, my chin resting thoughtfully in my hands as I pondered the complexity of the code that I was cutting. Or that's how it appeared to my bosses. In reality I'd simply trained myself to sleep with my eyes open. This technique works particularly well at meetings, which, as anyone from the corporate world knows, are the practical alternative to work. Simply superglue your eyelids open and allow yourself to drift off. And if you throw in the occasional nod along the way, so much the better. The tedious hack who has the floor—"At the end of the day, we need to get back to the coalface and synergise a win–win situation"—will think that you're agreeing with him.

For all that, it was a struggle, and an exhausting one. So now, whenever I fly anywhere at someone else's expense, just before takeoff I allow myself a moment of smug contentedness that I made a relatively successful, if highly improbable, career switch. Such moments of self-satisfaction don't linger, though, as those residual macho genes kick in with: "Get a grip! Have you won the Booker prize? Are you flying first class? Have you been nominated for, let alone won, an Oscar for best original screenplay? Had your remains scattered round Westminster Abbey? No. Then pull yourself together!"

The aircraft was half empty (or half full depending on how you look at the world) and I thought for a moment that I was going to score three seats to myself. But no such luck. Just prior to rollback the last passenger joined us and of course he happened to be sitting next to me.

As he took his seat I was interested to note that he had exactly the same mobile phone I did and was immediately worried that it might become a talking point at some stage of the journey. Worried, because I generally like to keep to myself on long hauls. I want to be left alone to read, listen to my Walkman, or watch the movies in peace. Apart from anything else, you never know who you'll have to trample on to get to the emergency exit, or whose whistle you'll have to steal, when the plane suddenly plummets into Mt Fuji, so it's best not to get too friendly with anyone.

It was only after we'd levelled off that I realised I might have had a live one on my hands. My travelling companion was examining his mobile phone as if it was the most extraordinary thing he had ever encountered. He had the look of someone who's just split the atom and is now considering how he can use this incredible achievement to get more women to sleep with him.

I have absolutely no interest in mobile phones, and had only recently, and somewhat reluctantly, taken to carrying one. I'm certainly not in the business of giving my friends impromptu demonstrations of its many features. For a start, I wouldn't have a clue what they are. I once entered a restaurant and found four men sitting at the same table all talking on their mobiles—probably to each other. 'I've been under a lot of stress lately so I'm going to be spending the weekend in an isolation tank at an undisclosed health resort in the Blue Mountains. If you need to get in touch I'll be on the mobile.' What, have we all suddenly become brain surgeons and need to be on call twenty-four hours a day? Turn the bloody things off! The world will get back, get back to you, sooner than you imagine. And there's that peacock-strut guys do when they're talking on their mobiles. A strut that's just short of a goosestep. 'Look at me, look at me. They won't stop calling me on my ten-dollar mobile phone.' Probably the talking clock.

I tried to ignore Mobile Guy and get back to my book, but he started to do something that was so stupid I wanted to hit him over the head with my pillow. He was trying to turn his seatback entertainment system on with his mobile phone. I can still hardly believe it. He was pointing the thing at the screen and pressing random buttons, but the screen remained frustratingly blank.

Fortunately a flight attendant happened along at that moment and showed him the correct way to operate it with the controls on his armrest, but not before hitting him over the head with a pillow for being so utterly stupid.

After dinner, Mobile Guy found himself three empty seats on the other side of the aircraft and, after gathering up all his possessions—with the exception of his mobile phone, which, strangely, he left behind in the seat pocket—he settled down to what I hoped would be an extremely disturbed sleep.

Around this time I began to wonder where my own phone had got to, because I hadn't seen it since we boarded. I assumed that I'd tossed it into the overhead bin with the rest of my stuff, but a quick rummage around proved that this wasn't the case. I checked my seat pocket, jacket; I even got down on the floor and started to hunt frantically under the seats. Nothing.

I looked across at Mobile Guy, who was dozing fitfully. I considered taking *his* phone and dialling mine in the hope that this would reveal where it was. Then I censored *that* thought in case it caused the aircraft to suddenly veer into a ravine.

'What sort of moron moves to another part of the plane and deliberately leaves his phone behind?' I grumbled as I upturned cushions and seats.

I slumped back into my seat and sulked. Great start to my spiritual journey. Spirituality could go and bollocks!

I decided to retrace my steps from the moment I got on board: I'd put my backpack in the overhead bin, having first removed my book, writing pad, and Walkman. Then I'd taken my mobile out of my jacket pocket, placed it on the aisle seat, and stuffed my jacket into the locker. Then I'd sat down. Then...there were no other "then"s, at least none that involved the phone. Mobile Guy came along, played with *his* phone for a while, which was identical to mine, and then tried to use it to operate his seatback entertainment system. Then, after dinner, he moved to a new seat and made a deliberate point of leaving his phone behind and...

I don't know if you've ever tried to beat your own brains out with a British Airways pillow, but I can assure you the results are less than satisfactory and all you end up doing is drawing alarmed looks from everyone round you.

JOHN LARKIN

With an exasperated sigh I retrieved my mobile from the seat pocket and tried to determine whether I was the one who'd just met the stupidest man in the world, or he was.

Four

Fag Ash Lil and the Tarantula

I arrived at Heathrow Airport completely exhausted and with a headache that felt as though someone had recently macheteed my brain in two.

Although the aircraft was largely empty for the leg to Singapore, it had been packed from there on, mostly with British short-break holidaymakers. For the fourteen hours to London we were stuffed into our seats like overweight sardines.

'Could they cram any more of us in here?' I remarked to the fresh-faced couple who were now sitting beside me. The legroom in economy is bad enough, but add to it the obligatory six-year-old behind you who bangs his tray table closed at least a dozen times every five minutes. Then of course there's the bastard in front who immediately reclines his chair as far back as it will go so that he is effectively asleep in your lap, and you end up like a piece of underdone bread popping out of a toaster.

When you take all this into account, the amazing thing about air rage is not that it happens, but that it doesn't happen more often.

•

Perhaps you already know that one of the Monkees' mothers (Mike Nesmith's was it?) invented Liquid Paper. But you don't know that my mother, bless her, in a moment of extreme pique, invented air rage. The year was 1979 and she was taking me and my younger brother Paul on a holiday back to England. I think she was entertaining serious notions of our returning there to live, and perhaps wanted the two of us along to see how we felt about it. The aircraft was practically empty for the first leg, so I was able to stretch out across three seats and read or listen to my Bucks Fizz tape. When we arrived in Kuala Lumpur, however, we were joined by the Malaysian badminton team, which was on its way to London to compete in the world championships. We weren't allowed to leave the aircraft while it was in transit and as it became hotter and hotter my mother's tolerance threshold dipped lower and lower. No sooner had the badminton team taken their seats than the player in front of my mother (foolish man) reclined his seat to the point where his head was in precisely the position it shouldn't have been. Subtlety is not among my mother's many endearing qualities, so she calmly reached for her in-flight magazine, casually rolled it up, and proceeded to beat the man vertical. To this day I have never seen another member of my species move with such alacrity. He was like Jack leaping out of his box because someone had hurled in an incendiary device. Paul and I just looked at each other with shock in our eyes and a half-smile etched across our faces that said, *Boy, I'm glad that wasn't me.* To the man's credit he didn't say a thing; he just spent the rest of the journey with his head so far forward it was practically on his knees.

On the return flight, following a blazing row in Singapore Airport, I was almost on the end of my mother's rolled up in-flight magazine myself. What happened was this. She'd been buried deep in the duty free shop, obstinately ignoring my warnings that our plane was about to leave. I've always been a bit anal when it comes to punctuality and I'd been watching the departure board with growing unease. She finally emerged, clutching about seven cartons of cigarettes and a look in her eye that said, *Don't mess with me!* Then she sat down and began the long process of ignition. I was practically hyperventilating by this point so I yelled to her through the fug that our plane was about to leave, with or without us. She blew an aggressive smoke ring at me and told me to bugger off because she was having a bloody fag and that was the end of it, you anally retentive little pillock!

Although there were still smoking sections in those days, Paul and I had nagged her to let us fly non-smoking because we wanted to be alive when we got home. I grabbed Paul's hand and told him that we were leaving and that Fag Ash Lil would be catching the next flight, just as soon as the fire brigade had beaten back the worst of the blaze around her. Not only was it pre-air, it was pre air-bridge, so the two of us ran for the escalator down to the transit buses on the tarmac. We'd just reached the bottom when we were summoned back to the peak by Medusa in a brown crimplene pants suit, with a Winfield Red on the go and speaking in tongues.

'Come back here, you little swine!' A couple of snakes twirled around her head might have made a more startling impression, but only marginally. Paul and I sprinted for the last shuttle bus while Mum descended from the fiery summit, more Moses now than Medusa. With scant regard for rules, let alone the highly flammable nature of aviation fuel, she threw her half-smoked fag onto the tarmac and hauled herself onto the bus just as the doors closed behind her. It was one of those wide transit passenger buses designed specifically for tarmacs so all but the aged and infirm stood, and I went and hid behind a couple of loud American tourists who were wearing even louder shirts. This gave me some protection from Fag Ash Lil's frontal assaults, if not her withering stares.

•

I'm just over six feet tall in the old scale, as were my two companions for the rest of the flight to London. So we were all going to spend the rest of the journey with our knees up around our chests. Or in their case—each other's chests.

'Perhaps they could wedge a couple more of us into the overhead bins. There's still a bit of room up there,' I suggested to the three inconsiderate bastards in front of us who were snoozing peacefully around our groins. Being something of a teeth gritter and head shaker when it comes to self-assertion, I was surprised to hear myself uttering this tirade and began to suspect that I was completely rat-faced.

Just before dinner and our arrival at Singapore Airport, the booze buggy had been wheeled around and I'd asked politely for a glass of red wine if they had one to spare. With the sort of smile that flight attendants alone can bestow (it generally requires more than one face) she handed me a quarter bottle of the Hunter Valley's finest. Then, almost as an afterthought, she passed me a second for the meal. She obviously had me tagged as either a connoisseur or a complete pisshead because along the way I somehow acquired a third and a fourth bottle ("You might like a sip after your coffee and another when you settle back with a movie"). So by the time we landed in Singapore I was surprisingly happy with proceedings.

I wandered around Singapore Airport in a bit of a daze and found myself in a souvenir shop where I briefly contemplated moving from admiration to ownership of an enormous, petrified South American tarantula.

Despite the fact that my back teeth were floating I was still lucid enough to talk myself out of actually going through with it. Although I intended to spend this holiday (if that's what it was) taking a break from myself and doing things that I wouldn't normally consider, this new age philosophy mercifully didn't stretch to keeping dead arachnids as pets.

I suppose that's one of the benefits of having your own philosophy, you can just make it up as you go along. It's a bit like forming a splinter religion—you just keep the bits you want. Then you can have literally hours of fun writing up your church's charter.

'What about free love?'

'Oh, yeah. Compulsory. I haven't been on a date for a while so let's have bucketloads of that.'

'Why don't we go for polygamy?'

'Why buy a book when you can join the library?'

'Good point. Technology?'

'Well I can never get my PC to interface with my service provider, so let's say the internet is banned.'

'Cash flow?'

'Ten per cent of our followers' gross salaries, including GST.'

'And will women be permitted to be ordained as priests?'

'Only if they look good in a satin cassock.'

The fact of the matter is that I live in abject terror of spiders. The closest thing we have to tarantulas in

Larkin about in IRELAND

Sydney is the huntsman, which is a large, grey, rapid-mover that turns up in your bathroom, shed, sock drawer, sock, or lunchbox when you least expect it, and leaves a revolting green gooey blob on your wall. Or at least it does when, after a fifty-metre run up, you hammer it through extra cover with a cricket bat. If you live in Sydney you've got a huntsman story, which generally involves a sunset, a hastily pulled down visor, and a car veering into the oncoming traffic

My friend Stuart has, or at least *had* before he moved to Queensland, the best huntsman spider story. Stuart was riding to work on his motorbike when he noticed that there was something in his crash helmet with him. There obviously wasn't room for the two of them, so almost languidly due to the cramped conditions, the huntsman made its way around to the front of the helmet and perched itself across Stuart's face—perhaps hoping to convince him that one of them had to go. If it had happened to me I would have ridden straight to the nearest home for the bewildered and spent the rest of my life etching landscapes on a rubber wall with a crayon and dribbling.

I'm writing these words balanced on a hammock in the backyard of my leaf-strewn home. The mainly illegible notes beside my laptop were scrawled on the back of a coaster over a coffee and a beer in the early hours of the morning at Singapore airport. It's clear, or at least it's become so after a little deciphering, that "big spid in souv shop" is there to remind me to write something about the enormous South American tarantula that I came within a whisker of purchasing. Whereas I can only hope that "huge cock size of house brick" is a reference to some of the other petrified insects I encountered that same night.

But I digress.

•

Back on board the aircraft, my companions for the Singapore/London leg were Debbie and Steve, a tanned and healthy-looking twenty-something couple who'd spent the week on a backpackers' trail in Thailand, discovering innovative positions in which to shag—or so their red faces implied.

Although I still wanted to be left alone to read and, if possible, sober up, it's extremely difficult not to be on first-name terms with people you find yourself in a *ménage à trois* with, every time one of you gets up to go to the bathroom.

The booze buggy had visited again shortly after take-off and I slurred out something along the lines of Boeing having cocked up the design of its aircraft. Steve and Debbie were completely enthralled by my lecture, or at least they would have been if they hadn't popped off to enquire about membership of the mile-high club part way through it.

Lulled by a combination of the wine, the drone of the engines, and the rhythmic banging of the six-year-old with the tray table behind me, I lapsed into a troubled coma for the rest of the journey.

•

I collected my bag from the carousel at Heathrow Airport and began picking my way through the maddening sea of trolleys towards Ireland.

Although my ticket to London included as part of the package a free flight to Dublin, I chose to forego this option and finish the journey by foot, train, and ferry. This wasn't entirely due to the fact that I was out of my mind, though that was a contributing factor; rather, because I had a strong desire to enter Ireland from the sea.

Given the number of souls who had been exported from Ireland by ship, I felt there would be a certain symmetry attached to making *my* "homecoming" the same way. I felt passionate about it, in fact. But then again, I'd once felt passionate about buying a Bucks Fizz record too.

I had arranged to meet my Australian friend Jon Appleton at Euston Station for breakfast, to hand over a manuscript and discuss book jackets. Jon now worked as an editor for my London publisher and I was really looking forward to seeing him. My excitement was heightened by the thought that handing over a tattered manuscript next to a hissing train would have been just the sort of thing Graham Greene might have done before heading off to Capri and embarking on affairs with married women. The fact that I had yet to start work on the very manuscript I was meant to be handing over did little to quell my excitement.

I made my way down into the bowels of Heathrow Airport and onto the Piccadilly Line for central London. Although that's a relatively inexpensive way to travel into the city, on reflection I wished that I'd taken the far superior Heathrow Express to Paddington and joined the underground there.

If there's a more miserable train journey anywhere in the world at six in the morning then I'm yet to encounter it. I've never actually travelled on the Calcutta suburban rail network, but even at its worst it couldn't be uglier than the Piccadilly Line on the London underground (or at least the bit that isn't underground). The houses all looked damp, deserted and uninviting, and were huddled together as if to stave off the cold. I suppose my mood was coloured by the fact that I'd just left my family in sun-drenched Sydney and had spent the last twenty-two hours or so hurtling through the stratosphere in a pressurised and cramped tin can, and having strange dreams about large South American tarantulas making off with my mobile phone.

I could, of course, have taken a cab to Euston Station, but given the exchange rate of the Pacific peso to the pound, the distance from Heathrow to the centre of London, and the congested state of the roads at that time of the morning, it would have meant handing over a large slice of my weekly budget, if not all of it, for the pleasure.

I'm also wary of talking to London cab drivers, at least in any great depth. For although they are generally courteous and *always* know where they're going ("I want to go to my aunt's house in Kent." "Mother's or Father's side of the family?" "Father's." "Right. I know the place.") one of them was responsible for one of the strangest conversations that I have ever had.

It was the mid-eighties and I'd recently hung up my soccer boots to pursue a career as a writer. I was wandering through London, ostensibly in search of inspiration and a writing pad, when I managed to help prevent a young woman from being robbed.

What happened was this: I'd just emerged from Sloane Square tube station when a mugger lurched out of a doorway at me and at once lurched back in again when he realised that I was a penniless backpacker. Moments later he lurched out again at the richer pickings to be had from a young Sloane Ranger who had followed me out of the tube station. I couldn't just walk away. I'd seen it happen and I felt involved. Besides anything else, she was seriously cute and might have invited me home with her. We could have lived off Daddy's allowance, had satin sheets and kept a pet finch called Michael Heseltine. Over wine and pizza on Friday evenings we would have had good-natured arguments about the class system and how I suddenly no longer wanted to smash it. Arguments that would invariably have ended in long and intense tickle fights. And while I penned witty, observational pieces for the weekend's colour supplements, Portia would have done whatever it was that Sloane Rangers did during the daytime, which, on the available evidence, appeared to be getting mugged.

Summoning all my mental agility—or at least the bits that weren't involved in fleshing out my extraordinarily detailed fantasy life—and bearing in mind that I couldn't fight my way out of a Wiggles concert, I half turned around, held out my hand, and, pretending that I hadn't seen the mugger lunge at her I said, 'Come on, Portia. Hurry up or we'll be late.' Fortunately Portia realised what I was doing, and with her would-be assailant momentarily caught off guard—*She's* going out with *him?*—she ran up to me and we proceeded along the street hand in hand, like a happy young couple on our way to a Wham concert.

Afterwards, over a coffee, Sharon (boy was *that* a disappointment) told me about how dangerous London was becoming. We both decided that Margaret Thatcher was to blame and left it at that. We shook hands and parted, but not before Portia (it was *my* fantasy) pressed on me the small bunch of flowers that she was carrying. They'd been given to her earlier by her live-in boyfriend, who I suspect drove a Bentley and answered to the name of Heath.

I felt extremely self-conscious and more than a bit downcast, walking along with my bunch of flowers that had come on the back of my intense but ultimately doomed relationship with Portia. So I hailed a cab to take me back to the guesthouse where I was staying in Russell Square.

After a brief discussion on immigration, with particular reference to the cooking smells that emanated from the house of the Pakistani people he lived next door to, the cab driver turned round and gave me a wink. 'Trying to get your leg over, eh?'

I didn't have the foggiest idea what he was talking about. 'Sorry?'

'The flowers. Trying to get your leg over?' Call me naive but I still didn't know what he was getting at. Get my leg over? Over what? 'Or have you been on the nest all night with something a bit tastier and the flowers are to buy off the old lady?'

The nest? Legs over? Something a bit tastier? Old ladies? Finally the penny dropped. The story of the flowers was too convoluted to share with anyone at that stage. I mean, apart from anything else, I hadn't finished embellishing it yet. So I just nodded. 'Yeah. Something like that.'

'Women these days. Can't figure 'em out. They want equality, so we give it 'em. Yet they still want doors openin' for 'em and flowers and Christ knows what else.'

'They're a hazy mystery.'

'Married thirty years me. My old girl's never answered me back.'

It was at this point I realised that the cab driver wasn't engaged in a conversation but a monologue. 'Well if she's been good, perhaps you should let her out from under the stairs occasionally.'

'None of this career woman stuff for her. Knows her place, she does.'

'Where's that, then? On your doorstep?'

'Terrific little homemaker, my girl. Knows that the way to a man's heart is through 'is stomach.'

'Through his lung with a meat-cleaver my friends in the Macquarie University Women's Room would have me believe.' Boy, I was enjoying myself. Or at least I was until he reached into his pocket and handed me a photo.

'Right little goer too, if you know what I mean.' He gave me another wink.

I took the proffered photograph, glanced at it and immediately reeled. 'Should she be doing that with a vacuum cleaner?'

'It ain't plugged in.'

I cocked my head to one side and examined the photo in greater detail. 'It looks like it is.'

'Into a power point I mean.'

'Oh. I see.' I handed the photo back to him and

wiped my fingers on the seat. I had a strange feeling that I was about to be invited to a party that evening.

'Where is it you're goin' again, guv?'

'Right here's just fine.'

Five

Shagalot Atlantic

As agreed, I met Jon under the departure board at Euston Station. There were rumours that my sister-in-law Karen, who was living in London at the time, would be joining us for breakfast too. The fact that she was largely nocturnal meant that she was rarely seen before midday or, whenever possible, three in the afternoon, so I didn't hold out much hope. With her return to Sydney imminent and her suitcase already bursting at the seams, Karen did, however, leave detailed instructions with Jon for me to pick up a bag of her clothes when I returned to London in a month's time. So at least I had that to look forward to.

Jon asked me where the manuscript was. I smiled, tapped my head and told him that it was safely locked away. He rolled his eyes and led me across to the ticket office.

I had recently taken to setting myself punishing deadlines and felt that Jack Kerouac was to blame. Excited by a long, rambling letter that he'd received from his former travelling companion Neal Cassady, Kerouac fed one end of a continuous roll of paper into his typewriter and, rarely stopping for tea, toilet or punctuation breaks, in less than a month managed to produce the enormous, single-spaced, 175 000-word paragraph that would eventually make his name. This incredible feat was to lead to one of the most famous putdowns in literary history when Truman Capote, the pretentious git, said that Kerouac's achievement wasn't writing but typing.

But Capote's long dead so Kerouac's work ethos is still my model whenever I discuss deadlines with my publisher. What I always fail to factor into the equation, though, is that being single and part of the Beat generation (ie unemployed and on drugs), Kerouac was able to lock himself away for however long he saw fit. He was always *On the Road* in some capacity. Not once did he have to break off to collect his daughter from school, walk the dog, buy a carton of milk, mow the lawn, perform stand-up comedy, assemble a trampoline, abuse telesellers, turn the hose on cable guys, buy more milk, sugar, bread, Nutella, etc; because if he had, the impact would be obvious on both the length and content of his work. And you can't tell me that Kerouac's masterpiece would be regarded as the definitive portrait of America in the late forties and early fifties had it been titled *On the Road to the Shops*.

It was in this frame of mind that I approached the

ticket counter at Euston Station and immediately hit trouble.

The young man behind the counter was exceedingly friendly but totally useless. He considered my request in a manner that suggested I'd just asked him for a non-smoking ticket to the Horse Head nebula.

He scratched his chin thoughtfully. 'You want to go to *Holyhead*?'

'Yeah, you know,' I remarked, trying to be helpful. 'It's in Wales.'

'Where the Irish ferries depart from,' added Jon. 'Or, more recently, haven't departed.'

I took this as a reference to the boiling Irish Sea and recent cancellations. However I chose not to comment on it, fearing that it would only confuse the ticket guy further.

He considered us for a moment longer and then disappeared into a back room, possibly for a cup of tea but more likely in the hope that we would simply give up and go away.

'Probably gone to look at an atlas,' suggested Jon.

After a couple of minutes he joined us back at the counter. 'You'll have to change at Crewe.' His tone implied that changing trains at Crewe would tax the limits of my mental dexterity. He obviously didn't think much of Australians.

'I think I can just about manage that,' I said.

Then he added. 'I don't fancy your chances, though.'

'What? Of changing trains at Crewe?' I was more than a little nonplussed. 'I'm assuming the train actually stops there. Or is that the difficult bit—leaping onto the platform from a moving train?' This immediately called to mind my former school friend John Averyham who, in a moment of inspired insanity while on the way back from an excursion to the Sydney museum, chose to leave the train we were on well before we'd arrived at the station. Anyone who grew up in Sydney in the seventies will recall the old red-rattlers that clattered about the suburban rail network like skeletons making love on a tin roof. The thing about them was that the doors were opened manually, so you could disembark at any point in your journey, sometimes quite unwillingly.

Anyway, this day the train we were on was just coming into Pendle Hill Station when John Averyham, in the interest of scientific enquiry and perhaps to alleviate the boredom, decided to see if he could half-alight and scooter one foot along the platform. Unfortunately for John his coordination wasn't very good and in attempting to only half-alight and skip his trailing leg along the platform, he fully alighted and ended up running alongside the train at a speed that was simply beyond him. Cheered on by the whole of year nine, John was propelled along the platform like a demented gazelle as he tried to stay upright and out of hospital—neither of which he managed. No one knew for sure what speed the train was doing that day, but the sparks that flew from John Averyham's school case as it thundered along beside him suggested that it must have been pretty fast. At one point John had even begun to overtake the train, presumably because even the old red-rattlers had a more sophisticated braking mechanism than the school shoes of a fifteen-year-old boy.

'No, it stops there all right,' said the ticket guy, interrupting my thoughts. John Averyham, by the way, died tragically young when, having been handed his driver's licence, he took the same empirical philosophy onto the road. 'It's just that the trains aren't moving very quickly and I'm not sure you'll be able to make the connection in time. I don't think you've got a chance in hell of making it to Ireland today, to be honest.'

This didn't come as a complete surprise. I knew that the trains were on a bit of a go-slow. It had even been on the news back home. The south of England was practically under water owing to heavy rains. Add to this the fact that some trains had failed to negotiate sweeping bends with fatal results, and it was a wonder that they were running at all.

I looked at the ticket guy and shook my head. 'But if the trains *are* running slow, then surely the timetables of the connecting trains would be adjusted accordingly.'

'Yes, well I can see why you *would* think that.'

Jon snorted. Having moved to London several years earlier, he'd taken on that sort of stiff-upper-lipness associated with his adopted home.

The ticket seller gazed at his screen. 'Now, which train will you be taking?'

'Pardon me, but isn't that the sort of thing *you're* supposed to tell *us*?' snapped Jon, his upper lip beginning to crack under the strain.

'There's one leaving in an hour's time at nine,' the man said. Then, perhaps because I looked like the sort of person who enjoys hanging around train stations, added that there was another departing at eleven.

I held Jon at bay with a hastily extended arm. 'I think I'll take the nine o'clock if it's all the same to you.' Then with a wildly optimistic flourish added, 'How long will it take to get to Crewe, do you suppose?'

He shrugged his shoulders and held out his arms, cocked his head to one side, sneered and raised his eyebrows. Then, just in case his body language had left us in any doubt, added, 'Given the current circumstances, I'd hate to commit myself.'

'He ought to be committed,' mumbled Jon.

'Take a wild guess,' I said. 'I won't hold you to it.'

He leaned forward conspiratorially. 'About five or six hours.'

That did it. After twenty-two hours crammed into British Airways economy like a sock down a homeboy's pants at a nightclub, there was simply no way I was going to handle a further six cooped up on a train and still retain what little sanity I had left. I asked him to sell me a first class ticket and tried my best not to cringe when he mentioned that it would be a hundred and fifteen pounds (about three hundred and fifty dollars at that time).

'And how will you be paying for that, sir?'

I looked him in the eye. 'By selling a kidney to the highest bidder.'

•

My ticket gave me entry to the first class lounge so Jon and I went there directly and set about the tea and muffin trolley like a couple of half-starved weasels. We availed ourselves of all the facilities afforded the upmarket rail commuter, which primarily meant the tea and muffin trolley and a man in a coat and tie handing out towels in the toilet.

About an hour later I settled back into my extremely comfortable seat aboard one of Sir Richard Branson's smart new trains. Having read the Virgin head's, so to speak, autobiography just months earlier, I had been amused by his heightened sense of irony when it came to choosing a name for his group of companies. But then again I suppose *Shagalot Atlantic* doesn't quite roll off the tongue the way that *Virgin Atlantic* does. Neither for that matter does *Shaftaround Megastore*.

When the last of the plebs had been cattle-prodded into the boxcars at the rear of the train, we began our long, slow chug northwards out of Euston Station.

We hadn't gone all that far, in fact we were still in sight of the station, when I noticed a man on an overhead bridge, wearing a worryingly bright anorak and jotting notes down as we clattered by beneath him. As much as I enjoy travelling by train in Britain and Europe, it isn't by itself enough to make me want to abandon the real world for a place on an overhead bridge or grassy bank with a timetable, a notebook, a flask of coffee and a packed lunch. I try for all I'm worth to imagine conversations at a gathering of such enthusiasts, but I always come up desperately short:

'Well, you can picture the excitement in the shunting yards when the five-thirty-four from Exeter arrived nine minutes early.'

'Oh, aye. It was meant to be coupled to the engine of the three-thirty-three from Doncaster, but as that was running approximately twelve minutes late owing to a signal failure at Luton, the yard manager took the controversial decision to switch to the second engine from the four-twenty-two-and-a-third out of Edinburgh in the hope that no one would notice.'

I don't believe for one minute that such conversations have ever taken place. I reckon train spotters stand around like most men, fantasising about who they would most like to shag. The only real difference being—apart from their outrageously uncoordinated clothes—that they also discuss, at great length, which overnight sleeper they'd most like to shag them in.

'Well, of course, on the leg between York and Newcastle, the line is so unstable, that, for all intents and purposes, you only have to lie there and the heaving of the train does the rest.'

'Oh, aye. Rung a few bells on that journey myself.'

Although I would happily rank London in my top five cities in the world, much of its urban squalor is clearly the work of successive town planners who were clinically insane. Parts of the city make you think that the architect, in the pursuit of artistic experimentation, has taken a protracted and painful dump on his drawing board and simply handed it over to the building contractors. Although many of the inner city suburbs are heart-thumpingly beautiful (and heart-attack-inducingly expensive) most of those that you view from any of the lines out of London are plain ugly. Decaying high-rise slums sit alongside abandoned factories and derelict buildings smothered in graffiti, on streets that are liberally doused with dog-shit. This glorious city deserves better.

Although the Luftwaffe did everything in its power to redesign London in the early forties, what the city clearly lacks is the picturesque sweeping boulevards of Paris. Up until the reign of Napoleon III, inner city Paris was itself a maze of crowded slums and narrow twisting streets. This intricate network of escape routes out of the city made it impossible for the authorities to arrest potential revolutionaries and insurgents. So, on officially becoming emperor in 1852, the (till that point) breathtakingly incompetent Napoleon III, nephew of

Napoleon Bonaparte, handed Baron Georges-Eugène Haussmann the inner suburbs to redesign as he saw fit. Baron Haussmann got to work with gusto, clearing the slums and replacing them with wide, open, tree-lined boulevards—ostensibly so that Napoleon III could see when anyone was attempting to sneak up on him. (Ironically, he himself had been swept to power by the revolution of 1848.)

As the train increased its pace from a trudge to an amble, I couldn't help but feel that what London lacked was a little French paranoia. Having finally left the urban decay behind, however, we were now rolling along through the outer suburbs.

Apart from one horrific moment in my early teens, which we will come to in the next paragraph, I generally enjoy peering into backyards from the safety of a moving train. You can learn a great deal about the people who live there. For instance my own backyard, with its hammocks, deck chairs, and wildly overgrown trees, would tell the casual interloper or persistent cable guy that I am a lazy git who doesn't care much for gardening, and you wouldn't be a million miles from the truth.

Once during the school holidays on the way home from Luna Park, I happened to witness a woman sunbathing nude in her backyard on the western suburbs line and I *really* wished I hadn't. It wasn't just that I thought she was too old to be doing that sort of thing, though I suppose, thinking back now, that she can't have been much beyond forty. It was more that she had the sort of body that could only be negotiated with a team of highly experienced Sherpas. Why is it that the people with a desire to appear naked in public generally have the sort of bodies that should automatically disqualify them from ever being allowed to do so? Which I suppose raises the interesting question of whether she was in fact "in public".

Whatever. We can dress it up in all the eye-of-the-beholder, all-bodies-are-beautiful, pompous political correctness that we like, but let's be honest for a moment: some bodies are nice to look at, and some are best kept covered (my own, for a start—any six-pack I once had having been long since replaced by a keg). Whenever there's a news item or lifestyle segment on tv about a nudist colony, or the entire population of some country town walking naked down the main street to commemorate the hundredth anniversary of old Bill Saggybutt walking naked down the main street, you never get a shot of some svelte twenty-something. It's always some sad old thing whose body is not only incapable of defying gravity: it now appears to positively relish its embrace.

The outer (leafier) suburbs gave me a brief glimpse into the lives of the more affluent Londoners but mercifully it was too cold for any of the circumferentially enhanced to be scampering about unclothed. One or

Larkin about in IRELAND

two householders I was surprised to note, had, installed built-in pools, which in Northern Europe makes about as much sense as a haemophiliac taking up boxing.

Whenever I see backyard swimming pools from a train or from the air, though, I'm immediately reminded of that wonderful and disturbing film *The Swimmer*, which I watched one lazy afternoon after I'd skived off school as a fourteen-year-old for about the zillionth time. I don't remember the exact details of the film, though what I do know is that it disturbed me for reasons I've never quite been able to understand. In *The Swimmer* Burt Lancaster plays a man who, having popped into town to do a bit of shopping, decides to swim home through all the backyard pools between the village and his house. He sets off on his bizarre quest and arrives home several hours later to find his wife and daughter gone, the house boarded up and that he's barking mad. The haunting image of the screen-door banging as a mid-evening gale sweeps in has stayed with me and was, at the time, enough for me to get my idle arse off the lounge and back to school the following day.

As the train clattered on, the gaps between the houses grew wider and wider until eventually it was all just gap. I was only about twenty minutes out of London, the heavens still the texture and colour of wet blankets, when I found myself involuntarily uttering my first British-ism. Spotting a small patch of blue through the sodden gloom, I couldn't stop myself leaning across the aisle and saying to the businessman seated there that it 'Might turn out nice.' Unlike the Irish, who expect it to be miserable the whole time (and are in fact rarely disappointed), the English have this perverse sense of optimism when it comes to the weather. The sky could be black and dripping blood, the four horsemen of the apocalypse have just hoven into view, but somewhere in the country, someone will be looking up to the heavens and saying, 'Mmmmm. Might turn out nice.' I've watched relatives pack up their car with towels, windbreaks, beach-balls, sunscreen (had to hold a snort in there) picnic baskets and flasks of tea, and become genuinely and deeply mystified when, ten seconds after setting out, it started bucketing down. 'Well, that's a bit odd. The weather man said that it might turn out nice.' Sometimes I feel like getting hold of an atlas and saying, 'Look! There's the Sudan. There's the equator. And *there's* Sheffield. Now it's generally quite warm in the Sudan; and that's because it's about as close to the equator as Sheffield is to say the Arctic Circle. Get it?' But of course you can't, because the English optimism about the weather is an article of faith and you'd be lynched for being an infidel or a smartarse.

I don't know what it is about railway catering in this country (pre- and post-privatisation) but clearly something happens to food in England when it's moving. Our first class catering officer (a woman with a trolley) for the Euston/Crewe leg informed us that there was a problem with the day's cuisine (it had been prepared by somebody English, I imagine) and that as a result there would be a selection of bacon and egg toasted sandwiches available instead. I felt quite sorry for her in a way. I mean, she had all the drawbacks of being a flight attendant—cramped working conditions, a job description that required her to have a permanent maniacal leer, and so on—without any of the benefits, such as flight.

From where I was sitting, it seemed that the bacon had only recently been removed from the pig, whereas the toast was being served at something well short of room temperature. I was flirting with vegetarianism again as I tried hard not to imagine a one-legged porker hobbling around a field and shaking his little trotter at the train and yelling 'Bastards!' as it trundled past, so I settled for a coffee instead. I should have asked for a cup of mud and left it at that, because that's what I ended up with. And this was first class! I couldn't imagine what was happening back in economy; probably had some weather-beaten old babushka wandering up and down the aisle with a ladle and a steaming cauldron of brussels sprouts.

I know how to fix the catering problems on British railways: employ the French. They could do it while they're running up a town plan. The year before, Jacqui and I had taken our daughter, Chantelle, to Paris on the EuroStar. As a joint venture the Anglo–French

JOHN LARKIN

EuroStar is excellent proof of what can be achieved when people are allowed to play to their strengths. Early in the piece it was obviously decided to let the English get on with whatever it was that they were good at: queuing, making cups of tea, finding new and interesting ways to lose at cricket, while the French were allowed to stick to their speciality, which meant the catering and being invaded by Germany every once in a while. The coffee alone was worth the price of the ticket to Paris. I've never tasted anything like it. My tastebuds had obviously remembered the EuroStar experience because the moment they were hit by the Virgin equivalent, my tongue rolled out of my mouth like carpet off the back of a truck and my upper lip curled into an involuntary sneer. This wasn't coffee, or if it was, it had clearly been filtered through Richard Branson's tennis socks on its way to the urn.

We passed through Birmingham, Britain's second city, which was, from where I sat at least, designed to show people how the world would look in the event of nuclear holocaust. Now I don't wish to appear too negative and I know that there are people who love Birmingham dearly—and may I take this opportunity to apologise to both of you for the last sentence and for the one that follows. But, to be honest, Birmingham is a bit of a shit-hole. I remember once seeing a tourist commercial on the *Clive James Show* advertising to Americans Birmingham's many virtues. It had been shot some time in the seventies and appeared even then a little light in content, focussing as it did on sunken pedestrian precincts. The voice-over was by Telly Savalas and it was clear to all but the completely brain-dead that old Kojak Birmingham-that's-my-kind-of-town had never so much as set foot in the place. Travelling through it now I could see his point—about not going there, that is. To my left was a series of derelict factories beside a canal that was so murky and polluted you could have walked on it. There were a couple of men fishing from its banks (obviously on day release from some institute for the bewildered). Unless used condoms and shopping trolleys were part of their staple diet, I can't imagine what they were hoping to catch—dysentery perhaps.

I have a friend whose father used to be a policeman in Birmingham, and I remember him telling me that the Birmingham/Worcester policing border ran down the middle of a canal—perhaps the very one I was now staring at. One evening my friend's father and his partner came across a dead body floating face down on their side of the canal. With the end of their shift imminent, however, and the pubs still open, they fashioned together a large pole from the debris on the bank and prodded the corpse back into Worcester jurisdiction.

I looked from side to side, my mouth gaping at how utterly repulsive and miserable the city appeared. I must have looked like one of those laughing clowns that you can still find in sideshow alley. Certainly the man sitting across the aisle from me, after I'd interrupted him again just so I could tell him how miserable Birmingham was, seemed eager to ram a couple of balls down my throat.

Birmingham, or at least the bit I saw from the comfort of the train, looks ripe for a bit of gentrification, though considering what's still to be done to London, it could be quite a while coming.

•

I stood on Crewe station, dizzy with exhaustion, cursing the British rail system and my own romantic idiocy at wanting to arrive in Ireland by sea. I must admit my getting-there-is-half-the-fun theory was wearing thin.

There was an information office and a queue leading into it that stretched halfway along the platform. I wasn't in any particular need of information—I figured that there would be departure boards and announcements about times and destinations—but at least it would give me someone to talk to, so I joined the end of the queue.

'Coomfar?' said the woman in front of me, swivelling around. She was wearing one of those dour old ladies' coats that have been handed down from Dickensian times.

'Sorry?'

'Coomfar?'

Australians travelling in regional England should know that most of its inhabitants lead such hectic lives they tend not to bother with linguistic trivialities such as pronouns or their preceding verbs. For a moment I thought "Coomfar" might have been a village in Wales, but then I realised she'd simply omitted the superfluous "Have" and "you" from the sentence. And had "Coomfar" been a village in Wales, it would have been spelt "Cymghmfmeefrggheeffrrdrhyrrggfggyyhhghh".

With Crewe possibly Sydney's true antipodes, I had come about as far as it was possible to. In fact I figured that if I took one more step, I'd technically be on my way back home.

I decided to play it cool, like a man who, for reasons of abject hilarity, wanders around with a light bulb in his pocket for twenty-five years, waiting for the day when somebody in a pub asks him for a light.

I chewed a non-existent piece of gum and blew an imaginary smoke-ring out of my left nostril. 'Sydney.'

For some reason this totally failed to impress her. Still, I suppose she realised that travelling halfway around the world "these days" simply involved sitting down for a day and, where possible, getting drunk while they rotated the world beneath you. I may have come a long way, but I was hardly Scott of the Antarctic.

'Whereyofftothen?'

I did a quick translation in my head. 'Ireland.'

'Whatyouguintherefor?'

I chewed my gum at her. This was a question that I was still coming to terms with myself. What was I to tell her?

- "I'm trying to find my spiritual home."
- "I'm hoping to finally make sense of the world and my place in it."
- "I'm undergoing a midlife crisis and if I backpack around Ireland for a month it's cheaper than buying a shiny red meno-Porsche."
- "Fuck off, you nosy old bag and leave me alone!"

'I'm hoping to join the professional Morris-dancing tour. It's just finished a sell-out season in England and it's now working its way across Ireland and on to the States.'

'Youreadancer?'

'Yeah. I used to be in Riverdance actually.' I bowed my head sadly. 'But I was turfed out for using my arms.'

Six

The Paddy Wagon

Having been told by the man dispensing wisdom at the information booth that my train would be leaving from platform nine in about an hour, I dragged my weary carcass and my bag up and over the footbridge and down onto the platform, which was completely deserted.

Platform ten, where I had been standing until now, had not only the information booth, but a café, the occasional train, the old lady who thought I was a Morris-dancer with professional aspirations, and who'd left suggesting that it might turn out nice, and, well, everyone else.

The people on that platform were staring at me as if I'd just taken a break from French-kissing a nun. I suppose there was little else to draw their gaze so it was, *Hey, everyone, there's a guy over on that other platform now. Let's all stare at him.* I was thinking about doing a moonwalk, but after twenty-two hours on the plane I didn't think my knees were up to it.

I contemplated one of my stand-up comedy sets, but

the acoustics weren't up to that and there was a fair chance of my being carted off in a net.

As time passed and I was still the only one on the platform, I started to think that I might have been given the wrong information. Or that the information was right and I'd just misheard it. Either way I surely couldn't have been the only one travelling to Holyhead that day. Taking a good look around, it was clear that my platform, with its rusting baggage trolleys and tumbleweed blowing through, hadn't serviced a train in years. So I felt even more self-conscious and suddenly very English. If my train was to arrive now on the other platform, I would be forced to pick up my bag and scamper back over the footbridge like a complete pillock and everyone would be laughing. I didn't know what was happening to me. I'd stopped caring what people thought about me when I was fourteen, on the day that I'd fainted with heat exhaustion.

•

As a teenager I was extremely thin. Painfully and self-consciously so. I acquired the nickname "Spaghetti Legs" shortly after starting at Pendle Hill High School because my mother, like most mothers, had a seriously misguided idea of where the hips are, and insisted that I arrive at school, on my first day, with the waistband of my trousers up around my chest. This of course accentuated the length of my spaghetti legs. I was suddenly looking at the world through my fly. I must have looked like Big Bird as I loped across the quadrangle and I might just have survived the experience had I not been so thin. But the truth of the matter is that I was skinny enough to stand outside in a tropical downpour and remain dry. Some of the guys in my year used to tell me that although they appreciated my efforts for charity, I really ought to come off the forty-hour famine before malnutrition set in. And there was nothing worse for a self-consciously thin teenager growing up in Sydney in the seventies than walking onto one of those electronic door opening mats and have it fail to register your presence. I used to have to loaf around outside the building until someone with a better body came along whom I could follow in—the doors snapping at my heels like a hungry crocodile.

But just after I'd turned fourteen, I developed a crush on a dental nurse and felt that I needed a larger body so I could avoid having sand kicked in my eyes in the event that we found ourselves on the beach, in the desert, or at a cement plant. Showing perception that I didn't think he possessed, my father, bless him, bought me a Bullworker for my birthday. The Bullworker was a sort of medieval torture device designed to build muscle and false hopes in the seven stone weakling. I had trouble lifting the thing out of its box. After a week of intensive use, however, I was disappointed that my chest had failed to appear hewn from granite, and had not sprouted even a single hair. In fact it was starting to look more and more like a birdcage—and a birdcage that had been heaved out on council cleanup day at that.

I suppose it was a bit optimistic, expecting to look like the guy from the Bullworker instruction booklet in time for my next appointment with the dentist, especially with the hole in my tooth getting bigger by the minute and the guy in the booklet having a porn-star moustache and everything, but you can dream, can't you? Since my new body had refused to materialise, though, I did the only thing you could do under the circumstances. On the morning of my appointment I slipped on six jumpers and admired my Brutus-like reflection in the mirror. Now this was more like it. Who needed Bullworkers, weight-gain powder or a gym membership when you had a grandmother who was an accomplished knitter? Why bother with putting on "six ounces after only ten weeks' exercise" when you could crochet your way to a newer you? I was huge. I was immense. Sure, my legs were still a problem, but I figured if I wore my baggiest pants, once I sat down on the dentist's chair and they billowed out to the side it would be impossible for the nurse to tell where the pants ended and my legs began.

I paid the bus driver my fare and cast him a look that said, *Don't mess with me, pal—I'm encased in wool!* and walked down the aisle to the back seat as if I was carrying a couple of soccer balls under my arms. All the stitching in my armpits made it tremendously difficult to hold my hands to my sides. They kept floating up into the air as if someone had tied bunches of helium balloons to them. Not that this mattered overmuch—if anything it made me appear even bigger. And so what if I clunked a couple of passengers on the head as I sashayed past? My elbows were well padded.

The plan might have proved successful had it not been the height of summer and about thirty-five degrees in the shade that day. The liquefying asphalt shimmered on the horizon as the sun baked tyres to road. At the back of the bus, sitting just above the engine, I began to wilt like a tulip in a jacuzzi. When we finally reached Parramatta I only managed to make it about a hundred metres from the bus before I collapsed in a heap. I eventually scooped myself up off the ground, with the aid of the Salvation Army, and somehow arrived in time for my appointment. Much to my disappointment, however, my new body made absolutely no impression on the nurse, largely because it was her day off, and to make things worse the dentist wrote a stinging letter of complaint to my parents because I'd devoured a Chiko roll just before I got on the bus and still had large chunks of cabbage, carrot and gunge wrapped around my teeth.

When I arrived back home I ripped off my woollen sauna and gazed at my sweating corpse in the bathroom mirror. In my effort to appear bigger I'd lost about five kilograms. Here I was, then, fourteen years old and I'd just discovered irony—so at least the day hadn't been a total waste.

I lay in bed that night feeling the first faint symptoms of malaria and decided that once I was discharged from the tropical diseases ward I would no longer care what people thought about me, if only for the sake of my health. People could take me as I was or not at all. I would no longer give the remotest shit. And up to this point it had mostly worked.

•

But now, standing on my deserted platform I suddenly did care what people thought of me. Complete strangers who I would never see again held the key to my immediate happiness and sense of self-worth. And I was prepared to stand there all night if necessary rather than risk the humiliation of admitting my error and haul myself back over the footbridge for their amusement.

The woman I'd met waiting for information, let's call her Violet, was standing with another elderly woman who was also wearing one of *those* coats. They both chose that moment to wave at me so I gave them a little wave back. Several other people waved back at me.

To my immense relief a fast approaching freight train offered me a way out of this insane little dilemma I'd got myself into.

The thing is, I don't think my own view offers the best perspective on what happened next. But the narrative form I've chosen doesn't allow me to simply cut away and observe myself from the other platform. It'd be the same if this was a novel: convention dictates that I can't simply switch to a minor character's perspective even though it would serve the story better. A far better medium for this scene would be a film script—so let's run with that:

EXT.   CREWE RAILWAY STATION.   DAY.

John, a thirty-something Australian writer and performer, is standing alone on what is evidently the wrong platform. Opposite him is a large crowd of commuters, all on the correct platform. They are staring at him and making fun of his Gore-tex jacket—or at least through some jet-lag induced paranoia, John believes they are.

CUT TO:

John. Staring back at the crowd.

CUT TO:

Two shot of Violet and Mavis—a couple of elderly women who are on the correct platform. They are looking across at John.

[VIOLET]

Wonder what he's doing over there, the daft bugger. They haven't used that platform since the war.

[MAVIS]

Second World War?

[VIOLET]

Crimean.

[MAVIS]
And is that Gore-tex he's wearing?
[VIOLET]
You know, I believe it is.
[MAVIS]
He's probably one of them train spotters.
[VIOLET]
Let's mess with his mind.

Violet and Mavis wave at John.

CUT TO:

Violet's POV as John, somewhat reluctantly, returns their wave.

CUT TO:

Shot of freight train hurtling past between the two platforms.

CUT TO:

Violet's POV. John is obscured by the freight train.

CUT TO:

Two shot of Violet and Mavis.
[VIOLET]
Will you look at that?

Violet and Mavis appear quite shocked.

CUT TO:

Violet's POV. The freight train has gone but so has John.

CUT TO:

Two shot of Violet and Mavis looking up and down the deserted platform.
[VIOLET]
What do you suppose happened to him?
[MAVIS]
Maybe it's like one of them *Harry Potter* things.

CUT TO:

John sitting in the station café. There are a couple of empty coffee mugs on his table as well as a half-eaten slice of carrot cake and the shell of a meat pie. It's obvious that he's been there for quite some time. He is making notes on his writing pad.

CUT TO:

Two shot of Violet and Mavis looking thoughtfully up at the dark sky.
[MAVIS]
Might turn out nice.

•

In times of extreme stress the human mind can process vast quantities of information at a greater than normal rate. Thus to the person undergoing the trauma it appears as though the events are being slowed down. This means that anyone who inadvertently finds him or herself in the midst of an erupting volcano, car accident, earthquake, flash flood, or game show can sometimes miraculously escape before any real damage is inflicted.

Once the freight train had concealed me from the crowd on the other platform I was up and over that footbridge in the blink of an eye. I bounded down the steps eight at a time like bionic Lee Majors in *The Six Million Dollar Man*—there was even an accompanying electronic *boooooiiiiiiiiiinnnnnnggggggg* coming from an unidentified source (quite possibly me) as I flew along the footbridge. I managed to get a seat in the café, consume a couple of cups of coffee, a meat pie and half a slice of carrot cake long before the freight train's caboose had even entered the station.

About an hour or so later, when normal mental services had resumed, I took my seat on the British equivalent of a boxcar. The train was so meagre in its appointments and so utterly depressing that I half expected a hobo to appear in the doorway of my compartment clutching a sack, a dog, and a workable theory on economic reform. It made any of our own long-since decommissioned red-rattlers look like the first class dining car on the Orient Express. It was as if the urban planners of London and Birmingham had got together, opted for a career change and wouldn't be deterred from moving into railway carriage design.

The car was broken up into compartments, so,

clutching my ticket, I entered the one designated first-class. If anything, it was worse than the others. A yellowed and faded picture of Stonehenge decorated one of the walls which were splintered and damp like the inside of a child's abandoned cubbyhouse. That the walls weren't festooned with huntsman spiders the size of dinner plates was the carriage's only saving grace.

There was one other passenger in the compartment: a well-dressed young man of about thirty who immediately struck me as the sort of guy who read James Patterson novels and phoned his wife to let her know that his train was almost home and ask, if possible, could she pick him up from the station.

'Excuse me,' I said, 'but is *this* first class?'

The man put down his mobile phone and his James Patterson novel, took one look at my cargo pants and my bedraggled been-on-the-road-for-the-past-thirty-six-hours-and-crossed-several-time-zones features and said, in a thick Welsh accent, 'Yes. But don't worry, they probably won't throw you out if they catch you.'

I slumped into my soiled and slashed seat.

So this was one of the infamous paddy wagons. I'd heard of them certainly, but, like the Bermuda Triangle, UFOs, wailing banshees, and the music of Human Nature, I wasn't prepared to accept its existence until I'd encountered one for myself.

I don't for one nanosecond believe in conspiracy theories. The idea that somewhere there exists a shadowy elite who know what's best for us and will stop at nothing to prevent our getting to the truth is a concept that I frankly find laughable. Take UFOs for example. There isn't a single scrap of evidence to support their existence. They are the fairies at the bottom of the garden. Yet there are some conspiracy theorists who want so desperately to believe in them that they insist there has been a government and military cover-up since the 1940s.

"I'm telling you, my cousin Virgil's got this Polaroid of four alien corpses on a secret military base in the Mojave desert."

"Is that the one where the aliens are wearing those flared satin jumpsuits and the 'I Love Lucy' badges?"

"Yeah. How'd *you* know?"

"Saw it in *America's Most Gullible Wanker* magazine."

Now let's just suppose for a moment that a race of hyper-intelligent beings *have* discovered a way to cross the sickening void between their planet and our own. Are we really expected to believe that a race so technologically advanced would arrive here in the dead of night but forget to switch off their hazard lights, and then spend their time leaping out from behind trees and yelling "boo" at a succession of Alabama farmers and highway patrol officers before getting to work with their anal probes?

Okay let's flip it around. Let's imagine that SETI (Search for Extra Terrestrial Intelligence—a serious investigation into the possible existence of alien life which scans the heavens for radio signals rather than little green men in Alcoa foil suits) discovered a habitable planet in, say, the Andromeda galaxy. And let's suppose that NASA scientists and engineers managed to bang together a shuttle that could get us there in a relatively zippy hundred million light years. Then let's say NASA were able to recruit and train a couple of dozen astronauts who wouldn't object to being cooped up together for the requisite hundred million years—the cast of *Big Brother* perhaps (and I for one would love to see them blasted into the stratosphere. Though there are, of course, problems inherent in using a communal swimming pool in a weightless environment). Or maybe the scientists could find a way to put the astronauts to sleep for a hundred million years—a perpetually looped tape of the entire *Big Brother* series ought to do the trick. Whatever the method, let's just hypothesise that such a journey is achievable.

So finally, having spanned the seemingly infinite nothingness between Earth and the Andromeda galaxy—a journey that constitutes a mere blip in our ever-expanding universe—our intrepid star trekkers remember to switch off the hazard lights, and manoeuvre the undetected ship carefully down into a backwoods field. But, rather than exchange ideas on science, technology, art, culture, philosophy, and health with the inhabitants of this strange planet, all they can think to do is to insert a probe up an unsuspecting farmer's bottom (now *that's* a close encounter), steal a cow, turn around and fly off home.

One of my Irish uncles once told me about the paddy wagons that supposedly ran between England and Holyhead and that it was all part of a conspiracy to discourage tourists from travelling to Ireland and to generally piss the Irish off. And I remember rolling my eyes rather shamelessly at such an absurd theory. Looking about my first-class boxcar now, I was forced to admit that it all had a distinct whiff of the Smoking Man about it.

Seven

Have You Ever Been across the Sea to Ireland?

Having resigned myself to spending the night in Holyhead, I got off the train and was pleasantly surprised to find a ferry smouldering away at the dock, ready to leave. Of course I shouldn't have been surprised. The ticket seller at Euston Station said that he didn't think I had a chance in hell of making it to Ireland that day, so I should naturally have assumed that I would.

A succession of uniformed men along the railway platform, their arms rotating like windmills in a gale, tried to hurry us along to the ferry.

I remember when I was a teenager watching late one night this appalling footage of the Nazis herding Soviet Jews off a bus and then making them run, at gunpoint, into a mass grave before they executed them. The calculated cruelty of this act of sheer barbarism shocked me—it's not enough for us to take your life, we're going to deny you any last semblance of dignity in the process. From that moment I resolved never to run again if someone was shouting at me. Although such naive idealism achieved exactly nothing, besides infuriating one psychotic soccer coach after another, it stayed with me.

So while the other dozen or so passengers hurtled down the ramp like the coyote pursuing the roadrunner over a cliff in pair of jet-powered ACME roller-skates that he was still coming to terms with, I ambled along behind. One of the runners was Mavis, Violet's friend from Crewe railway station, whose legs were clearly not up to the pace—not with that much baggage anyway, and certainly not without a good solid warm-up and stretch. A desperate clutch at the back of her leg about halfway down the ramp suddenly told me that she had torn a hamstring, quite possibly off the bone.

I was meant to be travelling with the Stenna line, but when I presented myself at the Stenna check-in desk I was immediately handed over to the Irish Ferries company because that was its ship out there in the fast-descending gloom. Apparently it was too rough for the zippier Stenna boats.

'Okay,' said the check-in woman, examining my ticket. 'If you go through that door and down to the bus...'

'Bus?'

'The shuttle bus that'll take you out to the ship.'
'Oh, right.'
'You'll have to run, though.'

What was it with this country and running? Part of some perverse Welsh fitness program? 'Excuse me,' I said. 'I've been travelling for the past thirty-six hours. I haven't slept in over a week. I'm tired. I'm cross. I'm hungry. And I've just watched Wile E Coyote's great grandmother damage a major muscle group because she was instructed to run. I'm not running for anyone—particularly not Nazis,' I added quietly.

She threw me a hoity look, 'They're about to close the stern doors.'

'Well, that'll make the crossing immeasurably safer.' I smiled, proving to everyone present that I was a complete smartarse.

I shouldered my backpack, strolled down to the bus, and stepped on board, just as the doors closed behind me. I was too cool to be allowed to go on living.

I glanced round and saw that Mavis hadn't made it onto the bus. Either her injuries weren't up to the crossing, or she wasn't going to Ireland at all and had simply been caught up in the moment.

As we headed along the wharf towards the ship, I was actually a bit disappointed that things had worked out so well for me and I realised that I had been rather looking forward to spending the night in Holyhead. I had passed through the town several times now, and it had always struck me as an agreeable enough sort of place because, apart from anything else, I really like port towns. There's still a tremendous sense of adventure in them, and as you look out on the ocean you start wondering about the romance of the sea and the life of a merchant seaman. Though, I suppose, having an ocean view isn't the same if you're in it.

I would have liked to wander through the town and down to the docks to have spontaneous conversation with weather-beaten old sailors. Men who seem to conform to every seafaring stereotype: wooden leg, parrot on the shoulder, flowing grey-white hair and beard, and who finish every sentence with '...aarrhh aaaarrrrhhhh, matey.' I must admit that my nautical reading hasn't extended much beyond Long John Silver.

But on second thoughts, I was probably lucky to have made it onto the ferry after all. Cruising the docks in the hope of meeting sailors could very well end up being alarmingly misinterpreted.

•

I made my way up through the bowels of the ferry with the other "foot passengers"—a strange term for those of us who had taken the ferry but left our motorised transport behind. There seemed to be an endless number of decks, so that the ferry was almost as high as it was long—or that's how it felt. It was like sailing inside a wedding cake.

At last I was on the main deck and I checked the

layout of the ferry on a wall map near the foot of the stairs. I wanted to find somewhere relatively quiet—a restaurant or bar—where I could sit in comfort for a while, gather my thoughts and write up the notes I am working from now.

Several children, who had been sensibly dosed up on sugar for the crossing, hurtled about and around me, while their parents sheltered in the duty free shop, no doubt intending to get well dosed up themselves. Now I adore children as much as any parent—or, to be more truthful, what I adore are my own children. Others I prefer to admire from a safe distance protected by an electrified field. I've wiped up my own children's poo and vomit and snot with my bare hands and thought nothing of it. (They're not neglected—I'm just making a point here.) Yet when my nephew accidentally drooled on my neck during a shoulder ride at the Easter Show last year, I was so repulsed that I had to be physically restrained from killing myself with a fairy-floss stick.

These lovely children had graciously incorporated me into their chasings game—I was "B.A.R." apparently, whatever that was. Something to do with their parents' attempts to disguise their whereabouts, I imagine.

'Yes, yes. Cute,' I said to one precocious brat who'd crawled through my legs to render me safe. 'You know if you lean right out over the railings, you can sometimes see the propellers.'

Checking the wall map again, I noticed that there

was a bar called the Sky Lounge on the top deck, up eleven steep flights of stairs, probably at the insistence of those travelling without children. With the prospect of panoramic views over the Irish Sea and a child-free environment, I immediately cramponned my way up and found to my delight that the Sky Lounge was almost empty. I soon discovered that this wasn't due to the fact that it *was* up eleven flights of stairs, though that had to be a contributing factor. Rather it was because the Irish Sea is notoriously wild and the further you move away from the waterline, the more violent the pitch and roll and heave of the ship appear.

As I entered the lounge a couple of young backpackers were stumbling out, their faces a startling shade of green. They had their hands clapped over their mouths as if they were about to utter what some of my countrymen refer to as a technicoloured yawn. As I settled back into one of the plush lounges by the window, I couldn't help but feel sorry for these poor girls. They were clearly in for one hell of a crossing, because at this stage we were still tied up at the dock.

No sooner had we slipped out to sea than the bar opened for business and all the passengers in the Sky Lounge, most of them sea-hardened truck drivers, descended on it like crows onto carrion.

There were only about twenty of them, and although I fancied a drink and perhaps something to eat myself, I decided to hold back for a while. The speed at which the truck drivers hit the bar suggested that they were seriously thirsty and intended to arrive in Ireland completely rat-faced. I didn't want to be flattened in the race and as I waited I was thinking it wouldn't do a lot of harm for the Irish police (the Garda) to set up a random breath testing unit around the port.

Eventually I made my way to the bar, held onto the counter for dear life and wondered how the hell I was supposed to get a drink back to my seat without tipping it all over the floor, or worse, a tattooed trucker. Suddenly I understood the truck drivers' haste. They weren't alcoholics; they were seasoned crossers and knew they had to get their drinks back to their table before we sailed out beyond the breakwater and the real fun began.

We weren't far out of the harbour—in fact I could still make out the shine on the shuttle bus driver's scalp, and he was at home eating dinner—when the ferry began to roll about like Stevie Wonder's head when he's at the piano. The only option seemed to be to drink my coffee at the bar and save face by getting into some small talk with the barman.

After an initial exchange he asked me a question that I was to be asked throughout my stay.

'What the feck are you going to Ireland in November for?'

For some reason the Irish assume that people visit their country for the climate. My uncle maintains that there are two states of weather in Ireland—either it's raining, or it's going to rain. I'd figured that I would be asked this question quite often (though not as often as it turned out), so before I left home I had the answer ready.

'I'm not on holidays; I'm working actually.' I slurped casually on my coffee, but the ferry suddenly hit a trough, and it washed out of my cup and over the bar.

'Don't mind that. I'll mop it up later. So what is it you do, if you don't mind me asking?' continued the barman, dabbing at the spill with a tea towel.

'I'm in the music business.'

'Really? What are you—a talent scout or something?'

I nodded. 'Yeah. Something like that.' I leaned in conspiratorially. 'I'm on a mission...'

'From God?' The barman was obviously a fan of *The Blues Brothers*.

'You might say that. It's a secret assignment.'

'Surprise me.'

'My role, and I'm prepared to die for it if necessary, is to prevent the formation of any more boy bands.'

He looked up at me and smirked. 'I'll drink to that, all right.'

Five minutes later I was back in my seat, staring at my second cup of coffee that the barman insisted on paying for and carrying back to the table for me. 'See if you can get those feckin Westlife gobshites to disband while you're at it, can you?'

Larkin about in IRELAND

I took a slug of the coffee and fiddled with my pen. The sea was far too violent for notes to be committed to anything other than memory. A huge shudder ran the length of the ship as we crashed through the heaving swell. It wasn't just wild out there any more; it was dangerous. The Sky Lounge was strangely silent. I had to time the surges in my coffee cup if I wanted to keep drinking, so I nodded and baulked like a child trying to join a skipping game.

When my family emigrated to Australia at the end of the sixties, we did so on the Italian cruise ship the *Achille Lauro*, which sadly now rests on the bottom of the Indian Ocean off the coast of Somalia. It was on this fairly intense seven-week voyage, quite often through wild and brutal seas, that I acquired my sea legs. Apart from a brief cruise on *Fairstar The Vomit Ship* when I was nineteen, my seafaring since has been limited to an occasional trip across Sydney Harbour on the Manly ferry, but my sea legs have somehow remained sturdy.

Jacqui and I once took a day cruise out from Fremantle to Rottnest Island on a prawning boat. It was soon clear that I'd chosen the wrong sort of day to be out on the Indian Ocean, particularly with someone who gets seasick in the bath. The smell of raw prawns didn't help much either, so when we arrived at Rottnest, Jacqui's face was the colour Dr Seuss used in his story about green eggs and ham. As I was carrying her up to the island's hospital, I rather foolishly made this observation and everyone around us was immediately forced to leap back several paces. I waved her off at the airport on that afternoon's mail flight, and had to make the return journey alone. It was even wilder but I slept pretty much all the way back.

Looking about the hushed bar now, I didn't sense that kind of sturdiness in some of my fellow Sky Loungers.

To pass the time, I decided to run a little book on which of them would be the first at the helm of the porcelain bus.

Perhaps arrogantly, given the presence of the truck drivers, I ranked myself least likely to bolt off for a hurl. Although I believed that the truck drivers could go the distance, twenty minutes into the voyage their numbers had halved, and they'd halved again shortly afterwards. There was no way they were going to outlast me. The remaining few had been playing cards with some enthusiasm when I finally sauntered up to the bar for that coffee, but they had since abandoned their game and were now busy staring out at the black horizon. I ranked them accordingly.

There was a young Italian guy a couple of lounges along from me who didn't look at all well. He was having his hair stroked tenderly by his Irish girlfriend as his head lay groaning in her lap. But considering his girlfriend's drop-dead looks and the position his head was in, I suspected a cunning Latin ruse. (Did you hear the one about the Italian honeymooner who was so tired he fell asleep as soon as his feet hit the pillow?) The girlfriend made occasional "There, there. The ship's not sinking. You won't be going down" noises. But I wasn't entirely convinced she was right. At any rate he was immediately disqualified from my sweep for not playing by the rules.

On the next seat along were a couple of Australian women in their late twenties or early thirties. One of them never uttered a word for the entire crossing, mainly because she couldn't get one in. The other woman, Ms Shutthefuckup, could have talked underwater with a mouthful of marbles. When we sailed out of Holyhead she said (and I can hardly bring myself to record it), "Well there goes Wales. I can't say that I had a *whale* of a time." See what I mean? It wasn't the appalling pun itself that got up my nose, but her need to emphasise the punchline and share it with everyone in the lounge. This may have had something to do with the mass exodus of truck drivers. Tragically, though, she'd hit such a rich vein of humour she was clearly determined to mine it to exhaustion. 'I wonder if Ireland's where they made *Gilligan's Ireland*?' 'I bet Germaine Greer's never been to the Isle of *Man*!' 'Do you know why the Ku Klux Klan never drink Guinness?' The world held its breath. 'Because it's *black*.' I noticed the red trainers she was wearing and thought that perhaps if I could get her to click her heels together three times, she might just fuck off to Kansas.

Fortunately her brain was so preoccupied talking the legs off chairs there was no way it was going to have enough cells to recognise seasickness. So we wouldn't be seeing her lean out over the railings and heave into the ocean. Though if her puns continued, the rest of us might.

I must admit to being wary of Australians overseas anyway. I mean let's be honest—we are embarrassing. Example: we don't speak French but we think it will help matters if we speak English in a French accent. I was in Paris the year before and had watched, in utter bewilderment, one of my countrymen swagger up to a local and say, "Yeah. G'day, mate. Could you tell me ze way to ze *Arca da Triomphe*?" I mean you don't get French people coming up to you in Sydney and saying, "*Excusez-moi, monsieur. Could you, ar, tell me the way to the, ar,* **Rewty Heel RSL club**?" What was he thinking?

The previous year I'd visited Stonehenge for research and watched agog as a bus load of young Australians pulled up in the car park and immediately unfurled a large Southern Cross and a boxing kangaroo flag and hung them out the windows of the bus. A couple of them, who hadn't yet rendered themselves completely brain-dead, went and had a look around the "rocks and stuff", while the rest took out a footy and had a bit of a kick around one of the nearby fields. I don't know what was on their minds, but it probably wasn't much.

As soon as we travel overseas we feel obliged to uphold cultural stereotypes: maybe because we're unused to the attention of an international audience; perhaps hoping that the stereotypes will somehow bring us closer to home. Following my brief relationship with Portia the Sloane Ranger, I was walking through Earls Court to meet up with a friend for lunch. As I sauntered down the street to my friend's flat (I'd taken to sauntering after the break-up) I noticed a bunch of blokes wearing Drizabone coats, Akubra hats, and drinking cans of Foster's, leering down from a first floor balcony and sneering at passers-by.

'Hey, here comes a good-looking pommy sheila.'
'G'day, love! Want a shag?'
'She's ignoring you, Davo.'
'Muff tucker for sure, I reckon.'

I once included that exchange in a story, and the editor deleted it because it wasn't believable.

My conversation with these balcony boys was equally succinct.

'Check out the pommy poof in the purple ski jacket.'
'I'm from Sydney actually.'
'Are you *actually*? Whereabouts then, mate?'
'Toongabbie.'
'Well, come up and have a beer then.'

'No thanks. I'd rather eat the arse out of a dead wombat.' Sec? I was doing it myself.

'Must be a poof.'

'Reckon.'

'Another beer, Davo?'

'Are Kiwi sheep nervous?'

We must have been about three-quarters of the way across the Irish Sea—the rocking of the ferry so violent now that even Ms Shutthefuckup was down to a subdued thousand words per minute—when a new starter in the Lounge had me rewriting the odds. Although he'd taken the table next to mine, I didn't notice him at first—either because I was dozing or because I was still trying to figure out how I could knock the pompom off Ms Shutthefuckup's silly ski-hat with a croquet mallet and not get arrested.

The new entrant was a well-heeled American who looked like a cross between Grizzly Adams and Bill Bryson—if such a coupling were agreeable to both parties and to ultimately prove fruitful, that is. He was reading one of those books that Americans go for, *How to Make a Zillion Dollars While Protecting Your Inner Child* or something similar. Looking at him again, though, I was forced to relegate myself to second rank in the hurling odds. Not only was he reading his book as if this was a pleasant afternoon on solid ground, he had a couple of pints of Guinness on the go and was eating something out of a brown-paper bag that didn't look or smell much different from the aforementioned green eggs and ham.

Despite my sea legs I could feel the colour rapidly draining from my face.

An open-air deck that was possibly a passageway for the crew led off from the Lounge. I ignored the "No Passengers Beyond This Point" sign, opened the door, stepped into an arctic gale, and immediately let out an involuntary high-pitched yelp, like a chihuahua having its testicles seized by a vet. Several other Sky Loungers joined me, no doubt driven outside by Grizzly Bryson's wrought-iron stomach and constitution.

The sea mist stung my face like a flight of kamikaze mosquitoes, but the pitching of the ferry wasn't as furious as it had been earlier, and although the air was so frigid that I sounded like an asthmatic duck whenever I inhaled, I still felt considerably better.

The ferry had slowed slightly and in the distance I could make out the lights of Dublin stretching from Howth in the north to Sandycove in the south.

I'd made it.

Approximately forty hours and thirty thousand words after setting out, I'd arrived.

I stood on the deck and strained to make out some detail of the coastline through the heavy night air. The plummeting temperature soon drove everyone but me and a man who was wearing a hollowed-out sheep back inside. The wind-chill factor had frozen my lips solid and I found myself chatting to the sheep in what sounded like a Swedish accent. Bearing in mind the volume of Guinness I intended to consume in the following weeks, it seemed like an appropriate homecoming.

PART 2
There

Eight

Spanners

Oscar Wilde is credited with saying that wherever he journeyed he generally found that "Ireland is everyone's second favourite country. A notion that is often shared by the Irish themselves."

Actually he said no such thing. But it's the kind of remark he might have made if someone had been following him around with a notebook and a pencil with the intention of compiling a desk calendar.

There are something like fifty-five million Irish people scattered throughout the world. What *is* said, though not by Oscar Wilde, is that the fifty million who live overseas want to live in Ireland, whereas the five million who actually live in the place want to live overseas.

It's a land of contradiction and confusion, as anyone who has stood on an Irish roadside next to a swaying and rotating signpost knows. St Patrick, for instance, the most famous Irishman of them all, was actually Welsh. A Welshman with an extreme phobia of snakes.

One thing that confused me even on my first visit

as a three-year-old was the way the Irish would sing heartfelt, sob-inducing songs about how much they missed the place. These songs generally included misty mountains rolling down to the sea, low-lying fields, the desire to wander about with a shillelagh (a polished hardwood stick handy for beating someone's brains out), and the consumption of vast quantities of whiskey and porter. Songs that invariably culminated in the singers lying fairly low in a field themselves.

The thing is these songs were generally sung by people who'd never left the place.

Oh, the fields of my childhood, so dewy and green. I yearn to lie down in them again 'fore my spleen...

'You mean those fields over there behind the car park?'

'Feck off!'

As I opened my bedroom curtains on a day that might have turned out nice (and did) I was determined to discover whether any of these stereotypes were true. I still wasn't certain exactly what my journey to Ireland was all about, but this seemed as good a task as any to be getting on with.

I could feel the dark shroud wrap itself round me as I drank my coffee. I tried to shrug it off and dismiss it as jetlag, but it wouldn't quite go.

For the past decade or so I have been afflicted with the condition that Winston Churchill called his black dog: a condition that has claimed the lives of writers whose pens I'm not worthy of refilling—Hemingway and Woolf, for a start. In its mild form it is extremely exhausting and takes a gargantuan effort just to complete the simplest of tasks such as getting out of bed, paying a bill, or attending to the needs of a crying child. At its worst it becomes a soul-destroying emptiness that leaves its victim craving oblivion. Although it is fairly easy to diagnose, it's not so easy to cure. Some drugs are successful but have side effects. Other drugs are successful despite the fact that they were originally designed for different purposes and lead you into strange conversations with psychiatrists. "Trials in Uzbekistan have found that this one works quite well if taken in sufficiently large doses. It was originally designed to increase the libido in young bulls, but it has proved successful in treating cases like yours. A word of caution: be careful if you happen to find yourself on a dairy farm." Little wonder, then, that after years of feeling like a six-foot tall lab rat, I've chosen to ride it out and simply retreat to the spare room when the dark shroud descends.

But that's only been possible because I've always had my family there for support: Jacqui, who is a tower of strength and knows when I need to be left alone, and our daughter Chantelle, who wants me not to go away on tour so much and is prepared to sell lemonade out in the street to cover the shortfall. How was I going to survive without them if things turned ugly?

I tried not to think about it too much and returned to the task at hand. Tracking down the clichés.

One thing I would definitely *not* be doing on this trip, though, was going off to look for leprechauns.

Back home, I have this program about Ireland: one of the many produced each year by the lifestyle and holiday shows that we've been inundated with in recent years. Their main function is to give the producer an all-expenses-paid holiday, and the host the chance to bestow his oh-so-hilarious Irish accent on anyone who isn't fast enough to get out of his way: "See you, Jimmy. Och aye the noo." Called *Sodding Off*, or something similar, it starts promisingly enough with a brief investigation into the history of "The Troubles" in Londonderry. Five minutes later, though, having run out of ideas, the documentary crew pack up their minibus, head out into the country and, to the lasting shame of everyone associated with the program, spend the rest of the time wandering around fields, across streams and through abandoned castles looking for leprechauns with a view to capturing one and securing his crock of gold. Highly ironic, given that most of the program was a crock of something else entirely.

While, as I've said, I wasn't sure what I was looking for on this trip, I was determined that it would at least have a basis in reality.

But having written all this over breakfast and a plunger of industrial strength coffee on my first morning in Ireland, I suddenly had this vague recollection of a leprechaun squatting in the corner of my bedroom at some point during the night. He wasn't handing out crocks of gold or fishing from a toadstool or engaged in any such stereotypical endeavour; he was working on something in the wardrobe with a monkey wrench the size of a sledgehammer.

The previous evening I had been collected from the Dublin Port ferry terminal by my friends Richard and Paula. Richard was an old pal from Sydney who had temporarily settled in Dublin with his Irish wife Paula, partly because as a cultured young man he wanted to experience life in another country, but mostly, I suspect, with a view to retiring at forty, after making a killing in the information technology industry—Dublin had become a sort of second Silicon Valley.

I'd been meant to arrive at Dun Laoghaire (pronounced "Dun Leary") a smaller tourist and leisure craft port on Dublin Bay a few kilometres south of the city itself, and a far more agreeable point of entry to Ireland than the more industrialised Dublin Port at which I *had* in fact arrived. But unfortunately the woman at the Irish Ferries check-in desk had neglected to tell me about the change of destination. If she had, I might have decided to spend the night in Holyhead after all.

Although I had stayed with relatives on previous visits, Richard insisted that I stay with him and Paula this time. After two Dublin winters I guessed that he was starting to feel the first faint pangs of real homesickness and perhaps he thought that having me there might have helped offset some of it. All in all, then, it was a good deal for everyone concerned. I got a free base in Dublin for the length of my stay. And Richard and Paula, for their part, got someone to occupy their spare room, lie on their lounge, raid their fridge, borrow their cars, and make disparaging comments about the weather.

Despite being a native of Ireland, Paula felt the cold as badly as if she had been raised in the Bahamas. Having finally collected my bag from the Irish Ferries' carousel (they must have been using it as ballast because it took about three-quarters of an hour to turn up) I slumped into the back seat of Richard and Paula's car and immediately started to hallucinate camels. I have never known heat like it. My eyes were sweating and my tongue lolled out of my mouth like a pervert's at a peepshow.

Paula was wearing the sort of ensemble that might occur to someone making an attempt on the upper slopes of K2, or a love-struck teenager visiting the dentist, but despite this she started to make prolonged *bbbbbrrrrrrrrr*-type noises. 'Could you turn the heat up a bit, Richard?'

My eyes widened to the size of the London millennium wheel. *Turn it up?* Turn it up, all right! There were already flames from the aircon vent lapping at Richard's hand like thirsty dogs. Unlike me, though,

Richard was an accomplished handyman. Unfortunately. A total wiz with a toolkit and a soldering iron, he liked nothing better than poking about inside computers, car engines, and other bits of technology. Clearly, he'd fitted the car's heater with a nuclear component, which explained the radioactive isotopes in the boot. So up the heat went a couple of notches. Now I don't know if you've ever accidentally found yourself driving through the Simpson Desert at midday with no air-conditioning and the windows up, though I suspect not. But let me tell you that would be a damn sight cooler than going on the road in Ireland with Richard and Paula. I felt myself starting to disintegrate like an ant under a magnifying glass.

I was prepared to put my strange visitation that night down to the lingering hallucinogenic effects of having driven in an imploding sun. There was also the possibility that it might have been due to a couple of bottles of wine and six-pack of beer we'd consumed to celebrate my arrival. A cocktail of jet lag, alcohol, and heat exhaustion was bound to have an impact on anyone's mental agility.

It was only when Richard phoned to apologise a short while later, as I was making my way towards UCD (University College Dublin), that the mystery was finally cleared up.

My nocturnal guest hadn't been a leprechaun at all (now that I thought about it, he'd probably been kneeling); it was Spanners, a genius plumber and handyman who Richard and Paula had employed to assist with their ongoing renovations. Spanners was a true Mozart of the pipes, but his brilliance with a wrench and angle-grinder was matched only by his staggering unreliability. Whenever he *did* turn up, he would casually brush aside complaints that it was three in the morning, or Sunday afternoon and proceed to tear about the house like the Tasmanian devil in those old Warner Bros cartoons. If he encountered a problem that couldn't immediately be beaten into compliance with a heavily wielded claw hammer, he would scratch his head thoughtfully, pack up his toolbox and disappear for weeks at a time. I had apparently caught him towards the end of one his frequent sabbaticals, when he'd hit on the notion that the best way to deal with a troublesome wardrobe-based water heater was to thump it repeatedly with one of my hiking boots.

Over the phone Richard told me that he had staggered to the door around midnight but had been unable to prevent Spanners from racing up the stairs like a greyhound out of its trap.

It all came flooding back now.

'Spanners!' Richard had hissed from the doorway to my bedroom, having finally heaved himself up the stairs in Hurricane Spanners' wake. 'Can you do it in the morning?'

'Just need to make one final delicate adjustment.' THUMP. WHACK. GRIND. CLUNK.

'It's just that...'

THUMP. WHACK. GRIND. CLUNK. 'Oh, there's someone in here,' said Spanners, turning around and surveying the corpse-like thing that passes for my body. 'Sorry about the noise.' THUMP. WHACK. GRIND. CLUNK.

Nine

Horizontal at the Forty Foot

My destination was James Joyce Tower in Sandycove about five kilometres or so to the south of Dun Laoghaire, which itself was a good five kilometres from Richard and Paula's house.

Opened in 1962 as a museum by Joyce's publisher Sylvia Beach, it is a must see for all lovers of Joyce's work or those of us who like the idea of James Joyce and stock our bookshelves with his oeuvre to impress dinner guests.

Note 1: Be warned: the museum is closed more often than it is open and may only be viewed by appointment during the winter months.

Note 2: That last paragraph was starting to take on the tone of a travel guide for a moment, and I do apologise.

Larkin about in IRELAND

My choice of transport for the journey was good old Shanks's pony. I always find that you miss a lot when you are behind the wheel of a car. And I'd adopted a sort of Buddhist ethos for this trip in that the journey was more important than the destination. I also firmly believed that every decision I took would turn out to be the right one.

So, brimming with confidence, or at least brimming with as much confidence as only a man wearing Goretex can be, I made my way through the grounds of UCD surrounded by cocky young undergrads, relieved that my undergraduate days were long behind me. You think you know it all when you start going to university—or at least I did—and it's only when you graduate and gain some experience in the real world that you realise you knew next to nothing. And although now (most of the way through my fourth decade) I still don't know the difference between my arse and my elbow, I at least have a vague idea where they are.

There is a tall structure like a toilet brush standing watch over UCD, an enormous concrete sentinel. I can't imagine what purpose it serves other than as a postmodern sculpture intended to entice passers-by to stare up at it and wonder about its purpose. It's alarmingly phallic and may have even been the sculptor's self-portrait. Or at least it might have, had the sculptor spent most of his life with the business end of his tackle wedged in a novelty ice-cube maker.

Leaving *The Artist's Knob* behind, though I could still see it poking through the trees for several kilometres, I continued on through UCD and made my way down to the waterfront at Booterstown DART (Dublin Area Rapid Transit) station to begin the trek along the front to Sandycove.

I crossed the DART tracks over a footbridge and sat on the sea wall for a while to gather my thoughts and make some notes on *The Artist's Knob*. A bitter easterly wind was howling in off the Irish Sea and chopping up Dublin Bay. But the sun was out and, looking south to the ferry terminal at Dun Laoghaire, I could see that the Stenna ferries were operating again, which meant that it must have been calmer at sea than it had been the day before. Cotton wool clouds swept across the sky and once you were out of the wind it was actually quite pleasant.

All seemed right with the world as I sat back with the sun on my face to enjoy the notion that I was at large in a country that would, under different circumstances, have been my home—had my father not left it or had he returned, as I'm certain he often yearned to do, with the lot of us in tow.

There is a foot/bike path running between Booterstown station and Black Rock. After a few minutes' reflection by the water, I followed the path and was nodded to several times by a number of well-heeled elderly people who'd taken their dogs out for a daily dump.

Pretty much all of the picturesque south side of Dublin Bay, from Black Rock, where I was at the moment, to Sandycove, where I was heading, was doing rather well for itself and it didn't care who knew it. Looked at from a ferry or even from the seawall, the south side of Dublin as it sweeps round the bay seemed to me the sort of place that Postman Pat might retire to.

Thanks to a number of EU grants, generous business and tax incentives, and the creation of its own Silicon Valley, Ireland had become extremely wealthy. Following centuries in the poorhouse the Irish could now look the world in the eye and tell it to feck off! Suddenly the fifty million overseas were moving back "home". The character and culture that was lovely to have but which couldn't usually be dined out on, was now enhanced by something that *could* be dined out on, namely wealth, and Irish expatriates were on their way back in droves. There was still an enormous amount of work to be done on public works infrastructure (the roads, for instance, which were a joke) so that the country could handle the influx of returning immigrants and refugees. But there was no doubt about it: given the number of BMWs and Audis sashaying about the place this particular morning, Ireland was out there, moving and shaking, cutting deals, talking bollocks on mobile phones, and generally going through a period of vast transformation. Even the winos were staggering about in Armani.

The south side of Dublin, though, had always been wealthier than the rest of the country. It was just that now the rest of the country was catching up, and good luck to it.

I followed the path between Salthill and Monkstown DART stations and tried to enjoy the view and take in the air, but focussed more on stepping cautiously round the steaming piles of dog crap that were liberally scattered and smeared along the path. Now why, in a place as evidently wealthy as this, couldn't the council find the necessary funding to clean up the shit? Or, better still, educate people as New Yorkers have been to Scoop the Poop. (In Sydney you practically get lynched if your dog looks like it's about to even break wind in the street, and I'm all for it. Nothing quite ruins your day like going for an impromptu twenty-metre slide before you crack your head a vicious blow on the pavement.)

There was a sign along the path saying that graffiti "artists" would be fined 1500 Irish punts for their endeavours. Myself, I'd make them clean whatever it is they have defaced and then force them to spend a year at art school—oh God, I'm starting to sound like one of those demented callers on talkback radio shows who phone in with an opinion on everything from capital punishment to single mothers. Looking at the sign now, though, I couldn't help but feel what the sign needed was another one next to it to warn that the owners of dogs caught shitting on the path would have their noses rubbed in it. [I am now, more than ever, convinced that I'm nothing more than a pawn in the God of Coincidence's game. Yesterday, as I was writing the piece on Spanners' strange midnight visitation to fix Richard and Paula's water heater, my own water heater expired and needed a costly service call. And today, having completed my slightly tangential but imperative tirade on dog shit, I made myself a coffee, wandered down the garden path to have a ten minute break in one of my hammocks, and what did I tread in? I then spent an energetic ten minutes hurling abuse at the dog and shaking my fist at the sky.]

Like a character in some computer game I finally negotiated Dog Shit Lane (you save time and score more points if you walk along the narrow wall separating the train line from the path) and found myself at Dun Laoghaire's picturesque port. Across the road near the west pier was an eclectic collection of buildings, all of which looked brand new or recently sandblasted in keeping with the generally affluent vibe of the place. One of them was a sort of Mediterranean apartment block that should have looked out of context and yet curiously didn't. In fact the whole vicinity had a distinctly whitewashed feel of southern Spain about it.

Next to this was a semicircular office block that should have looked out of place too, and did. Given the location and the superb view, the cost of leasing was obviously expensive, and the companies who had set up there had to be doing extremely well for themselves. One of the occupants, I was interested to note, was the Berlitz Publishing Company. As anyone who has seen their display racks in airport bookshops knows, they specialise in pocket size phrase books. I reminded myself that I had to learn another language before I turn forty, a resolution I make every New Year's eve.

It is a constant source of shame to me that I have come this far and I'm still completely monolingual. In a rather pathetic attempt to offset my embarrassment, I tend to joke, in a variety of accents, that I may speak only English, but I speak it really, really well, and stuff. Particularly galling when the person I am trying to impress with the gag doesn't in fact understand English. So I end up shouting it, because as all tourists know, English is made instantly comprehensible if it's bellowed. I'm surprised that Berlitz hasn't yet incorporated this methodology in its language programs: "Forget the subtle nuances and wonderful melodic sounds of the French tongue—they're for the French. Turn the cassette volume to maximum (preferably attach a sub-woofer) and repeat in ever increasing intensity:

Where is the train station?
WHERE IS THE TRAIN STATION?

WHERE IS THE (Insert expletive) TRAIN STATION?
YOU KNOW! (Make gesture with hand)
CHOO CHOOO?

If communication remains elusive and you happen to be English or American, now would be a good time to remind them just who saved their worthless French hides in the war." Although I might not be able to speak French, I've discovered that communication is improved immeasurably by waving your arms about. And on a recent visit to Paris when a waiter in one particular café off the Champs Elysées informed me that my two cups of coffee and a pastry cost the equivalent of fifty Australian dollars, I found I could gesticulate quite fluently.

I've been fortunate enough to visit Paris several times, but the best use I've found for my English/French phrase book so far was to hurl it at the windscreen of a taxi whose gesticulating driver seemed eager to despatch me to the next life.

Phrase books are of little use to you in Paris. The same unfortunately cannot be said of dogs, which are integral to the way of life there. Even the ones that aren't surgically attached to the left breasts of old women are still pretty much given, if not the key to the city, then certainly the doggy-door to it. They even seem to bark with Gallic attitude. And while my pocket translator rather cheekily contained the phrase for inviting someone home with me, *"Est-ce que tu veux finir le soir?"*, it was remiss in neglecting to include the exclamation, "That was either one sick dog, or horses are now allowed to travel on the Metro!"

My phrase book, then, was next to useless, even if it was possible to expand the invitation home with the instruction, *"Déshabillez-vous jusqu'à la ceinture, s'il vous plaît"* (*"please undress to the waist"*)—courtesy of the medical section.

For those lacking the requisite linguistic or gesticulating skills, a well-timed sneer can be useful in dealing with homicidal cab drivers or postcard sellers. The intensity of the sneer should be directly proportional to the level of irritation. For instance: if you find yourself being honked at for having the audacity to attempt to cross the road on a zebra crossing, the right side of your upper lip need only curl slightly—this is Paris after all and zebra crossings are provided for zebra use only. Conversely if you happen to be in or around the red-light district and a man dressed like a golfer offers you a night with his sister/brother/poodle in exchange for your laptop/watch/wallet/wife/husband/doberman pinscher, your sneer needs to reach such a level of intensity and vigour that you can actually feel your ear move.

Take a simple request for directions and you'll

understand why I fail to see the value of phrase books. After searching frantically through your book, you finally find the necessary translation and ask a local to furnish you with directions to the station, museum, doctor, laundry, brothel, soup kitchen, whatever. This *local* then lapses into a protracted and detailed response about how you haven't got the slightest clue what's being said and which generally includes a significant amount of arm waving, shoulder shrugging, and invariably culminates with a request to sit on your girlfriend's or boyfriend's face.

An entire and evidently prosperous wing of the publishing industry has built its success on the knowledge that people purchase phrase books as gifts for friends/relatives/work colleagues who are going overseas or might one day.

•

Now I don't know if the sculptor of *The Artist's Knob* had been busy again, or perhaps there was a one hundred year lease or similar legal loophole that allowed such a travesty, but on the waterfront at Dun Laoghaire, on what must surely have been one of the most sought after locations in the whole of south Dublin, there squats a wrecker's yard. Featuring a macabre display of dead engines and the twisted skeletons of exhaust systems, it is as ugly and depressing as only a wrecker's yard can be.

Not wishing to linger by this morbid scene a moment longer, I hurried along to the east pier and strolled out into the bay for its entire length, which was, I would guess, well over half a mile. At one of the docks, there was a ship that seemed to be attracting everyone's attention. Although by no means huge, it was certainly large enough to warrant being called a ship rather than a boat. Several men were standing alongside it, scratching their heads and pointing as if they didn't know what to do. And several tourists on the pier not far from me were taking photos. Although the ship appeared normal in most respects, it did have one striking peculiarity: it had capsized. Its hull bobbed out of the water like the carcass of a whale that had suddenly found itself in Japanese waters, through some sort of gross navigational error. It was such a surreal scene that I thought perhaps the Irish film industry, buoyed by recent successes, was remaking *The Poseidon Adventure* and any moment now Gene Hackman, dressed as a priest, would tap on the hull and yell at the rescuers to get them the feck out of there.

I was standing next to an elderly gentleman who was out taking his dog for *its* daily shit along the pier and *his* daily flirtation with emphysema. I asked him if he knew what had happened.

He scratched his head thoughtfully, then, after a time, removed his pipe and pointed the smouldering wet end at me. 'I tink it's capsized so it has.'

Oh Buddha! 'No. I was sort of wondering *how* it capsized.'

He gazed at me as if he'd never actually encountered anyone from Reality before. 'Well how should I be knowing that?'

I shrugged like a Parisian pimp. 'Papers. Radio. News. Rumour mill.' Goat entrails.

'Ah not at all.'

His dog was scratching its arse backwards and forwards like one of those guys about to take off in the luge, so with a nod he re-ignited his pipe, kicked his dog up the clacker, dragged it off and left me floundering by the dock.

Perhaps having a ship capsize out on the Irish Sea and then hauled back to Dun Laoghaire was such a common occurrence that it no longer warranted a mention in the daily news—like the Pope falling out of his bath. If this was the case I was glad that I'd decided to fly back to London at the end of my Irish odyssey.

Leaving the cast and crew of *The Poseidon Adventure II—Guess What? It Happens Again* to complete their filming, I continued on my way to the end of the pier where the anemometer announced that it was currently nine degrees and the wind was gusting at seventy-nine kmh. I wasn't sure if the nine-degree temperature included the wind-chill factor. I was just delighted that I wasn't a brass monkey.

Although Sydney occasionally throws up the sort of storm that has you scanning your home and contents insurance policy (and your collected essays of Frederick

Nietzsche) for the precise meaning of "Act of God", it is usually "Mostly fine". Actually the climate, apart from the odd summer's day when the dogs melt, is pretty close to perfect. I prefer the cold, though, so one of the enticements of coming to Ireland in winter was (and put the Thorazine on standby) the weather. I enjoy the idea of big weather, which is, I suppose, one of the reasons I've always been attracted to Europe. I like the concept of living in a place where you can pop out for a carton of milk and a paper and your body doesn't turn up again until the spring thaw. I'm sure it lends each day an exhilarating sense of *je ne sais quoi*, which is, of course, French for "haven't got the remotest clue"—check your Berlitz phrase book. I popped my head up over the parapet of the pier wall, looked out to sea and immediately my head was almost blasted across several counties. Brilliant!

The other reason for visiting a country out of season (apart from the lack of crowds) is that you catch the place with its guard down. It's a bit like knocking on the front door of Buckingham Palace only to find it answered by the Queen with a racing guide under her arm, a smoke on the go, and her hair Medusaed in rollers.

With the wind at my tail I hurtled back along the East Pier on the return leg like an out-of-control sailboarder. I was literally carried through Dun Laoghaire

Larkin about in IRELAND

itself and soon found myself approaching Sandycove and James Joyce Tower.

As I was about to peel off the path and head on down towards the actual cove and the Forty Foot Men's bathing area beyond, I encountered a couple of young guys who were having one of those conversations in which the more macho of the pair is the one who can pepper his conversation with the greatest number of expletives.

'He fookin, fook, fookin, fook, fooker.'
'Me fookin bollicks he fookin did.'
'I fookin swear, you fookin fooker.'

Naive of me, I know, but given the literary traditions of Ireland, and the fact that I was so close to James Joyce Tower, where arguably the most esteemed and unread novel of the twentieth century was born, I expected a bit more of them.

Sandycove is a jaunty little bay (actually it's a cove but you can't write "cove" twice in the one sentence). The kind Popeye might seek shelter in and then decide to stay in forever. It is full of cheerful people who look like they're about to embark on cheerful escapades such as doing up an old Captain Pugwash boat or setting off on a brisk kayaking adventure to Wales.

I stood on a rocky outcrop and gazed into the sea. The gusts were so strong that I had to tilt at a forty-five-degree angle just to render this possible.

Unaccountably there was a (what's the collective

noun?) ~~scone~~, ~~tracksuit~~, ~~botheration~~, ~~tea cosy~~, ~~bingo~~, ~~Steradent~~, dither of elderly people undressing in the lee side of the rocks, all jabbering climatic clichés like you'd expect of anyone who's suddenly found that beige has become an essential part of their wardrobe.

'It's a bit fresh out, all right.'

'Should have been here yesterday.'

'Oh, aye. It were a right pea souper.'

'Freeze the balls off a brass billiard table,' said one guy stripping down to his Speedos.

I slogged up to them with a scarf wrapped round my head and my Gore-Tex coat flapping in the gale like the spinnaker of a racing yacht. I must have looked like Captain Oates on his tragic final walk.

'You're not going in there, are you?' I asked of the man in the Speedos.

This brought a raucous round of *haw hawing* from everyone.

'It's a lot warmer in than you'd think,' offered a lady who was wearing the sort of ill-advised swimsuit that had obviously needed the use of two hot spoons and a close friend for her to have been able to take up occupancy. Her thighs must have really looked something around the time Noah's wife said, "Might turn out nice."

'Warmer in than out,' said someone on the edge of the group.

'Yes but it's even warmer in the pub,' I suggested,

and pointed to nearby Dalkey which has a number of warm and welcoming pubs.

Someone had obviously picked up on my accent. 'From Australia, aren't you?'

'No,' I mumbled quietly to myself while staring at the water, which appeared to be covered by a thin sheet of arctic slush. 'I come from Reality.

'Yes, I am. Sydney actually.'

'Well you've got those Bondi Icebergs.'

'Who are all barking mad.'

This brought a fresh round of *haw hawing*.

'It's good for the circulation.'

'So's aspirin,' I suggested helpfully, but I no longer had their full attention. They were throwing off towels and lowering themselves into the freezing floe, screaming all the time at a pitch that could only be heard by the many shitting dogs.

One much younger guy—who had to be a newcomer to the group because he was wearing a wetsuit—touched the water with his big toe and his testicles immediately retreated up around his ears like mice up a grandfather clock. I have never seen a face contorted in such agony (except perhaps my own reflected in the television screen when I inadvertently change the channel to *Judge Judy*). And here's the thing: he didn't have to be in there.

It is, of course, a writer's function to (where appropriate) show, not tell. With this in mind and in order to show you how cold the water was, I want you to do something for me.

- Get up from the lounge, bed, hammock, or wherever you happen to be reading.
- Go into the bathroom and fill the bath with cold water.
- Return to the kitchen and remove all the ice cubes, frozen peas, etc from the freezer and tip them in.
- Turn the air-conditioning to its coolest setting (if it's winter where you happen to be, so much the better).
- Set up a series of fans just outside the bathroom door and gun them to the max.
- And just so we get the mood right, have a couple of dogs shit in your hallway.
- Now lower yourself into the water.
- Remove (where appropriate) testicles from behind ears—your own ears that is unless you happen to be doing this with a partner.
- Repeat.

They were good-natured enough to encourage me to join them, but I declined by telling them that I was shortly due back in Reality.

I realise I am being a bit harsh because the truth is that I did have my swimmers and a towel with me in my daypack. One thing I promised myself I would do before I left for this trip was to go swimming in the Forty Foot Men's bathing area, which had been made famous in *Ulysses* and which was just beyond the next rocky outcrop.

Leaving my teeth-chattering friends behind, I made

my way around the rocks and over towards the Forty Foot Men's bathing area so I could have a bit of a poke around—perhaps not the best verb, given that the Forty Foot Men's bathing area is nude. I knelt down to touch the water and immediately let out an involuntary high-pitched yelp. Given the temperature, I knew at once that—along with learning the cello, climbing Everest with a trombone, and kneeing Peter Costello in the nadgers for slapping a GST on books—this was yet another dream that would go unfulfilled.

I've always found the name slightly ambiguous. Are the men who bathe there forty feet long? Unlikely, given the water temperature and the shrinkage factor.

There is a tradition on St Stephen's Day when hordes of people, generally university students, go swimming at the Forty Foot Men's bathing area and then repair to the nearest pub to drink hot whiskeys until such time as their bodies attain room temperature or they are assisted from the premises on a stretcher.

There was no one swimming today, though looking further along the rocks I could make out the bobbing heads of a couple of men undressing in a sheltered area that had been painstakingly carved out of the rock by erosion or by someone with a lot of time on their hands or a deep interest in men's bodies.

Given that this *was* a designated nude swimming area, I felt that sooner or later someone might get the wrong idea about a man lurking about with a camera, a notebook and a Gore-tex coat, so I hastened along to James Joyce Tower, which was only a towel flick up the road. I made it just in time to see it being shuttered up for lunch.

A worryingly thin man in bicycle clips (there was no evidence of a bicycle) was having tremendous difficulty with the roller-door security shutter. He'd half-closed the thing but now it was stubbornly refusing to go the rest of the way to the ground. He climbed on the lock and jumped up and down on it repeatedly, but this didn't seem to help. In fact the door suddenly turned into one of those roll-up blinds that never quite work and on his third bounce it shot up into the air and caused him to leap interestingly aside like a stuntman out of a balloon.

'Feck it!'

I figured that the floorshow was drawing to a close so I offered my assistance. 'Can I give you a hand?'

'Ah no,' he said, clambering to his feet. 'I've done it a thousand times.'

So it would appear. 'Do you mind if I take a photo then?' I mumbled.

'Sorry?'

'Do you have any photos inside?'

'Postcards? That sort of thing?'

I nodded.

'Yeah, we have.' He gave the shutter another yank, only this time it got with the program and clattered to the ground with a noise like that of the Tin Man being hurled off the back of a rapidly moving ute by the Wicked Witch of the western suburbs. 'We're just closing for lunch now, though, I'm afraid.'

We? Perhaps he was referring to himself and the roller-door, whose acquiescence was evidently required before lunch could begin.

'That's okay,' I said. 'I'm not exactly on a tight schedule. I'll go and sit in the pub for an hour or so.'

'We'll be back at two.' With a couple of nods and smiles they picked their bikes up from around the corners and pedalled off for their lunches.

I strolled up the road into Dalkey, which was so quaint I wanted to scream.

Jaunty shops, stylish restaurants, elegant architecture, welcoming pubs, and tight, twisty well-groomed streets are the order of the day in Dalkey, as the travel guides might say. You'll thrill at the brightly coloured houses. You'll delight at the affability of the locals. You'll reel at the language of the young men passing by ("He fookin, fook, fookin, fook, fooker."). And you'll leap about in frustrated rage following an impromptu twenty-metre slide on a dog turd.

Although Dalkey is where the rich and famous often come to hang out, it's not as pretentious as Monaco or Double Bay.

I fell in love with Dalkey when I first visited it in the mid-eighties. I wanted to move there, buy a house with an atrium, a writer's studio and views of the sea, and use my status as a writer with his own atrium and studio and views of the sea basically to meet women. Unfortunately, however, several other authors had a similar idea and what's more they had the added advantage of having actually written something. So with Dalkey falling well outside my limited means, I was forced to return home to Sydney and start my assault on the literary world from there. But Dalkey remained with me. I would mentally escape to it whenever things weren't going so well in my life or I was forced to sit through a lecture on structural linguistics or Chaucer's arsing *Canterbury Tales*. When the dark shroud descended, Dalkey became my safe place and I would visit it often.

Dalkey is still popular with writers—Maeve Binchy and her husband Gordon Snell live next door to the immensely popular Flanagan's pub. While more recently it has become the chosen retreat for grand prix drivers—Damon Hill and Eddie Irvine have houses there, so too apparently does Michael Schumacher. Writers and grand prix drivers? You wouldn't think there'd be a lot of crossover, but there you have it. Meanwhile, nearby Killiney Hill is popular with musos: Bono, The Edge, and Chris Rhea for a start, and Enya is busy building herself a castle. I think she *must be* actually building the thing herself—lugging the bricks and bags of cement up from Dun Laoghaire by hand—because there's been very little progress on it since I was last there. Out the back of Bono's place on his big, black, fuck-off gate, some brain-dead teenager had scrawled "Show me the way Bono". Now I don't know Bono personally but he seems like a decent chap, and his tireless efforts to abolish third-world debt should not only be applauded but actually listened to. Then again, we have to remember that this is the same Bono who once strutted about on stage with a flag, cowboy boots, and that stupid bouffed up mullet that made him look like a horse with a perm. So I'm not entirely convinced that I would rely on Bono, or any other rock star for that matter, to "show me the way" out of a Westlife concert.

I made my way along to the renovated Club, which is a pub with a tardis-like situation happening to it. From the outside it looks quite small and fairly nondescript. On the inside, however, it is enormous, with high ornate ceilings that give it the air of a scaled-down Sistine Chapel. In fact so disorientating is the size of The Club in relation to what you expect, that I actually popped back outside a couple of times to try and see where all the space comes from.

Although Flanagan's is the pub to be seen in, I always feel slightly deflated by the disappointed looks etched across everyone's faces whenever I enter and they realise that I'm not Bono, The Edge, Damon Hill, Eddy Irvine, Maeve Binchy, Michael Schumacher, or Enya with a hod of bricks slung over her shoulder. Which is why, whenever I'm in Dalkey either mentally or in person, I prefer

The Club. Of course there's also the inherent problem of meeting, say, The Edge, and then getting involved in a shout with him. I mean what would you call him? You couldn't say, "Fancy another one, The Edge?" It just doesn't work. Nor for that matter does, "Are you going again, The?" And while "Your round, The-man-who-thought-that-going-by-his-nickname-in-his-late-teens-was-provocative-and-radical-but-now-sounds-faintly-ridiculous-and-more-than-a-bit-embarrassing" is closer to the mark, it still lacks a certain something.

I had a pleasant lunch of cod and vegies while tucked into the cosiest and warmest corner of The Club. I then made the mistake of washing it down with three monumentally ill-advised pints of Guinness.

I'm not the greatest drinker in the world, but having yearned for so long to be at large in Dalkey as a professional writer, and having finally achieved my ambition, I foolishly let the moment go to my head.

When I staggered out of the place about an hour or so later, the sun almost blinded me—I hadn't been expecting it up so late; it was almost two-thirty, after all. My pupils immediately shrivelled to the size of distant pinpricks, while my legs seemed to be having a serious disagreement about which way I wanted to go.

I eventually made my way back to James Joyce Tower. The man with the bicycle clips had told me that he would be opening up again at two o'clock, but I decided to give him an extra half hour in the event that he'd slept in or was having as much trouble opening the shutter as he did closing it.

Fortunately Mr Bicycle Clips had made it back and had managed to sort out the recalcitrant shutter. I entered the tower with what I felt was the appropriate amount of reverence, telling myself to "Shush" and my legs to behave themselves. Mr Clips was behind the counter, sorting out souvenirs and postcards. I took a closer look at him and immediately reeled. Now I've heard it said that married couples sometimes grow to look like each other, and that a dog will often take on the appearance of its owner (or is it the other way round?), but I never knew it was possible for people to resemble their jobs. Yet there was no doubt about it: Mr Clips bore a striking resemblance to the great one himself. He even spoke with a soft, lilting west Britain accent.

'How, may I enquire, did you know that we were open today?'

Again with the "we"? Perhaps there was a cleaner upstairs. 'I didn't. Just popped down on the off.'

'You're very fortunate then.'

'No. I'm a Buddhist.'

Mr Clips looked at me as if one of us had gone insane. I just shook my head. Some people are happy drunks. Some are angry drunks. Some just talk complete bollocks and assume that everyone knows what they're going on about. I fit mostly into the first and third categories. Fortunately I was aware that I was talking bollocks so I made a valiant attempt to clarify the situation.

'For this trip I mean. I'm not usually a Buddhist. I'm RC. Or at least that's what it says on my birth certificate. Or at least I think it does. I seem to have misplaced it. Atheist now I suppose, but you say agnostic just in case, don't you? I'm probably more into the Sartre and Camus branch of existentialism to be honest. But then again Sartre was a short Frenchman and Camus was a goalkeeper.'

Boy, I was glad I'd cleared that up.

'Anyway, we close at four.'

I nodded and made my way through the displays and up into the tower itself.

Joyce Tower is one of twenty-six Martello towers that were erected as part of the coastal defence network. It is number eleven of the fifteen on Dublin's south side. The idea was that you would fire hotshot from the towers' cannons into the rigging of attacking vessels or the yachts of record company executives looking for boy bands.

Although the tower was possibly the inspiration and definitely the setting for the opening of *Ulysses*, in fact Joyce only spent a couple of nights in the place. On September 14, 1904 he was asleep in the round room with his friends Trench and Oliver St John Gogarty. At some point during the night Trench woke from a dream about a black panther, reached for his gun and discharged it at the fireplace, where he believed the panther was crouching. Not surprisingly, Joyce and Gogarty immediately leapt out of bed like startled whippets. But although the explosion from the gun was still reverberating around the walls, Trench was already back sound asleep.

A short time later Trench again woke from a similar dream, but this time Gogarty said, "Leave him to me", took out his gun and promptly starting firing at the collection of saucepans that were sitting above Joyce's bed and which came crashing down on top of the young author. Perhaps not surprisingly Joyce went screaming out into the night, never to return.

All I can say is that the three of them must have had one hell of a session before turning in.

A short while later a coach load of Spanish students (the reason the museum was opened) turned up. So, not wanting to share the experience with anyone, I beat a retreat from the round room—there was a porcelain black panther sitting by the fire which, in the hazy half light, I almost took a swipe at myself—and returned to the ground floor.

Having been reassured by Mr Clips that the Forty Foot Men's bathing was no longer a nude area, I made my way back down from James Joyce Tower to the Forty Foot to take in a little fresh air. My head was still spinning and I had no idea how I was going to get back to

Richard and Paula's place. But for the moment that was the least of my concerns. A combination of Guinness, jetlag, and thoughts of Joyce, Gogarty and Trench's famous piss-up were all drifting in and out of my frontal lobes, and making it extremely difficult to remain vertical.

I sat back on one of the stone seats like a starfish on a rock, and, given what takes place here on St Stephen's Day, was doubtless not the first person to find himself horizontal at the Forty Foot.

Ten

Christzone

From the moment I picked up Joe Simpson's wonderful book *Touching the Void* I've wanted to climb a mountain. I always feel inspired by people who laugh in the face of adversity, leer up the nose of danger, gouge at the eyes of Death and climb mountains. Or, in Joe's case, fall off them.

The mountain I had in mind didn't have to be all that big or involve grappling hooks, ice axes, base camps, satellite phone calls, and hastily arranged press conferences to explain the loss of my climbing companion down a three-hundred-foot ravine. In fact, given the state of my knees, I was quite content for it to be nothing more than a robust hill.

The mountain that I had my heart—or my knees—set on, then, was Croagh Patrick in County Mayo on the west coast. I'd heard of Croagh Patrick from relatives who'd climbed it on the holy pilgrimage, which takes place on the last Sunday in July. I had also read about it recently in Pete McCarthy's excellent book *McCarthy's Bar*.

The Reek, as it is known, sits 2510 feet (765 metres) above sea level and it is said to be the place where, after a fast on the summit that lasted forty days and nights, St Patrick issued his famous proclamation banishing the snakes from Ireland, presumably after they'd devoured his sandwiches.

County Mayo was a long way from the Forty Foot and the problem was how I was going to get there without a car. I returned to The Club, spread my map across one of the tables, and over a much-needed coffee or three considered my options. There was the bus to Galway and then another north to Westport. Then I'd have to take yet another bus or a cab out of Westport to the base of Croagh Patrick, which is about eight kilometres out of town. This seemed feasible enough in theory, but even allowing for straight bus connections, which in Ireland is something of an oxymoron, it would be extremely time-consuming. So I decided to go with the flow and let serendipity (with a dash of Buddhism) lead the way and hope that something would turn up.

Something did.

When I arrived back at Richard and Paula's place, Paula told me that her old Trinity College friend Angela and her husband Iain had invited them to their daughter's christening in Sraheens, County Mayo, the following day. And to the post-christening piss-up in

Angela's sister's pub, Clew Bay Lodge, which was (wait for it) at the foot of Croagh Patrick. Paula said she vaguely recalled me talking about climbing Croagh Patrick, and that perhaps the three of us could have a go at it on the Sunday morning.

This was almost too perfect. I couldn't believe it. Richard and Paula could drop me at the pub while they went to the christening. I might even be able to climb Croagh Patrick twice: once by myself on the Saturday, and again with Richard and Paula on the Sunday. I envisaged an invigorating day of hiking, yodelling, and perhaps an evening spent by the pub's fire in a turtleneck sweater with a plate of Irish stew, a hot port and a tale to tell.

Then Paula told me that they weren't staying at the pub but with Angela's parents. I'd been invited to go to the christening with them and there was a bedroom for me at Angela's parents' house.

'I can't gatecrash a christening,' I said.

'Of course you can.' Paula turned up the heat in the lounge room, which was already sweltering like Sydney on Christmas Day. 'This is Ireland. You'll be made very welcome.'

•

The following morning when I woke I didn't have the faintest idea where I was. I hadn't slept much lately but I'd certainly crashed and burned the night before, wherever that might have been. I was aware that jet lag could hit you like this, especially if you didn't give yourself time to acclimatise. And I'd certainly hit the ground running once I'd got off the plane at Heathrow.

Mentally I tried to retrace my steps. The last vaguely coherent thing I could recall doing was trying to work out how I was going to get to Westport in County Mayo and then to the base of Croagh Patrick. It all sort of fell in a bit of a blurred heap after that.

I looked around the room that the eerie dawn glow had lit with all the intensity of a ten-watt bulb. There was a picture of Jesus on the far wall and a statue of Mary on the chest of drawers. Whoever I was staying with was obviously a worshipper of the big guy, though I believed that to be true of a number of Irish people, so this didn't exactly narrow it down.

I raised my hand into the air and let it fall back onto the bed. The force appeared to be pulling about 1G. This was good. On that basis it seemed reasonably safe to conclude that I was on planet Earth, which came as a bit of a relief. I'd recently read somewhere that about three million Americans woke up feeling this way—missing memories, unsure as to their whereabouts—having been abducted by anal probe-wielding aliens.

I crawled out of bed and opened the curtains. There were several cows outside my bedroom window, chewing cud and just generally looking big and gormless. It was so not what I was expecting to see that I immediately let out a blood-curdling scream like a banshee having her nipples fried off on an electrified fence. Several of the cows bolted for the horizon, legs splayed out at all angles, never to return. Strangely, though, no one in the house stirred.

At least the cows, or what remained of them, had given me a reference point. I was obviously in the country.

Thoughts began to reassemble. I could remember drinking hot whiskeys the night before with Richard and Paula, Angela and Iain, and Angela's mother. In that wonderfully hospitable Irish way, Angela's mother had kept disappearing into the kitchen for tea, scones, cake, and barrels of whiskey, and who'd been happy to turn the spare room over to a man from the other side of the world, simply because his friend had married a girl her daughter had met at university. What a lovely country. What wonderful people.

After the port, the dark shroud descended and so, missing Jacqui and Chantelle, I went off to bed. I remembered Iain (his tongue so firmly in his cheek that he was in danger of severe facial injury) telling us about nearby Knock, which was apparently ranked third, after Lourdes in France and Portugal's Fatima, on the pilgrims' greatest hits.

In the late 1800s, with the famine still a recent memory, Knock was the setting for a divine apparition of the Blessed Virgin and a couple of her friends. Fortunately it was a time that Knock, and indeed the entire west of Ireland, needed an economic leg-up. Iain likened the event to an ecclesiastical Area 51—and indeed the completion of an international airport (to receive pilgrims from America) in 1985 has often been referred to as the second miracle of Knock. It's easy to be cynical, and certainly Knock has dined out on the event, real or imagined, ever since. There is even a "Pilgrimage Season" stretching from the last Sunday in April to the 2nd October. But there's no doubt that the people of Knock are convinced that something quite extraordinary happened on that cold, rainy night so long ago.

Iain also said that Knock had some of the tackiest souvenir shops in the known world.

I wanted to go there.

After rudimentary ablutions I shuffled out to the lounge room and found Richard hurling the equivalent of a medium size deciduous forest onto the open fire, obviously preparing for Paula's imminent rising.

I walked over to the front window and gazed out at the morning. The sun was up but was rather anaemic as if it really shouldn't have been out on a day such as this. And a ferocious wind was whipping along the lane and howling through the trees. Not as much despite the weather as because of it, I wanted to be out there, striding stoutly along the hedgerows and through the bracken.

I expect at some point in the future there will emerge

from me (in the strictest metaphorical sense) an elderly gentleman who likes nothing better than to traipse off over hills and dale with a stick, a dog, a packed lunch, and a penchant for lively knitwear.

I asked Richard if he fancied going for a walk.

He stabbed at the firestorm with a titanium poker that looked as if it was beginning to melt.

'Yes. Yes. We could do that.' The gale lashed the house and the windows shook violently. 'But then again *not* being out there has its advantages too.'

So we sat quietly by the inferno, drinking coffee and occasionally shouting to each other over the roar of the flames and exploding branches about our proposed cycling tour of the Ring of Kerry.

Richard studied my map and fed more of the local woodland to the hungry blaze, which was more or less a continuous process.

'I think these squiggly lines,' he said, pointing at our proposed anticlockwise route round the Ring of Kerry, 'are to indicate that it's quite hilly.'

'I thought they meant it was scenic.'

'Maybe it's hilly *and* scenic,' he suggested.

'Have you ever encountered hills that weren't scenic?'

'The Hills District of north-western Sydney,' he replied.

'There are some nice parts of the Hills District.'

'Yes. The houses and some of the suburbs. But not the hills themselves. They're fairly nondescript, as I'm sure you'll concur, John.' He really talks like this. 'That's the thing about the Hills District of north-western Sydney: the ascent is so gradual that you can't actually tell when you're in them.'

'Why do you keep saying, "the Hills District of north-western Sydney"? I know where it is. I used to live there, remember?'

'Yes, John, you did. But not all your readers are in such a position.'

I looked at Richard and wondered whether he was suffering from heat exhaustion.

'You're writing a book about this trip, aren't you?'

'That's the theory.'

'Well that's why I said, "the Hills District of north-western Sydney". So if people in Ireland, or anywhere else other than Sydney for that matter, read it, they'll know where it is. If I'd just said "the Hills District" they wouldn't have a clue what I was talking about, would they? They might think I was referring to the Hills District of Outer Mongolia, or the Hills District of the Sea of Tranquillity.'

I looked at him and sighed. He is, without a doubt, one of my favourite people on the planet, though he does tend to go off on these exhausting conversational tangents that leave you exasperated if you're foolish or naive enough to take the journey with him. In fact so gifted is he in the art of winding someone up during a conversation that when we first met I thought he spelt his name with an exclamation mark.

So I had enough experience to know better than engage with him, but unfortunately I was past the point of no return. 'I see what you're saying, Richard! But people don't talk like that.'

'Yes they do. I just did.'

'Okay,' I relented. 'Normal people, people who you don't want to hit over the head with that blazing branch over there, don't talk like that.'

'And I'll say again, John, I just did.'

There was a maniacal smirk on his face. It was a smirk I knew well and found impossible not to warm to. Later on this trip, after a meal in an Italian restaurant in Dalkey, Richard and I wandered down to The Club for a couple of pints. Manchester United was playing Panathinaikos in a European Cup match and the pub was full of vocal Man U supporters. We took our seats at the bar and Richard started yelling, 'Come on the greens!' 'Go, the other team!' 'You're hopeless, Man United!' 'The green team rules! Whoever they are.' The United supporters turned around as one, ready to dismember him. As soon as they saw his smirk, though, they wanted to buy him a drink—just as I was poised to land a left cross on him myself.

'Okay, Richard! You *did* just say it. But it's not as if I'm going to transcribe every single conversation I have, is it? I'm not going to include this one for instance.'

'Why not?'

'Well first of all it's not interesting enough, and even if it was, I couldn't include it because no one would believe that it actually took place. "The Hills District of north-western Sydney"? I mean, I don't believe it myself and I'm actually in it!'

Fortunately at that moment Paula hopped into the lounge room wrapped in about five doonas, and things returned to normal.

It was eight in the morning and the rest of the house wouldn't be up for about four hours—the Irish enjoy a bit of a lie-in on Saturdays. So with Paula vetoing my plan for a brisk amble in the country—'You must be bloody joking'—we left a hastily scribbled note to explain where we'd gone and promptly headed off to Knock.

It was the pilgrimage off-season, so there were plenty of car spaces in the main street. We parked near the shrine, which was a bit inconvenient because we had to walk back up the road to the souvenir shops—which were the destination for our particular pilgrimage.

We entered the first shop to the strains of (no kidding) Kylie Minogue's *Better the Devil You Know*. But before I go into detail about the souvenir shops, which were everything they were rumoured to be, and more, I'd better first tell you a bit more about "The Miracle of Knock". In the interests of responsible journalism.

In the early evening of 21st August, 1879, quite possibly around the time the pubs closed, Sister Margaret

Beirne noticed an unusual brightness over the church as she went to lock up. It never occurred to her that she was witnessing the start of an apparition that would shortly make Knock world famous—"Ahh, that'll be herself again"—so she returned home without giving the eerie glow a second thought. Shortly afterwards the priest's housekeeper, Mary McLoughlin, was on her way to visit her friend, who had just returned from holidays with perhaps a couple of bottles of duty free for them to sample. Passing the church Mary McLoughlin saw three figures, which she immediately took for statues, thinking that perhaps the Archdeacon had won them in a poker game in Dublin or something. She later said that she thought "the whole thing strange" but nevertheless hurried along to her friend's house and, once there, said nothing about the statues.

Later, Mary returned to the church accompanied by her friend's daughter Mary (I realise this overabundance of Marys, though factual, is confusing and needs to be rectified).

Later, Mary returned to the church accompanied by her friend's daughter Kylie. On closer inspection of the statues Kylie cried out, "They're not statues, they are moving. It is the Blessed Virgin!" After a brief discussion, possibly about the sale of film rights, Kylie raced home with the news and was soon back with her whole family in tow. Kylie then tore off around the streets like a whirling dervish and in no time a small crowd had gathered. They stood gazing at this apparition of the Blessed Virgin, St Joseph, St John and a lamb.

The fact that livestock accompanied the visitation is what throws me. I mean isn't there a passage in *The Book of Darryl* or something about animals having no soul? If the kingdom of heaven is open to "beasts of the field", and the lamb's incarnation in Knock that evening would seem to indicate that this is the case, then there must be billions upon billions of the things up there. And as for chickens, well there must be a hell of a racket in the mornings.

Why is it that sheep are always associated with religious events? Why, in the interest of not conforming to Biblical stereotype, couldn't the Blessed Virgin have turned up in Knock with St Joseph, St John and an aardvark?

One of the witnesses, seventy-five-year-old Bridget Trench, attempted to kiss the feet of the Blessed Virgin and ended up with a face full of wall, while half a mile away a farmer out in his field saw the glow above the church and figured that there was a bonfire in the churchyard.

The apparition lasted for approximately two hours and was witnessed by up to twenty people, though only fifteen gave testimony at the subsequent commission. In fact there were two commissions: one immediately following the apparition, and another in 1936. The commissions, both of which were held by the Church, found that "the testimony of the witnesses, taken as a whole, was trustworthy and satisfactory".

So what *did* the people of Knock see that fateful night? Well I suppose there are four possibilities:

- A mass hallucination brought on by the power of suggestion on encountering something the witnesses did not expect—statues perhaps, swamp gas, aliens armed to the teeth with curling wands.
- A cunning ruse designed to bring prosperity and fame to the town and possibly a return in numbers to the Church; all of which followed.
- An elaborate hoax that quickly got out of hand.
- An authentic apparition that simply cannot be ridiculed or dismissed by a cynical writer with a strange fondness for aardvarks.

•

Growing up in the western suburbs of Sydney in the seventies, I had a much-loved cat called Bobby who would keep me company on cold winter nights. In England we'd always owned cats (or they us), to keep out rodents. My father never cared much for cats, but he cared even less for rats owing to a childhood phobia brought about by a coal shed, a hastily wielded stick, and a rat flying through the air at him. As a result he'd learned to tolerate cats. When we moved to Toongabbie, though, we immediately upgraded to dogs—an odd decision, really, as none of us knew anything much about them. And we didn't believe in messing around with puppies—we wanted the full-on dog. So every once in a while (twice in fact) we piled into the old Holden and drove out to the RSPCA dog pound at Yagoona and returned, several hours later, with what was essentially an idiot in a dog-suit. The first one we brought home was an insane boxer, which had to be dragged out of its cage like Scooby Doo into a haunted house. While it stubbornly remained seated, the handlers yanked on its collar and that caused all the skin on its head and neck to be pulled forward until its entire face was compressed into an area the size of a fifty-cent piece. Then it had to be cattle-prodded into the back of our car.

Once Dad turned the car out of the pound and onto the main road, however, the boxer exploded in the back seat like a tornado. Sucked up by the vortex, we three kids were hurled over the front seat and into Mum's lap. Luckily she managed to placate the beast with a shoe that she kept on the floor next to her to assist with crowd control in the back. The boxer eventually settled down but spent the rest of the journey eyeing us suspiciously while it chewed on a bone that later turned out to be one of its legs. Its stay with us was so brief that we didn't actually get around to naming the thing—its departure followed so soon on the heels of its arrival that for all intents and purposes they were the one event.

Over our back fence, in a house we called "The Geese Tin", there lived an old Ukrainian woman named Dora. Possibly due to her rural upbringing, or a passion for the British sitcom *The Good Life*, Dora was completely self-sufficient—she was like Felicity Kendall with a thyroid problem. Not only did she grow all her own vegetables, her backyard was a real menagerie: ducks, geese, chickens and those strange birds with the black beaks that have free reign at the zoo, all had free reign at Dora's. It was impossible for the night to pass without being woken at some point by a honk, cluck, cackle, or quack, a raucous territorial dispute involving a clash of beaks, or a heated debate concerning an egg that had been sufficiently fertilised thank you very much. It was all rather charming and lent our rapidly growing suburb an agreeable semi-rural feel and sound.

Enter the boxer. With alarming speed it set about turning the area into a vast ornithological wasteland. Unable to scale the fence because of its height, the boxer launched itself headfirst at it like a battalion of knights at a castle door. What had been a semi-rural suburban idyll now took on a distinct medieval feel thanks to a lobotomised battering ram in a flea collar. The only thing missing from the scene was Dora leaning over the back fence with a cauldron of boiling oil. Twenty minutes after he arrived there were more feathers flying about the place than in a pillow fight at a *Brady Bunch* reunion Christmas special. Thirty minutes after arriving he was back in the car. He was repatriated to the dog pound or the wild; I can't remember which. Though

Dad's solo trip to the dog pound did seem quicker, unencumbered by three screaming kids in the back.

About a year later a collie-like thing joined us and even managed to make it past the naming ceremony. Rex might have stayed longer if he hadn't been so fond of dangling teeth-first from the clothesline, and going for the earth's core via our flowerbed. Again, the return journey seemed markedly quicker.

Even though children generally love animals, I wasn't in the least bit upset by the departure of these two. I looked upon them as you might a psychotic half-brother who's taken away in the middle of the night to join the army for his and everyone else's benefit.

A few years later my sister Trish was given a corgi pup as a Christmas present. Her name was Suzie—nicknamed Too-pongs because Trish was basically off her head—and despite our appalling track record she managed to stick around for seventeen years. Until Suzie arrived, and possibly owing to a black ban by the RSPCA, we went back to cats.

Although Bobby technically belonged to the family, he was mine. A big lug of a tabby, he was more like a small mountain lion than a domestic cat. On cold winter nights I'd pull back the flyscreen, let him in through my bedroom window and he would snuggle in beside me. He purred so deeply that he sounded like the blades of a helicopter coming in to land. He was an electric blanket with talons. Lying on my chest he would knead me with his claws until I was forced to muffle my giggles or screams with a pillow. With the menagerie over the back fence restored to full voice following the boxer's departure, I'd never known happiness like it. On rainy days I would sneak out of school at recess or lunchtime and race home to let Bobby in. Because I moved like The Flash I would be back at school before anyone knew that I'd gone—and that included the kid I was playing handball with.

I just didn't like Bobby being outside. I could never relax until he was safe under my blankets. I don't know why I felt this way; I just knew that something bad would happen to him if he was left outside.

Something bad happened.

The worst place for a cat to try and nap in is a yard with a pit bull terrier. The second is under a parked car.

Trish finished primary school and was off to her sixth grade dance; I went along for the ride. Somehow the three of us managed to climb into the car and didn't disturb him or notice him snoozing there behind the back wheel.

Mum reversed the car out, completely oblivious of the fact that we'd snapped Bobby's spine in several places. From the back seat, though, it felt like we were in a golf cart going over a speed hump. Bobby leapt into the air and tore off up the side of the house. In a state close to hysterics I tried to convince Mum that we had run over him, but she was having none of it—hadn't I seen him run up the side of the house?

Decades later I learned that what Bobby underwent that day was called "dead cat bounce". The sheer weight of the car would have crushed all life out him. He was probably already dead as he ran up the side of the house. He was certainly dead when we arrived home.

Dad buried him in the back corner of the yard. Even the ducks, geese, chickens and those strange birds with the black beaks that have free reign at the zoo remained silent throughout the ceremony.

As night fell and a storm blew in from the south, I spent the hours before bedtime gazing through the kitchen window and up at the back of the yard. I prayed as hard as I could that Bobby would appear one last time; just so that I could say goodbye, so I would know that there was room for cats in heaven and that he'd be up there waiting for me one day, claws unsheathed and ready to knead my chest again until we were both sound asleep and purring.

And sure enough there he was, sitting on top of his own grave busily preening and cleaning himself like the pernickety old thing he was. With the tears running down my cheeks I beckoned him to come around the side of the house to my bedroom window, so I could peel back the flyscreen and he could sleep safe under my blankets forever. Either he didn't see me, or misunderstood what I meant, because moments later he stood up, and with his tail held high in the air like the conducting rod of a dodgem car, he disappeared into "The Geese Tin" and whatever lay beyond.

I'm utterly convinced today, as I was back then, that what I saw that night was genuine. The only real difference being that the ten-year-old was adamant that Bobby was out there in the garden, while the current version is equally unwavering in his belief that he was there all right, but in a ten-year-old's mind.

•

As I gazed out through the souvenir shop window at the glistening streets of Knock, the gale swept the freezing rain horizontal. Now if *I* was a Blessed Virgin—and I say this in complete knowledge that I lack a certain number of prerequisites that go with the job—the only reason I would appear in Knock would be to ask directions to somewhere else: Noosa, say, or Majorca.

The souvenir shops had everything your heart could possibly desire: apparition candles (real and battery operated), apparition RIP vases, apparition ceramic sacrificial lambs, apparition ceramic angels (real and battery operated), glow-in-the-dark crucifixes, glow-in-the-dark beasts of the field, new and old Testaments (hardback, softback, and CD-ROM), a plastic Scooby Doo fleeing what appeared to be the Holy Ghost, and stickers proclaiming the love of the Blessed Virgin, the forgiveness of the Lord, the wisdom of Jesus and the genius of Eric Cantona, whose presence in the shops was curious because he'd long since retired and turned his hand to acting.

While we're at it, could somebody please explain exactly what Eric Cantona was doing in the Cate Blanchett film *Elizabeth*? When I first heard that he'd hung up his soccer boots for an acting career I thought, *good luck to him*. I imagined years of devoted study, followed by small workshop productions and a tireless apprenticeship in local theatre, all of which might eventually lead to a television bit part or a walk-on in some independent film. Perhaps you shared my surprise when, a matter of weeks after announcing his decision to tread the boards, he turned up as a supporting actor in a major British production playing somebody incredibly French, his screen presence hewn from solid oak. What was that about?

Richard called me over to his corner of the shop, convinced that he'd just found evidence of the world's first boy band. He held up a poster of an angry looking Jesus who was leaning against a wall with a couple of his disciples, all of whom appeared to be gazing off into the middle distance the way U2 used to do on their album covers. It looked like the disciples had taken a break from the studio to appear in a knitwear ad for chunky jumpers. Dubbing this particular Jesus "Scary Christ" and the band "Christzone", the three of us left the souvenir shop doubled over laughing, perhaps just moments before we were to be physically removed.

I don't understand souvenirs. If I go somewhere exotic such as Paris or Rome, or somewhere else, say, Knock, I don't feel I have to prove it to anyone, least of all myself, with t-shirts, hats, calendars, glow-in-the-dark crucifixes, or life-size sacrificial lambs. The memory is enough. That and a ceramic Moses with interchangeable staff and light sabre.

On the other hand, here I am writing this book...

Knock may well have been the location for the apparition of the Blessed Virgin, St Joseph, St John, a lamb, whatever, but I'm afraid that once I saw the souvenir shops I just couldn't take it seriously. They cheapened the whole experience, although perversely I suppose without them I wouldn't have felt compelled to go.

I'd abandoned the Catholic faith the day, as an eleven-year-old, I watched a moderately deranged man thrown physically out of my local church when he stormed the altar claiming to have a message from God. If ever someone needed spiritual guidance, there he was. But he was tossed out onto the street like an old sack, crying the whole time. He took a part of me with him.

These days I think that after two thousand years if God doesn't put in another appearance soon, people will start finding other things to worship such as sport or money. Perhaps Knock was one such appearance. Who knows? Maybe what the world needs is a few more Knocks and a few less knockers, if you'll forgive the appalling pun.

While Paula returned to the beckoning warmth of the car, Richard and I headed for the information centre, where I bought a couple of books from a woman who was a dangerous cross between religious fanatic and used-car sales rep. She was particularly keen to show us the photos of all the crutches that had been tossed aside by the hobbling hordes who had been drawn to Knock immediately following the apparition.

I raised my eyes in what I hoped was appropriate admiration and then undid it by asking her whether by leaving their crutches behind the devout had forfeited their deposits.

Richard snorted in the background like a Colombian airport beagle.

To the woman's credit she didn't tell us to clear off, but continued to extol the virtues of Knock, quite possibly hoping to convert us to her beliefs or reaffirm her own. And for a moment I envied her her faith.

But I didn't go to Knock to undergo any such conversion or affirmation. I went there to remove a large dose of urine, and gaze down from the lofty perch of one who, while humble enough to accept that he doesn't know everything, is still conceited enough to suspect that he knows more than most.

Eleven
Pizza with Maggie

When I woke the next morning, my feet were dangling over the edge of a bed that was evidently three sizes too small. Meanwhile Thomas the Tank Engine chugged across my chest while the Fat Controller was doing something disreputable with a flag exactly where I wouldn't normally allow a controller to venture—fat, thin or otherwise. But at least I knew where I was this time: Angela's sister's pub, just near the base of Croagh Patrick.

After the christening feast and piss-up, I'd been generously given Angela's youngest nephew's bedroom and neither of us was completely happy about the situation. I felt that I'd inconvenienced the Comer family quite enough and Angela's nephew agreed. Tears fell all round.

Paula and Richard were ensconced in one of the pub's inviting guest rooms. The last one available. I immediately offered to buy it from them. Spacious and airy, the room had a big brass bed and its own en suite. I argued that I would be perfectly comfortable on their floor, or at the foot of their bed, curled up like an over-ripe and slightly sozzled cat. But my reasoning was brushed aside as utter nonsense, and I collapsed onto the Thomas the Tank Engine doona mid-argument—my finger still raised in the air like a Pompeii debater when Vesuvius erupted. I'd made the potentially fatal mistake of trying to go pint for pint with Angela's brother John.

When we returned from Knock the day before, we sat down to an enormous full Irish breakfast with the whole Comer family.

Afterwards John, who now ran the family property, took me and Richard down to another part of the farm to feed some more of his cows and to meet Maggie, a distant relative who lived in the cottage.

Maggie must have been close to eighty—she might even have been giving ninety a nudge. But when we arrived in John's old paddock basher, which was basically a four-wheel motorbike, Maggie was out stomping around the fields in her gumboots, and wielding a stick.

She told us there was a rogue cow in the shed that John would have to deal with. Despite the fact that I was only two generations away from Irish farming stock myself, I didn't have the foggiest notion how you would deal with a rogue cow. The phrase itself seemed like a contradiction. I tried hard not to imagine John dressed up in full matador regalia, posed at the entrance to the shed and waving his cape, but it wasn't easy.

He opened up the car's boot and handed Richard and me a pair of gumboots each. I slipped mine on, careful to use Richard for support in case my pristine white socks touched the cold and muddy ground.

Then we were both given a couple of buckets of what appeared to be wheat germ and were instructed to carry them over to the shed. Whether this was to supplement the diets of the cows there, or to entice out the rogue, I wasn't sure. My gumboots were so big, though, that I had to take several steps before they began to convey me anywhere.

As I squelched along in John and Richard's wake I found myself involuntarily uttering a strange mantra in rhythm with my steps.

'Icky. Icky. Icky mud,' was apparently what I intoned while holding my pinkie fingers parallel to the horizon. And although the soles of my gumboots were flat to the earth, I was, nevertheless, walking on tiptoes inside them.

'Icky. Icky. Icky mud.'

Slightly ahead of me Richard put down his buckets. 'Will you stop doing that?'

'Doing what?'

'Saying, "Icky. Icky. Icky mud".'

'I'm doing no such thing,' I replied, even though I was vaguely aware that I had been mumbling something.

'You *are* so.'

'It's a form of Tourette syndrome, then.'

'Well, stop it. It's embarrassing.'

Duly admonished I stepped into the shed and almost fainted. The smell was so intense that it immediately shot up my nose and cannoned off the inside of my skull like a startled foal. I wouldn't exactly call it unpleasant—a combination of cow shit, cow piss, cow vomit, and cow—it's just that there was so much of it, my brain didn't seem to know how to process it. And it was cold, too. Freezing in fact. I didn't know that an odour could have its own temperature, but there you go.

'Icky. Icky...'

Richard threw me a look that said I was about to wear his bucket of wheat germ on my head.

The cows, about thirty of them, were penned in on one side of the shed, while on the other side was the silage that would feed them through winter, the rogue cow, and the three of us. As soon as she spotted us, the rogue panicked and immediately tried to join the others in the pen. She did this by ramming her head through the bars so that it was in there with the other cows. Her plan might have even proved successful, had it not been for her five-hundred-kilogram arse sticking out on this side.

We shooed the rogue out of the shed. Or rather John did. Richard and I assisted as best we could by pinning ourselves flat against the wall as the cow came thundering past, her eyes wide open, but generally in control like Foghorn Leghorn fleeing Elmer Fudd.

'Icky...'

Richard quickly extended a finger.

And so we started to feed the cows. This involved pitchforking the silage closer to the pen where they could get at it through the bars. John seemed to be shifting several tonnes of the stuff with each stab of his pitchfork. While Richard, whose knowledge of pastoral practices, at least as far as I was aware, extended no further than MS Farmhand, wasn't doing a bad job either.

I stuck my pitchfork into the silage but it stubbornly refused to budge. The harder I tried to shift the stuff the more I ended up flailing about on the end of the pitchfork's handle, legs akimbo, like a recently skewered grasshopper on an entomologist's needle. The cows in my immediate vicinity stared at me in utter bewilderment.

Richard graciously showed me his technique, copied from John, but I just couldn't get to grips with it, and the most I could manage to shift was about three stalks at a time. The cows in my immediate vicinity stared at me with a look that seemed to say, "Top of the food chain, my arse!".

In the end I abandoned the pitchfork and attempted to handfeed the things. The cows in my immediate vicinity left it.

My forebears on my mother's side were all farming stock. And yet here I was, only a couple of generations down the track, about as useless as the proverbial tits on a bull. I could hear a heavy rumble in the fast-gathering sky. I expect it was distant relatives shaking their heads in disbelief. I was deeply ashamed. I really wanted to prove to myself, John, Richard, and the head-shaking ghouls in the sky, that I could put in a hard day's toil if necessary. And now I was forced to conclude that I couldn't. I know that if John had left me there the entire day with a pitchfork, packed lunch, and a thermos of coffee, I could have got the job done. But *he* did it in five minutes.

The thing is, though, that I'm no fifty-kilogram weakling. I am, according to all the available evidence, a ninety-kilogram weakling. As I've pointed out previously I'm not the hardest man in the world. It's just that I couldn't recall how and when I'd become so soufflé soft. I'd laboured before for my brother—shifting tonnes of soil with nothing more than a wheelbarrow, a shovel, and a bulk-buy bottle of sunscreen. And when I was going to university I used to run a supermarket night-fill crew, which at the end of the shift involved stacking pallets on top of one another without the benefit of a forklift truck.

'That was embarrassing,' I remarked to John and Richard as we made our way back to Maggie's house for a cup of tea.

John patted me warmly on the back with a hand that at first glance appeared to be encased in a couple of baseball gloves, while my own had obviously been transplanted from Snow White's sickly younger sister.

'Horses for courses,' said John. 'I couldn't do your job in a million years.' I thought that this was an extremely gracious thing for him to say, especially given that my job consists primarily of lying in a hammock with a laptop computer.

Maggie's cottage was so compact and musty that it immediately evoked images of long-dead gingerbread men. We had to be careful not to bang our heads a nasty blow on the ceiling, even when we were sitting down. A moth-eaten old cat was curled up by the fire and purring contentedly at the embers. Or at least it might have done had it not died during the De Valera administration.

Maggie drank milk straight from the cows, fuelled the fire with peat cut from her own field, in a cottage that was slowly being drawn back into the earth. Despite this, or possibly because of it, she looked in terrific health. Survival of the fittest.

Here was a reminder that although Ireland was going through a tremendous period of transition, not all the country was taking the journey with it. There was no jacking into the matrix here for Maggie. No internet banking. No phone. Possibly even no sewer, though I wasn't brave enough to check. And a microwave was a greeting offered by somebody barely visible on a distant hill. The tick-tock of the old clock on the mantelpiece seemed to mark time at a slower than normal rate. It even appeared to start slipping backwards.

Maggie was an anachronism. John said that her grandparents would have lived through the famine. Doing the maths I immediately saw that he was right. She was a throwback to earlier, simpler, more innocent, but ultimately harsher times. And for a moment I envied her that innocence. The days must stretch on for weeks. The weeks, years. You could get a lot done out here, without perhaps seemingly accomplishing anything at all. Maggie was over a hundred years from email. But then I realised that she was also over a hundred years from a takeaway pizza, and my brief flirtation with envy was over.

Those of us living in the twenty-first century can go Amish any time we wish. We can cast off the shackles of contemporary living, raise a barn, grow our own beets, and start calling our children Abner. But, here's the thing: we can return whenever we feel like it. Maggie could make no such journey because I doubt that she realised there was anywhere to go.

Maggie made us tea and spoke of times long past. Of pigs, of sheep, of cattle, of dance halls, and long journeys into a town that was only about five miles up the road. And I hung on her every word, because such words weren't going to be around for much longer.

It was wonderful to go back in time and visit rural

Ireland and see for myself how it used to be, and I will be forever grateful to John and Maggie for giving me the opportunity. But with thoughts of a pepperoni and chilli pizza with extra olives and cheese still melting deliciously in my mind like a Salvador Dali painting, it was even nicer to step out Maggie's front door and return to the present.

Twelve

Up the Reek

The day of the climb culminated successfully in the three of us perching on the summit of Croagh Patrick like Edmund Hillary, Tenzing Norgay, and, well, somebody else. Things, however did not augur well at the beginning when Richard and Paula almost left me behind in the pub.

The christening flowed smoothly, insofar as no one toppled over into the font in some kind of ecclesiastical ecstasy, and the post-christening celebrations failed to erupt into an orgy of drunken violence.

While Paula approached the altar with members of the extended Comer family, Richard and I knelt by the church's only functioning radiator to worship the pagan god of heat. You could tell how cold it was everywhere else in the old stone church, however, because Paula's teeth chattered like a nervous rattlesnake.

Afterwards a few of us joined John in one of the local pubs, which was so tiny that for a moment I considered giving the *Guinness Book of Records* people a call.

Larkin about in IRELAND

I decided to call on a different part of the Guinness empire instead and edged my way to one of only three tables in the place to join the members of my party. The bar was being propped up by about half a dozen or so weather-beaten old farmers, all of whom were involved in a heated discussion that covered everything from bringing down the government to whose round it was. Shortly after our arrival, though, they beasth a hathy retreath basx too the frields. Fielded a hasty beast bath to the hills.

John told us that what we had just witnessed was becoming an increasingly rare sight and that we really ought to have taken a photo.

Then he told us that there was one serious impediment to the modernisation of Ireland. Namely that the younger generation were standing around in pubs and talking complete shite.

I suggested to him that young people have always stood around in pubs talking shite.

The difference, he explained, was that in rural Ireland the older people were always there to keep the younger ones in check. It was like an elder system.

I asked where the elders had gone.

Apparently they hadn't gone anywhere. Didn't go anywhere anymore, and that was the problem. Because of a stricter drink-driving code, the old farmers were no longer coming in off the fields at the end of a day's toil to have a pint or eight in the town pubs, and as a direct result the younger generation, who were already in the pubs talking shite, were left to run amok.

Whereas in the past the Garda had turned a blind eye to a rat-arsed farmer at the helm of a piece of heavy machinery, be it on the road or out in the fields, now they were no longer able to do so. And so the farmers, who simply couldn't afford to lose their licences, or apparently come to grips with the concept of car-pooling, were staying home.

'Not so easy for you to be made aware that you're talking complete shite,' said John, taking a swig on his pint, 'if everyone around you is talking complete shite as well.'

The christening feast went extremely well, or at least it did until somebody set their table on fire. Okay, it was me.

I brushed my napkin a little too close to one of the candles, the subsequent inquest discovered, and unfortunately failed to notice it until the flames were reaching up towards the ceiling. The thing was, no one, including those at my table, would have become aware of the rapidly growing inferno either, had it not been for Paula's excited whoops and hollers. And even then, her near-hysterical cries for buckets of water and/or fire extinguishers didn't go against the mood of the restaurant, but rather accurately epitomised it. Several people held up their glasses in a toast, "Ah, that'll be Himself setting blaze to the table again".

Larkin about in IRELAND

With the speeches out of the way and the fire doused, we repaired to the bar for a little more dousing. Iain's father, a Scottish dentist, and Iain's mother, who wasn't a dentist (Scottish or otherwise) but whose choice of career eludes me at present, invited me to stay with them should I ever find myself Larkin about in Scotland. Here they were, almost perfect strangers, and yet they were willing to welcome me into their home simply because I had a friend who had married a girl who had once gone to university with a girl whom their son had later married. I've said it before: the Celts are wonderful people.

The following day, then, having divested myself of Thomas the Tank Engine and the Circumferentially Enhanced Controller, I packed my bag and checked in on Richard and Paula who were as fast asleep as hibernating bears on medication—or pretending to be.

I couldn't wait to get stuck into our assault on Croagh Patrick, but it would have been unfair and probably unwise to wake them just to pursue some folly of mine. It was only about seven o'clock and I imagined the words "Off" "John" and "Fuck" being hurled at me from the depths of the doona ravine, though not necessarily in that order.

The pub slumbered on, so I made my way down the stairs and back into the bar, which was deathly quiet—and it's not often you'll hear that said about an Irish bar. I found some light switches and, through trial and error, managed to light up my little corner of the world. Then I made myself comfortable at one of the side tables so I could jot down a few notes and start planning where I would go next. Surfing sounded good. It would give me a nice mountains and sea symmetry.

About an hour or so later I was found by a search party of children who'd been out scouring the area for me.

'There you are,' said Paula, returning with a couple of the children a few minutes later. 'We thought you must have got fed up with waiting and gone on ahead.'

'Sorry,' I offered meekly. 'Didn't know what to do, actually. I was going to wake you but thought better of it.'

'Why didn't you just go back to your room?'

'The Manchester wing of the Thomas the Tank conglomerate can only divert your attention for so long. Thought I'd come down here and make a few notes.'

'Richard's convinced that you're halfway up the Reek by now,' said Paula. 'We were about to drive off after you but I thought I'd send the kids down here to have a look first.'

We thanked the kids for their efforts and headed for the car. I could tell that Richard was tapping his foot impatiently because the foot he was tapping was the one that operates the accelerator.

I tumbled into the back seat, apologising all the while for the confusion and thanking them profusely for not leaving me behind. And just for a moment I thought they might abandon the quest and return to Dublin. But then it dawned on me that Richard was as keen to climb Croagh Patrick as I was. Paula, on the other hand, would need to be enticed up the Reek, like a recalcitrant pack-mule into the jaws of an erupting volcano.

First we were off to Westport for breakfast, which is a meal the Irish excel at. It must be said that they don't offer much by way of choice (it's essentially an old-fashioned fry-up with all the trimmings), but by not casting their culinary net too wide, they are able to draw on their strengths, which unfortunately doesn't include coffee. For a nation whose consumption of liquid is legendary, it puzzled me that I wasn't able to get one decent cup of coffee the entire time I was there.

As we hoed in to our breakfast, washed down with a couple of cups of "coffee", I was relieved to note that Richard was calling on his familiar technique of using a thousand words to make a point that could otherwise take ten.

'Perhaps I'm being completely naive, John, but you would think being an established member of the literary fraternity, ie a writer, that inscribing a small note in order to inform your climbing companions, ie us, as to your whereabouts would be a relatively simple task.'

Evidently I was forgiven.

After breakfast I phoned home to tell Jacqui and Chantelle that I was about to climb a mountain. For a moment I felt like Edmund Hillary saying a tearful farewell to his wife before embarking on his expedition to the roof of the world. I told them I'd call them again in a couple of hours when I'd got back, or from a phone box on the summit, if there was one.

From Westport we made the short drive back along the coast road and turned into the Croagh Patrick car park.

There were about half a dozen vehicles in the car park—their owners already well on their way to the summit, or on their way back down.

There was an ice-cream van parked near the lane leading up to the point where the climb started. If we were still under any illusion that we were genuine mountaineers, it ceased the moment we saw the Irish equivalent of Mr Whippy. A closer look, however, and I discovered that this was actually Mr Walking-Stick, dispensing not ice-creams but knobbly sticks and bottled water. What's more he had shut up shop for the season. I was the genuine article again. I immediately started chewing on a non-existent wad of gum.

There was nothing else for it: I'd just have to tackle this mountain without a knobbly walking-stick. Back I went to Richard and Paula, who were busy dressing on the lee-side of the car.

Although it was relatively mild in the car park, we knew that once the wind whipped in off the Atlantic it could get bitterly cold up on the Reek, so we dressed ourselves for its onslaught.

I of course had my dreaded Gore-tex coat, borrowed, I might point out, from my friend Jeff Knapp, the king of confrontation. On a recent trip to Venice, Jeff had outdone himself by buying a GI Joe from a souvenir stallholder, who had apparently mistaken Jeff and his wife Donna for Americans. Why the stallholder felt that Americans on holiday in Italy should feel the need to buy a GI Joe who knows? Having negotiated a fair price and secured ownership, Jeff laid his GI Joe on the ground in front of the stall and jumped up and down on it repeatedly until the little commando was nothing more than a green smear on a Venetian sidewalk, and a small crowd had gathered. I should have taken him to Knock.

It looked as if Richard had bought his Drizabone coat from Banjo Paterson's estate, while his hat had obviously been conceived by someone recently made redundant by the condom industry.

There isn't sufficient space in the remainder of this book to go into Paula's rigout in detail. But if you suspend reality for a moment and mentally slip a stylish black overcoat onto the Michelin Man, you'll at least have some idea of the bulk. People have died of the cold on Croagh Patrick, but that wouldn't be happening to Paula.

And so to the summit.

The first part of the climb was relatively easy. I would liken the experience to a pleasant stroll up the road to the shops. The only real difference is that you are doing it up a steep incline that's been covered with marbles. That plus it's cold enough to turn your bollocks blue. *And* you've got to endure the constant *swish, swoosh, swish, swoosh,* of the Michelin Man's all-weather legs rubbing against each other with every step. Like the sound of parasilk-suited shoppers in a mall.

Paula found it hard going. Picking her way cautiously around the rocks, perhaps worried in case she suddenly slipped and found herself bouncing back down the mountain towards the car park and the sea beyond, like a wayward beach ball. I don't think her heart was really in it.

Richard found the going easy but stayed close to Paula to help her along with an extended arm or encouraging word.

I myself found that the slow going had woken up my football knees. If I moved fast the upward momentum meant that there was less pressure on my troublesome joints. But that was the problem: I could keep up the pace, alleviate the pain in my knees and risk them seizing up completely. Or I could wait around for Richard and Paula, who were, after all, only on the sodding mountain in the first place because of me, and suffer the consequences.

In the end I came up with a reasonable compromise.

I would shoot up ahead for about fifty metres, under the pretext of finding a better route for the next stage of the climb. Then I would sit down on a rock and wait for Paula and Richard to catch up, while I feverishly rubbed life back into my knees. And then off I'd go up the mountain again.

Despite the number of climbers each year, oddly enough there is no actual trail on the mountain. Instead you follow in the tracks of the millions who have gone before you—the erosion, natural and man-made, has turned the whole mountain into one enormous trail. And as you climb you pass discarded drink bottles, cans, cartons, and the broken glass of those who have thoughtfully mapped out your progress to the top—their god clearly no shade of green.

The loose scree that makes up the surface of Croagh Patrick means that you can never be sure of your footing. There's a metaphor in there for tourists and locals alike. And, once you have negotiated the first part of the climb and found yourself on the mountain proper, there is a steep drop on either side that's claimed the lives of those unwary pilgrims who have, for one reason or another, strayed, no doubt without a torch. This is because the seriously devout take on the Reek barefoot and in complete darkness, just as St Patrick himself did. Considering the sharpness of the rocks and the tenderness of the average Irish foot, I can't imagine how anyone ever came up with such a notion, let alone actually putting it to the test. The screams you can hear ripping out onto the night air in the pilgrimage season are not coming from any flagellants having a grand old time on the summit, but rather from climbers who've just stubbed their toes on yet another shiteing rock.

The first part of the climb took about thirty or forty minutes. It may have been longer, though it certainly wasn't shorter. The fact was that I'd simply lost track of time. Abandoning myself to the rhythm of the climb, the banality of pop lyrics playing in my head, I forged on while shouting back encouragement to the others that we didn't have far to go, this next bit was easy, and just what on earth did Bob the Builder think he was up to by launching a music career.

I've got nothing against contemporary muzak, though when it comes to the lyrics of the average pop song I really think that someone needs to scrawl in the margins, in thick red pen, "Could do better". "Meaning unclear". "Does not make sense". "See me after class".

There was a song on the airwaves a couple of years back that had way too many babies in it. So as a full-time writer with a deadline on my hands, and in the interest of research, I sat down in front of my radio, à la *The Sullivans* circa 1942, and actually counted them. It would have been far more practical, of course, to visit my local music store, buy the single in question and program it on continuous loop until my figures agreed or I was carted off in a net. But writing full-time can mean putting prudence long before preference so there I sat in front of the radio for the best part of a day, surfing the commercial stations until the song finally bopped to the surface.

The song's called *Have a Look* (surprisingly enough, not *Baby, Baby, Baby, Baby I Want Your Baby*) by Vanessa Amorosi, and I can report that it includes something like fifty "baby"s, but it's not actually about a baby—as far as I can tell.

At some point in the sixties or seventies, about the time feminists were suggesting we should rethink our language, it was decided that a generic term was needed for someone you were going out with, loved, fancied, would give anything to shag, and after much heated debate "Baby" was given the nod over "Snookums", "Pumpkin," "Honey Pie" or "Flossy Rabbit".

There are of course problems with the chosen word, principally its ambiguity. Are you singing about the baby you're madly in love with in a romantic way or the baby you're in love with as a parent—a baby who turned up nine months after your being in love with your baby in the first place, only the seven-day-a-week, twenty-four-hours-a-day chemist shop was inexplicably closed?

"My baby's having a baby, yeah baby, baby." I suppose that pop lyricists are today's troubadours, but if it weren't for the considerable drag factor in his pantaloons, Shakespeare would be turning in his grave. No doubt thankful that the "baby" boom is a fairly recent phenomenon and that no one came up with the device in his day. "Soft what light from yonder window breaks, Baby?" It might work. But "Get thee to a nunnery, Baby"? It loses something. Admittedly, the Bard himself could bang on a bit, quivering forth such liquid crystal lines as, "How came'st thou hither, tell me and wherefore?" (*Romeo and Juliet*) when all he meant was, "How'd you get here and what'd you want?". But generally it's for his use of language that he's revered, so it's hard for us to imagine Shakespeare sticking fifty "baby"s in anywhere, even *if* Gwyneth Paltrow had been around at the time.

And on the subject of banal lyrics, while we're still running up and down the slopes of Croagh Patrick, wasn't the lead singer of Savage Garden recently singing about some perverse fantasy of morphing into a cannonball, albeit a gelled one in leather pants? Something about living like one and hurtling through the jungle? Now I don't doubt for one minute that, given the tragic history of colonialism, the African jungle has seen a few cannonballs hurtling through it down the centuries. But the bit about wind in your hair and sand at your feet: even allowing for the remote possibility that the occasional cannonball with a comb-over went into circulation, I can't in my wildest dreams imagine how Quality Assurance let the one with the feet get through.

Climbing over the lip at the end of the first stage,

the immortal words of Kajagoogoo were on a loop in the vacant lot where my mind used to be.

Paula and Richard soon joined me, and together we collapsed back onto a couple of rocks like otters in the sun.

As I've said, in mountain terms Croagh Patrick isn't all that big. However its size is accentuated by the fact that it thrusts up into the sky out of an otherwise flat landscape.

Looking up at the distant Reek as it peered back down at us through a break in the clouds, it did appear extremely impressive. But, despite the number of banal lyrics we'd slid and stumbled over along the way, we were only about a quarter of the distance to the top. In fact from here the first stage didn't even look like part of Croagh Patrick itself, merely a bit of a foothill leading up to it.

'Have we still got to climb *that*?' asked Paula. 'No bloody way!'

'Er,' I suggested, optimistically.

'You never said it was *that* fucking big, John,' offered Richard.

'I didn't know.'

'No,' he conceded. 'No you didn't. But you could have hired a reconnaissance team and sent them on ahead in order to ascertain...'

'Shut up, Richard!' Paula and I snapped.

The clouds rolled in off the Atlantic and obscured a

couple of climbers on the side of the mountain. The climb to get even as far as they had didn't look very inviting. In fact it looked downright terrifying. Looking at where we were, where *they* were, and where we imagined the summit to be, I was suddenly positive that I couldn't make it.

I'm not very good with heights—I've been known to hyperventilate while changing a light bulb—and even if I were dragged kicking and screaming to reach the climbers up ahead of us, I would only be about halfway. So I abandoned all hope of getting to the top.

With the rain threatening, Paula was all for returning to the warmth of the car and then on to one of the nearby pubs for lunch. This had a certain appeal. So what if I was writing a book about my Irish experiences? Perhaps failure could become the dominant theme. Centuries ago it was one of the first rhymes for "Australia" and could act as a link with my spiritual home. And if I failed to accomplish anything on this trip, that would be a perfect metaphor for those of us reaching our middle years—we may not have arrived where we intended, but we had, nonetheless, made it to somewhere pretty special. It would also tie in nicely with my Buddhist approach, in that the journey was more important than the destination.

With that resolved I was all set to head back down to the car with Paula when Richard suggested that we push on, if not for the actual summit, then a bit further up so that at least we could say we gave it a go. We'd made it this far, hadn't we? Our journey had been long, and not without hardship, but we had survived through grit and determination, and surely that which didn't kill us could only make us stronger. And what's more we might never pass this way again.

With Richard's monologue fast turning into the lyrics of a Seekers song, Paula and I readily agreed to carry on if only to shut him up.

At that point a young Canadian couple loomed up out of the gloom ahead of us like characters in a Sherlock Holmes novel.

'Are you guys going to climb it?' asked the woman brightly.

No. We're waiting for a bus. 'Yes.'

'We're going to give it a go,' said Richard.

'I don't think so,' said Paula. 'It's too high for me.'

'Don't give up now. You've got the hang of it,' offered the man. 'It looks steeper from here, and that's because it is. But that actually makes it easier as you're going up quicker. And because it *is* steeper you can use your hands as well.'

I pointed up at the climbers we could see through the clouds who were now about three-quarters of the way to the top. 'But what about where they are now? It looks...' I trailed off, trying to think of a better word than scary. 'Scary.'

'I know it looks like that from here,' said the woman.

'And that's exactly how I felt. But once you're up there it's different. You'll see. Believe me; if *I* can climb it, anyone can.'

Duly encouraged we bade farewell to our Canadian friends and started our assault on the Reek itself.

The man was right. By using my hands I was able to take some of the workload off my stressed knees. I literally scampered up the first part like a dog across a bindii patch.

Because what passes for the trail twisted left and right as I made my way up, I soon found that I had lost Richard and Paula. One minute they were right behind me, and the next I was alone about halfway to the summit.

I rounded another outcrop and spotted them sitting on a rock about fifty or so metres further down the slope. It looked as though they had given up. I called out to them but my voice was carried away on the wind.

Dilemma mark II: did I go back down? Or carry on? With the summit almost in sight I decided to carry on. Luckily I got chatting to a man who was on his way down. He agreed to pass on a message to Richard and Paula that I was going for the summit and would meet them back at the car.

I had enough sense to know that it wasn't safe to climb by yourself, but again my luck was in because just ahead of me was a father and son team from Chicago, Illinois (as opposed to Chicago, New South Wales).

Larkin about in IRELAND

They'd passed us earlier and had introduced themselves. The father was well into his sixties and once the climb had become steeper he'd slowed markedly. They'd embarked on this adventure as a sort of bonding exercise. Whether the bonding was with each other or the sweet Lord Jesus I wasn't entirely sure. Either way, I felt that it was rude to impose by climbing with them. Instead I overtook them and in doing so informed them that I was now on my own. They wished me luck and asked me to reserve them a table for two at the summit.

There is a scene in Peter Weir's masterpiece *Picnic at Hanging Rock* where Miranda and two other girls make their way up through a narrow opening between the rocks and disappear. The whole scene is played out in slow motion as if part of a dream sequence and is at once breathtakingly beautiful and utterly terrifying.

That's how I felt, as I looked up towards the summit, which was now less than fifty metres away. Although it was no longer visible through the thick cloud bank, I had caught glimpses of the small white-washed church that had been built up there and that I could feel myself irresistibly drawn to.

The Americans had gone. Either they'd fallen back through the gloom, or else had been spirited away by a bunch of aliens.

I scuttled up the last section of the climb, horrified by what might lie behind and ahead. If Richard and Paula *had* returned to the car and the Americans opted to descend, it suddenly dawned on me that I was alone on the mountain.

But then, as if by divine intervention, the clouds cleared and I was on the top of Croagh Patrick bathed in glorious sunshine. I walked up the short incline to the church and gazed down on the whale-like humps of the islands scattered about Clew Bay far below.

I took a couple of photos, had a celebratory drink of water and then wandered around the outside of the church and set to wondering just what St Patrick had against snakes.

Previously I'd looked upon St Patrick's banishment of the snakes as a metaphor rather than an actual venture into pest control. For some reason I'd always associated Adam and Eve's serpent with paganism. So when St Patrick brought Christianity to Ireland in 431 (or 432—accounts vary) I assumed it meant that paganism was duly banished.

Everyone I'd questioned about this immediately said that I was talking a load of shite. There wasn't any metaphor involved. St Patrick actually got rid of the snakes and it was this that had bagged him his sainthood. Had I ever *seen* any snakes in Ireland? No. But then again I hadn't encountered a whole lot of aardvarks or three-toed sloths on my travels either. Yet curiously enough we didn't get any St Garys or St Darrens wandering around seeking beatification for their banishment.

I walked around to the far side of the church looking for a way in, but the windows were frustratingly barred and there was a big, black, shiny, fuck-off padlock on the door. There was a slot next to the padlocked door into which you were asked to slip your donation.

I made a few more circuits, took a couple of additional photos, and relieved myself into the slot by the padlocked door (no I didn't, but I had you worried there for a minute, didn't I?). Then, with the thunder rumbling out at sea, I held out my arms and banished all the huntsman spiders from Sydney. With that done, I made a short but significant speech about conquering my fear of heights, but it was tinged with the sad thought that due to the state of my knees, I would never be back. With a lump in my throat I started the long, slow descent to the car park.

Twenty minutes later I was back at the summit.

No sooner had I started picking my way down through the rocks than I encountered my American friends from Chicago, Illinois who had kept on with their ascent and hadn't been abducted after all.

I wished them luck and continued down. Moments later to my utter amazement and delight I ran into Richard and Paula. Although he'd received my message, Richard hadn't been prepared to leave me alone on the Reek or let Paula go back to the car by herself.

I suddenly realised that, having got a whiff of the summit, I'd behaved selfishly and had left my friends in an awkward position. To his credit, though, Richard didn't make a big deal about it. He said that if he'd been in my position he would have done exactly the same thing. I just hoped that if I'd been in *his*, I would have done the same thing too.

They'd made it this far and there was no turning back now, and ten minutes later we were all together at the summit. But the weather had turned, and we were soon huddling in the lee of the church, trying to keep out the rain, and stave off the cold.

'What is the point of having a church on the top of this bloody mountain,' I yelled slipping into Basil Fawlty mode, 'if you can't get in? I mean what is the bloody point?'

'Jesus it's cold!' exclaimed Paula.

Richard examined the slot by the padlock. 'Perhaps if you stick your credit card in, the door springs open.'

'Now wouldn't that be appropriate!' said Paula.

Indeed.

In retrospect I would rather climb Croagh Patrick three times than descend it once. The return journey was one of the hardest things I've ever done. It was sheer agony, my knees swelling up like disgruntled pufferfish.

The human leg is designed to convey you up a mountain, not down it. A foot angled down and away from you offers very little means of support. Better product design would see our feet capable of rotating at the ankle through a hundred and eighty degrees, and our legs hyperextend to enable us to bend them as far forward as we can back. Such a person would be extremely difficult to beat at Twister.

On the last downward section, and with Richard and Paula already back at the car, I got chatting to a German gentleman, Gunter, who now lived in Ireland and regularly climbed Croagh Patrick.

'Did you find it hard?' asked Gunter.

'Coming down I did.' I replied.

'Yes. I think most people find that the hardest part.'

'There should be a ride back down to the bottom,' I suggested. 'Like an enormous collection plate that you could sit in and ride like a toboggan.'

'I don't think it's best if they make it too commercial,' said Gunter. 'We don't want a McDonald's up there now do we?'

'Perhaps just a small café specialising in hazelnut lattes and almond friands.'

'I take it from your accent that you're not from around these parts,' said Gunter.

I told him of my search to find my spiritual home, about being forced to leave England as a child, and how I'd never really come to terms with it.

'Your father is Irish, yes?' said Gunter.

I nodded.

'Then I think we'll be seeing a lot more of you in Ireland.'

Several hours later, while Paula ducked inside to bags a table in the restaurant, Richard and I stood by the entrance to the pub and gazed back up at Croagh Patrick. The sun was setting slowly behind the Reek, giving it a glorious aura that seemed only fitting.

We patted each other warmly on the back like the rugged mountain men that we now were. Then we disappeared into the pub and ordered a couple of steaming bowls of seafood chowder.

Thirteen
Behan's Final Hurl

Once we'd conquered Croagh Patrick, my plan had been to spend the night in Westport and then make my way down to Galway to meet up with my cousin Donal who had promised to take me surfing. Given that I lived only a short drive from some of the finest surfing beaches in the world, but had never actually hung ten, five, or however many it was you were meant to hang, I felt that making my debut in Ireland was about as ironic as it got.

Between courses and hot ports in the restaurant, I took my notepad out of my allegedly waterproof daypack. It was saturated. Although we had been hit by a couple of squalls on the way up, they were really nothing by Irish standards. But the notes that I'd made up there on the mountain had dribbled off the page, seeped through the bottom of my pack, and leaked back into the Reek. In retrospect I suppose there is a certain poetic symmetry to this, but at the time it just pissed me off.

I rummaged quickly through the rest of the pack

and everything else was sodden too, so that now the only dry clothes I had were the ones I was wearing: a very thin jumper, and a pair of swish-swoosh spray-pants.

I needed a laundry. So instead of staying in Westport, I settled on going back to base at Richard and Paula's house in Dublin so I could do a wash. The rugged adventurer returns. If I'd been with Scott en route back from the South Pole his diary would have read: "Captain Larkin has stepped outside to look for a laundromat. He may be some time."

The following day, then, having set the washing machine to a fairly aggressive full cycle, I went into town to visit the Dublin Writers' Museum. Although it was a good eight to ten kilometres away, I thought I'd walk rather than take the bus. This was partly due to the traffic—and the congestion was so bad that I kept up with the bus for all but the last couple of kays—but mostly because the guys in my soccer team had started paying me out about my rapidly expanding paunch. They'd threatened to start doing their warm-up laps around it, the bastards!

After an hour's hard slog, I'd made it to St Stephen's Green, a picturesque little park in the heart of the city. Wheezing like an asthmatic steam-train I collapsed onto one of the many benches that had been provided for "eejits" like me, who power-walked into town despite being seriously unfit and having climbed a mountain the day before.

Larkin about in IRELAND

I finally caught my breath, sat up and devoured one of the chocolate bars that I kept finding hidden in my coat pockets by Jacqui and Chantelle. Suddenly I seemed a long way from home.

There was a bust of James Joyce by one of the rubbish bins, so I wandered over to pay my respects and deposit my empty wrapper. He looked a bit forlorn, stuck out here in an almost forgotten corner of the park. Or maybe he was upset that so many of the dotcom Celtic Tiger Economy generation had never even heard of him, let alone read any of his work.

I studied the great one's face, hoping to draw some inspiration of my own or to understand what on earth possessed him to come up with:

> Sobs they sighdid at Fillagain's chrissormiss wake, all the hoolivans of the nation, prostrated in their consternation and their duodisimally profusive plethora of ululation. There were plumbs and grumes and cheriffs and citherers and raiders and cinemen too. And the all gained in with the shoutmost shoviality. Agog and Magog and the round of them agrog.

Refusing to bow to the constraints of English, Joyce hacked away at the language in much the same way that Vincent Van Gogh had done with his ear. And despite rumours to the contrary, *Finnegans Wake*, for so long known as *Work in Progress*, was completed over a marathon seventeen-year period and not, as so often seems, after a big night out on the tiles.

Leaving St Stephen's Green I came across a signpost that read, "National Library and Gynaecological Office". It seemed such an odd pairing that I resolved to go and check it out. I followed the directions, not completely sure what I'd find, but prepared to bet that it would be interesting. I tried to imagine what went on in such a place, and then thought better of it. It was only when I came across the third sign that I realised I'd been struck down by a momentary bout of dyslexia. What the sign actually said was, "National Library and Genealogical Office", a far more sensible symbiosis.

The streets were crowded with tourists taking photos and locals cutting deals and talking shite on mobile phones. I entered the library looking for sanctuary, only to find it staffed by security guards and the entrance hung with polite but firm signs intoning that bags were to be checked here, coats left there, and so on. I didn't like the idea of being frisked at the entrance to a library, so I mooched around the ornate foyer for a while, made some notes, and left.

These days we're forced to live with more security guards than ever, but it doesn't mean that I have to like them. The notion of giving an unemployed man a gun and a uniform is, to my way of thinking, just asking for trouble. They always seem to glare at me as if to say, "Try anything, buddy, and I'll fill you so full of lead you'll be able to use your love-wand as a pencil." (I'd settled on "love-wand" as a euphemism here, but I decided to insert "Penis", so to speak, in order to see what MS Word Thesaurus would have to say on the matter. Unable to locate a synonym, it suggested "Pen Friend". I can only conclude that in order to confuse these two vastly different nouns, somebody quite senior at Microsoft spends way too much time at the office, no doubt to the consternation of a spouse, a pen friend, or both.)

I wandered along to Trinity College but it was conferring day and the place was packed. So I lurched across the forecourt, trying desperately not to encroach on that non-space that exists between photographer and subject. I tried for sanctuary again in the Berkeley library but I didn't have a reader's ticket, so I was thwarted once more. For a nation so steeped in literary history, it was doing all it possibly could to prevent me getting to any of it.

I thought about having a look at the *Book of Kells*, but in the end decided against it. I'd seen it before and, besides, even out of season there's generally a queue leading into the sealed chamber where the book is housed. Once in the chamber, you have approximately twenty-eight seconds to admire the book's reflection through a smoked-glass mirror half-a-metre thick before your air expires. The *Book of Kells* has been guarded by the ninja warrior arm of a secret order of brothers for centuries. These brothers are so monumentally deranged that anyone suspected of looking directly at the manuscript, or uttering its contents aloud, is immediately taken outside and made to watch a perpetually looped tape of *A Very Brady Christmas*. Every six months, a specially trained and hairless orang-utan is lowered by its ankles into the chamber, where it painstakingly turns the page using telekinesis. If the brothers even suspect that the orang-utan has as much as breathed on the smoked-glass that protects the book's reflection, it is immediately taken outside and forcibly read the complete memoirs of the Reverend Ian Paisley.

I think it's overrated, myself. Since I'm a writer from a country whose literary history is so relatively recent that an ancient book is one without a barcode, you could be forgiven for thinking that the *Book of Kells* would leave me breathless. And you'd be wrong. That the *Book of Kells* is a great work of art is beyond dispute. But for me, the real magic of a book happens between the page and the reader, whether the book contains a barcode or not, the writer alive or dead. I'm not interested in a book that is a leather-bound, gold-lettered, limited edition *objet d'art*.

Crossing the forecourt in the direction of the exit, I overheard a conversation between two young graduates, degrees in hand, mortarboards set at a jaunty angle, gowns flowing on the morning breeze.

'He fookin, fook, fookin, fook, fooker.'

'Me fookin bollicks he fookin did.'

'I fookin swear, you fookin fooker.'

They're probably dotcom millionaires already.

Perhaps it was the mood I was in, which I'm forced to admit was rather odd, but walking up O'Connell Street towards the Writers' Museum, I couldn't help feeling that Dublin's fair city lacked something. Maybe it was soul. Ironic really, given that soul is something Ireland is known to have in abundance. Whatever it was that I'd come to Ireland in search of, I knew that I wouldn't find it here. I live in one of the best cities in the world, and if I was to move to another, it would be London, Paris, Rome or New York. Dublin just didn't cut it for me and suddenly I didn't want to be there anymore. I wanted to be out in the country again, dangling off a mountain, eating seafood chowder in an old stone pub, traipsing through the icky mud of a dairy farm.

I carried on to the Writers' Museum but my heart really wasn't in it.

Because it was a weekday and out of season, I pretty much had the place to myself. But I'm not sure that the idea of a writers' museum actually works. To me, as I say, the magic of the written word is a process that takes place somewhere between the page and the reader. The art should always be bigger than the artist. Which leads me to think that every single bookshop is a writers' museum.

I suppose a museum set up to commemorate a particular writer's life has a certain voyeuristic appeal: "This is the typewriter on which James Joyce wrote *Finnegan's Wake*. Notice how many of the keys are interchangeable, and some of the others are just, well, missing."

"And this perfectly preserved selection of diced vegetables was removed from Brendan Behan's final hurl, shortly after he'd consumed one too many glasses of carrot punch."

I was wandering round the displays and having a grand old time despite my reservations, when my solitude was rudely interrupted by the arrival of a tour group. It seemed they couldn't think for themselves or read, because each of them was wearing a Dublin Writers' Museum Walkman that advised them where to stand and told them what they were seeing, therefore saving them the tedious necessity of having to actually read the inscriptions. An audio tour of a writers' museum just makes me want to scream.

I'd been merrily reading about my old friend, the loquacious Oscar Wilde who, on his deathbed apparently said of the wallpaper, "One or the other of us has to go" and promptly expired, when no fewer than twenty people immediately crowded around me because their headsets had told them to do so.

In the spirit of Uncle Oscar I turned around and said, 'I have nothing to declare but your vacuity.' They couldn't hear me, of course, because right at that very moment the voice in their headphones told them to go into the toilet and take a dump.

I left the museum and returned to St Stephen's Green to check on JJ's forlorn-looking bust. I just hoped that in the economic revolution that was currently sweeping the land, he wouldn't end up being decapitated in the way that Lenin was when the Wall came down.

But as the Celtic Tiger prowls the country, it's not just Joyce who's being tossed aside by the sashaying dotcom generation. Wilde, Beckett, Yeats, Shaw, Behan, O'Casey, and Goldsmith are all being ignored in equal measure. Now I don't for one minute begrudge the Irish their new-found prosperity—and who would care if I did?—but I hope that in their haste to stuff their coffers and line their pockets, that they don't end up throwing the baby out with the bath water, because the baby is pretty wonderful.

Fourteen

The Geisha of Glendalough

I headed for Avoca to dispel a myth, but never made it.

Avoca is where the popular television program *Ballykissangel* is filmed. I had heard that the entrance to Fitzgerald's pub, the very heart of the town and show, was nothing more than a façade and that the interiors were actually filmed in a studio. And what's more the Fitzgerald's pub of Avoca was actually a hairdresser's and is simply decorated to appear like a pub for the exteriors. I resolved to find out for myself. As quests go I freely admit that it wasn't exactly up there with the search for the Holy Grail, or the pursuit of world peace, but at least it was going to get me out of town and back into the country.

Avoca is a difficult spot to get to by public transport, especially if your decision to go there is a spontaneous one. And making your way round Ireland by public transport, especially out of season, lends itself not to acts of spontaneity but hours of meticulous planning. So I abandoned my no-car policy and borrowed Paula's.

Although the roads were congested to the point of gridlock with inward bound traffic, I followed the signs out of town and, less than half an hour after dropping Paula at her office, I was, much to my delight, back in the country.

Pulled along by the rest of the traffic I was soon zooming south on the N11, my eyes as wide as startled hubcaps, watchful in case a genuflecting motorist should suddenly loom into my path and despatch me to the next life.

•

I must admit to being intensely wary of Irish drivers. On an earlier visit, one of my uncles kindly offered to take me on a cross-country outing to Sligo.

The uncle—who is about to get a pseudonym because I'm hoping to throw his immediate family off the scent—is a deeply religious man and attends mass every day and twice on Sundays. More Irish than a shamrock, Uncle Vladimir is mild-mannered—almost incredibly so. He once apologised to my sister Trish for giving her directions as he was showing her around the town, "Now over there behind the church, and excuse me for pointing...". He is one of the loveliest people you could ever have the pleasure of meeting. He is also one of the most reckless drivers outside the professional smash-up derby circuit. Add to this a certain religious enthusiasm, and you have a potentially lethal combination.

On the day of our trip to Sligo, Uncle Vladimir got me up so early that technically it was still the night before. For some reason the extremely devout do like to beat the chickens up (in a non-violent sense), even if their nephews are more than happy to loaf around in bed until midday. So while the roosters were still hitting their snooze buttons, we were blasting along the lanes of rural Ireland in Uncle Vladimir's ancient car. I was never sure of the make but it bore a striking resemblance to the old Batmobile—its tailfins slicing through the heavy morning air like a pair of dolphins gliding across a bay.

Careering through the town, Uncle Vladimir started to wave his hand around wildly like a bikie with a bee caught in his helmet and he mumbled something under his breath which I didn't quite hear but that might have been related to the subject of bees.

Every few kays, just as I was nodding off in the eerie pre-dawn glow, the car would lurch violently to the left as Uncle Vladimir continued with his incoherent mumbling and slashing. At one point I jolted back to consciousness to find him steering the Batmobile round a sweeping bend with his knees.

With my face pointed straight ahead, but my eyes locked right on Uncle Vladimir, I soon saw that the car lurched and fishtailed every time we passed a church.

Larkin about in IRELAND

I watched in stunned silence as Uncle Vladimir removed his hands from the wheel, eyes from the road, and paid homage to every single church we passed. Once, with the car practically airborne after we'd cleared a hump in the road, I heard him mutter, 'Mary, Joseph, and Jesus himself', while waving to a church on a distant hill. And that was an interesting thing: the amount of energy Uncle Vladimir put into his signs of the cross seemed to vary with the size of the church in question and our proximity to it. Passing an enormous old gothic greystone minster and round tower, Uncle Vladmir genuflected so vigorously that he was almost rendered unconscious by the dashboard. Fortunately the car didn't have airbags or they might have detonated. Meanwhile a smallish chapel down a side street would get just a cursory nod and wave as if to say, *we'll get you on the way back.*

Needless to say, at the speed we were going, and despite my existentialist leanings, by the time we reached Sligo I was muttering a few prayers of my own.

•

Not all that far from the Avoca exit, I came across a sign to Glendalough, which I'd heard from several sources was not to be missed. So, secure in the knowledge that every decision I'd made so far had turned out to be the right one, I turned off the N11 and headed to Glendalough instead. The inquiry into *Ballykissangel's* bar and hairdresser's I was prepared to leave till later or to a serious investigative journalist. I thought I'd give *Four Corners* a call when I returned home.

I hadn't gone all that far down the winding lane to Glendalough when, to my horror, I hit a patch of black ice. The car spun out along the road for the next fifty metres like the Batmobile suddenly encountering the Vatican.

Amazingly, just as I put my hands on the roof to brace myself for the car's imminent roll, the steering suddenly corrected itself and I carried on into Glendalough a bit shaken but otherwise unscathed.

I stopped at the smart-looking visitors' centre but unfortunately it was closed for the season. I hopped back in the car and made my way over the type of bridge that you could imagine leprechauns fishing from. A brook babbled away beneath it and under the Glendalough Hotel too. Although there was hardly anyone about and heavy rain loured off the Wicklow Mountains, a souvenir stall was opening up just beyond the bridge and hotel. Despite my experiences in Knock, I was actually heartened by this, because it meant that Glendalough, and the hills and mountains beyond, were also open for business, and that I wouldn't be the only "eejit" out in it.

Turning the car around, I made my way back over the bridge and parked beside the hotel. When I went inside, the aroma of frying pig bits filled the air. I'd only managed to consume a bowl of horse food before leaving that morning, so with my blood sugar level critically low, I was more than ready to go the fang again. Fortunately the hotel staff were more than willing to have me for breakfast, so with my mouth watering as if I were a rabid dog, I hurried along to the delightful dining room over the babbling brook.

I ordered a full Irish fry-up with coffee—determined to persevere with it—and took a table by the window. Apart from two elderly American women, the dozen or so other guests were middle-aged English couples who all seemed to know one another.

The view I had of Glendalough from the dining room was so breathtakingly beautiful that I insist you go there immediately. If the south side of Dublin is where Postman Pat might retire to, Glendalough is the place his soul will inhabit when he dies. The Wicklow Mountains leapt up behind the trees like a Mexican wave, while the wind whipped down the hills and through the trees, causing a strange, high-pitched sound that summoned me like Odysseus's sirens. I had no earplugs and no chums to tie me to the mast, so I succumbed to their temptation.

Not content to admire the view, I longed to be part of it.

After breakfast I went out to the car and slipped on my spray-pants, hiking boots and daypack. Although given the strenuous efforts of the past few days, I had resolved to take a day off from trekking, I was delighted that I had at least packed for the possibility.

I filled my water bottle in the hotel, hitched up my daypack, stared at the furthest peak, gave myself a brief pep talk on how to conquer these hills, stepped out the door, and promptly turned the wrong way.

It didn't occur to me that I was actually going the wrong way until I met Catherine, a friendly English woman who was walking along the path towards me.

'Good morning,' said Catherine. 'It isn't that way.'

'What isn't?'

'Anything.'

Around the back of the hotel there were two trails: one leading up into an old graveyard, and another that seemed to cut around the graveyard and up into the hills beyond. Like me, Catherine had taken the other.

'It doesn't go anywhere,' said Catherine. 'It just stops dead. We have to go through the graveyard.'

I'd had a day of solitude in Dublin, and there's nothing like a city to make you feel lonely. It was comforting to have someone to talk to again.

We made our way up the steps into the graveyard and down the other side to the trail beyond, which led down to the lough itself.

Catherine was married to an Irishman and now lived in Galway. She was on her way back from a conference in London, but when she'd alighted from the ferry at

Dun Laoghaire, rather than head straight to Galway, she'd opted to detour here.

I suggested that she'd added at least three hours to her journey.

'Sure,' she said. 'But look around us. How could you possibly come so close and not yearn to be out in it?'

My thoughts exactly.

Although she wasn't quite kitted out for hiking, Catherine walked with me the half kilometre or so down to the lough. We didn't say much; were both just thrilled to be out here while the rest of the population were out cutting deals or talking bollocks on mobile phones. We practically had the place to ourselves—the elderly English couples I'd shared the dining room with at breakfast apparently content to admire the scenery from the hotel bar.

I knelt down to touch the water and immediately yelped like a startled hyena.

'Invigorating?' Catherine smiled.

'That's one word for it,' I said. 'I think my finger's got frostbite.'

'People go swimming in there.'

'Yes. And then they're immediately carted off in a van to a climate-controlled environment.'

With her eyes set to the heavens, Catherine told me that there was a path somewhere high above that led to a very special place, and that I really ought to try and find it.

For a moment I thought she'd turned into a religious fanatic and was trying to convert me, but then it dawned on me that she was referring to a hiking trail, and at the same time admiring the view.

With the hills calling, and Catherine forced to head back to the road, we wished each other well, shook hands and departed.

Not far up from the lake, I came across a small information hut that wasn't just locked up for the season but sandbagged. I wondered what kind of information required such a level of security. Nothing that I'd been offered on this trip so far! Whatever it was, the informants weren't having nosey off-season types gaining access to it.

Duly warned, it was back to the trail and my solitude. The rain was falling steadily now but it wasn't going to dampen my spirits. I strode along in the hills of Glendalough just like someone who can call striding along in the hills of Glendalough his work. I tried to remember all the main roads that I'd gone down to get to this point in my life, but I couldn't and just considered myself extremely fortunate. In order to make a living I'd once pushed supermarket trolleys up a steep hill in the Winston Hills shopping centre, and then I'd worked in a factory, putting caps on bottles. Now, here I was, with those days more than half my life away, wandering about in my father's country and calling it a job. The gods, whatever form they take, were clearly looking after me. And who was to say? Maybe Uncle Vladimir was right: perhaps God was watching our every—

My epiphany was disrupted when a bird chose that exact moment to release into my hair the sort of bowel movement that would immediately lead other birds to take up a collection for its retirement due to ill health.

Back I went to the pristine waters of Glendalough, and, using my drink bottle, managed eventually to rinse out all the shit. Had anyone come across me just then, they would have assumed I was performing some bizarre self-baptism, and they would have been quite wrong. I was a committed existentialist once again.

Returning to the woods, I found an ancient graveyard. The headstones were so old they had been weathered back to the rocks they were originally hewn from. I wondered if St Kevin was buried up here.

If Croagh Patrick is synonymous with St Patrick, then Glendalough is the domain of St Kevin. I knew from my reading that in order to be canonised, you had to have at least two sanctioned miracles to your credit. St Patrick had got jiggy with the snakes and had brought Christianity to Ireland, but no one seemed to know what St Kevin had done—or, if they did, they certainly weren't telling. When pressed, one of my uncles (not Vladimir) said, 'Ah, you don't ask such questions.' Then he muttered something under his breath about colonial heathen.

I knew that St Kevin had a bed round here somewhere, carved into the hillside: St Kevin's bed curiously enough. But surely loafing around beneath the doona all day isn't, by itself, enough to attain sainthood. If it were, I'd be up for half a dozen of them.

I decided, on the strength of the little I knew about him, that St Kev was the patron saint of good blokes. The sort of guy who you could phone when your car broke down, and who not only lent you his ute when you were moving house, but would actually pitch in and help. St Kev was the first to get a round in at the pub, despite the fact that he was the designated driver for the evening and on lemon squash. You could always sleep on St Kevvy's lounge when your relationship had gone pear-shaped, you'd lost your job, or there were a couple of loan sharks out after for you. If you were desperate to go to the rugby league or AFL grand finals, the Davis Cup semi, or a World Cup qualifying match, the Kevster would always come through with the tickets, despite the fact that the event had been sold out months beforehand.

I liked him a lot.

Once out of the woods I found that I was on a sort of gravel track that zig-zagged further up into the hills. At the end, disappearing back through the trees was the trail that Catherine had spoken about earlier.

I don't know who is responsible for the walking trails in and around the hills of Glendalough, but I would like to thank them. The trail that I was now on wasn't simply an eroded dirt track, but thoughtfully engineered and well-maintained. The Irish enjoy a brisk stroll in the country, and whoever built this trail hadn't let them down. They had laid out a series of logs (longer than railway sleepers, but shorter than telegraph poles) in pairs and bolted them together. Obviously aware that the logs would become slippery in the wet, the builders had painstakingly wrapped each pair of logs with chicken wire. I thought it looked a bit precarious at first, but my boots gripped the wire and after a cautious start I was soon stomping along like Armstrong and Aldrin on the Sea of Tranquillity.

The logs became steps and I was soon climbing up through the rainforest—well it was a forest and it was pouring rain. Shortly I emerged above the line of trees and picked up the log trail again. I stepped over a fence and made my way across to the side of the hill (so steep it was really a cliff) and encountered a couple of goats who gazed at me in a dumbstruck manner as if to say, *Now how do you suppose* he *got up here?*.

I was a mountain man again. Lost in the cadence of my steps and the rhythm of the rain on my Goretex hood, I hiked without any sense of time or the notion that I had a care in the world—and I didn't. Ever cautious, though, where the trail meandered a bit too close to the edge for my liking, I stepped off it, made my way inland, and picked it up again a bit further along.

I sat down to take in the view and a Kit-Kat—the staple diet of hardy mountaineers. I thought I had the trail to myself, but looking back to where I'd come across the goats, I could make out the bobbing red anorak of a fellow hiker.

I didn't want to share this moment with anyone, so I pocketed the wrapper and off I went over the distant peaks, which, of course, were no longer distant. As I reached the top of the first peak the weather, which had only been menacing up until then, now turned downright hostile. The wind threatened to transform my coat into a sail and lift me helpless into the air before slam-dunking me into Glendalough far below.

With the horizontal rain all but blinding me, I hitched up my hood and must have looked like a Franciscan monk. I dropped into a crouch and edged my way cautiously back down the trail like an overweight and uncoordinated duck. Forget dignity; this was survival. Now I knew why I had the mountains to myself. I was the only one stupid enough to venture up this far at that time of year. I wished I was back in the hotel bar with the elderly English couples, admiring the view over a hot port and a jolly old game of dominoes.

As I waddled down the other side of the hill, I noticed that Red Anorak was now sitting exactly where

I'd stopped for a Kit-Kat. I stood up and, with the wind at my back, the trail sloping away from me and made slippery by the heavy rain, I was suddenly gathering speed at an alarming rate and any second was about to run right over the edge of the cliff like an expendable pleb in an *Indiana Jones* film.

I slammed on the brakes. Fortunately, with its back to me and unaware of my approach, Red Anorak didn't see my inelegant landing on my backside. I picked myself up slowly and quietly. I tiptoed down the trail with little pitty-pat steps like a geisha crossing an ice-rink blindfolded, with her best tea-set on her head.

I was worried in case a raucous 'G'day!' made Red Anorak leap into the ravine in surprise, so I coughed a gentle warning.

'Oh, hello there.' Red Anorak swung around and turned out to be a woman called Maeve. 'I had a feeling there was somebody else up here with me.'

'Not the nicest day to be out.' I didn't really mean this. It was just something to say.

'It's not too bad for Ireland,' Maeve offered.

'I can't believe that there are just the two of us up here,' I said. 'It's so magnificent.'

'It's a bit different in summer,' she sighed. 'Literally thousands of people along this very trail. You've practically got to queue up to get onto it.' With that she got to her feet and started walking towards the peaks that had just driven me down.

'Be careful up there,' I warned her. 'There's a bit of a breeze.' The mountain man goes for understatement.

'It's okay,' said Maeve. 'I hike this trail two or three times a week in winter.'

Looking down on Glendalough it was easy to see what it was that had drawn me to Ireland. But of course there was more to it than that. It wasn't just the scenery or the big weather. There was something else down there. Or was it in here? Something that I couldn't quite put my finger on. Something innate.

If you take God out of the equation, as more of us are choosing to do, what you are left with in the individual life is nothing more than a complex lump of organic matter. This could, I suppose, explain why as we enter what we hope is the second half of our lives, so many of us are somehow drawn back to the place of our birth, or the place of our forebears, like the Eloi into the Morlocks' caverns.

For most of my life I have lived in Sydney. And although it is so beautiful and vibrant, I still get pangs of homesickness for the mining town in South Yorkshire where I first experienced life. Though it is basically a damp, drab, miserable hole in the ground, there are times when I long to return, buy myself a flat cap and take out a subscription to *Coal and Pigeon Fanciers Weekly*.

Looking down on Glendalough, though, I found it hard to take God out of the equation.

With my epiphany completed after all, I stood up, buttoned my coat and headed back along the trail towards the car.

I was going surfing.

Fifteen

Staying at Ben's

When I woke early the next morning it was pouring. *Quelle surprise.* There was also a wicked wind howling in from what appeared to be every direction, and it sent the already teeth-chattering temperature plummeting. So the call of the waves was a distant one.

My plan had been to head for the Dublin terminal, catch a bus to Galway and meet up with my cousin Donal. Since my arrival in Ireland, however, I hadn't been able to contact him. Although he had an office in Galway, as a forestry inspector he was mostly out on the road—or in the forest at any rate—and although I wasn't surprised that he was so rarely in the office he never seemed to be in mobile range. Still, because things had worked out so well for me thus far, I figured that all I had to do was turn up in Galway at any given time and somehow he would be there.

On a whim, though, I decided to go to Tullamore instead and continue on from there to Galway at a later date.

I'd always intended to go to Tullamore. It was my father's home town, after all, and I still had relatives living there: Uncle Seamus and Aunt Veronica, and my cousins Mary and Fiona. My Aunt Margaret was now stationed in Mullingar (if that's the verb you apply to a nun), so unfortunately I knew that there'd be no tours of (or head banging in) the Tullamore convent on this occasion.

With that planned, I threw a few things into my daypack, skulled a cup of the Irish equivalent of coffee, and headed off for the bus stop. The rain blattered on my hood as I let myself out of Richard and Paula's house, but the garbage men were out—and in fine voice too. One of them was singing, well, *yelling* a curious Indian or Pakistani song about a woman who was sweeping her front step when what she really ought to have been doing was catching the next boat home to India or Pakistan. It may not have actually been India or Pakistan that the garbo was singing about—perhaps it was Bangladesh, I wasn't sure because his diction was so unclear—but it was clearly sub-continental. He was wailing and warbling as if his testicles had just been caught in his sitar strings.

I was immediately heartened by the garbo's willingness to embrace multiculturalism—a relatively recent phenomenon to Ireland—until I saw the focus of his song: an elderly Indian woman sweeping her front step. This wasn't the last overtly racist incident I was to encounter either. Later, on a shopping trip into town—a day that was far too mind-numbingly dull to recount in detail—I was waiting in a queue to catch the bus back to Richard and Paula's, and I listened agog while the driver tore into one of the passengers. He was enraged because the passenger was trying to pay his fare with a ten-pound note. I had a feeling that this was only part of the problem, and that the real issue at hand was the gentleman's West Indian heritage. As the man took his seat, the driver uttered a quiet but clearly audible "Black bastard!" under his breath. To further test my thesis—I was fast becoming the Stephen Hawking of social conscience—when it came to my turn to pay, I handed over a twenty-pound note.

'Sorry, mate,' I offered in a polite yet firm, take-it-or-bite-me voice. 'That's all I've got.'

'That's okay,' said the driver. 'I've got plenty of change.'

'Then what was your problem with that other guy?' I snapped. The garbage man had been huge but I was much bigger than the bus driver—which constitutes another kind of ism, I suppose.

'That's none of your business.'

'Well, I'm making it my business, buddy.' I was so rugged I could hardly stand it. I had climbed a couple of mountains after all. 'You're giving your country a bad name. Lift your game or I just might put you in my book.' I snatched back my twenty-pound note, stormed off the bus, and walked ten kilometres home in the driving rain. And that showed him.

It seems that the Irish, more accustomed to sending people out, were still coming to terms with welcoming them in. However, coming from a nation whose prime minister still refuses to apologise to our Aboriginal cousins for past wrongs, I can't, in all conscience, cast stones.

After being deposited in O'Connell Street by (let the record show) an extremely friendly and not the least bit bigoted driver, I made my way along to the Busaras bus station, which is Irish for Buses "R" Us. The streets of Dublin were swamped with people, traffic and rain, and I longed to be out of there. I wanted to sit in a country pub by a roaring fire and have lively conversations with old men in tweed coats. Tullamore was looking better by the minute. For although it wasn't exactly rural any longer—it was, more and more, becoming a satellite town of Dublin—it was, nonetheless, a gateway to County Offaly and Shannon Harbour beyond, the destination that I was steadily being drawn to.

I studied the departure board at the bus station but couldn't find even a passing reference to Tullamore. Somewhat dismayed, I made my way across to the information booth. I resisted the temptation to ask the occupant whether there was a god, and if so what form that god took, and asked instead about buses to Tullamore. I was told that there wasn't a bus all day until suddenly, around five o'clock, everybody got the idea they wanted to be in Tullamore and as a result there would be two leaving in quick succession.

I must admit that the idea of hanging around smelly and mouldy old bus stations for the best part of a day has limited appeal. Perhaps because of their transient nature, bus and train stations seem to attract a disproportionate number of loonies. The way to avoid being accosted by them, of course, is to act like one yourself, and a forthright opinion on God, economics and a penchant for lively anoraks and plastic carry-bags always help.

The Buses "R" Us terminal was about as miserable and depressing as these places can get. It had the appearance and odour of a public toilet. Returning to the departure board, I was approached by a gentleman who had directions to the Kingdom of Heaven and assured me they would be mine if I could see my way clear to giving him ten pounds. I was concerned that this might involve taking the journey immediately, so I rejected his kind offer and told him that as a practising Buddhist I didn't hold with the notion of a higher being.

Seeking sanctuary in the toilets downstairs, I was stunned to find that they were every bit as crisp, clean, hygienic and modern as the bus station wasn't. You had to pay to get into them.

I gazed at myself in the mirror. The bags under my eyes were fast turning into suitcases, and my hair looked like it had previously belonged to an astronaut's wife. I was definitely starting to look my age. Worse: I was looking like someone much older's age. The dark shroud was clearly taking its toll.

'Just in town?' asked a distinguished-looking man washing his hands next to me in one of the many pristine basins.

'On my way out, I hope.'

'Where to?'

'I haven't decided yet.'

'I can't place your accent. London?'

'Sydney.'

He shook his head and gave me a wink in the mirror. 'Well, I never! I wouldn't have picked it.'

That's because your exposure to Australian accents doubtless stretches no further than the Crocodile Dundee *movies or crappy soap operas.* 'Irish father. English mother. Tends to dilute it a bit.'

'Ah, so you're Irish. Where from?'

'Shannon Harbour, originally. Then Tullamore.'

'A fine drop,' said the man, referring to Tullamore Dew whiskey, the town's most famous export.

'I'll have to take your word for that. Never actually tried it myself.'

'Would you like to?'

'I suppose I should. Out of respect for my heritage at least.'

'Listen,' said the man. 'I don't live all that far and I've got a bar fridge in my...'

About now I suddenly realised that engaging in spontaneous conversation with men who hang around public toilets wasn't the wisest of moves. Someone was bound to get the wrong idea. Someone evidently *had* got the wrong idea. I immediately worried in case he was an undercover police officer and that perhaps, under some outdated and draconian Irish law, what he was proposing was punishable by public flogging, stoning, or being taken outside and forcibly read the complete memoirs of the Reverend Ian Paisley.

I thanked him for his kind invitation, was delighted that he had his own sauna and an extensive collection of imported magazines and videos, but I had a bus to catch. *Now!*

Returning yet again to the departure board, I realised that I was free to go wherever I wanted. I was like Arthur Dent arriving at an alien spaceport. The universe was mine. I could go anywhere I pleased. With the obvious exception of Tullamore.

A few hours later I arrived tired, cold and hungry in Galway. There'd been a coach for Galway leaving the Buses "R" Us terminal on the hour every hour, so it seemed that destiny was set for me to go there. Obviously Donal was in the office that day and not out inspecting the forest.

The N6 road from Dublin to Galway is so

breathtakingly dull that I slept most of the way. Although inland Ireland does have moments of stunning beauty, it is, for the most part, flat, uninteresting and full of bogs. High precipitation (it's pissing down pretty much all the time) and poor drainage have given the inland the look, and sometimes the smell, of an old waterlogged dishcloth that's been left by the sink in a student's flat for a couple of millennia.

I only stirred to life once in the crossing, when the driver, who could easily have been Ireland's entrant in the Nicest-Man-in-Europe competition, announced that we would shortly be stopping in Kilbeggan. For some reason the name struck a chord with me, though I didn't know why. Pulling out my map, I soon discovered the reason. Kilbeggan was approximately halfway between Dublin and Galway—but only about ten to fifteen kilometres north of Tullamore. Although Jacqui had made me promise not to hitchhike, it wouldn't have taken me any longer than an hour and a half to walk it. And with the couple of days' break in Dublin behind me, I would have enjoyed striding stoutly about the countryside again. Why hadn't the stupid woman at the Buses "R" Us information booth told me? Now, armed with this new information, though, I wondered did I get off in Kilbeggan and make my way on foot to Tullamore, or carry on to Galway? I felt like the Dice Man. But I'd paid my seven-pound fare to ride all the way to Galway so I decided to stick with it—I was on a budget and no one was going to get three-pounds-fifty out of me that easily.

My plan was to hole up in a B&B for the night, leave a message at Donal's office to let him know I was in town, and then see what transpired.

With the rain hammering down, I got off the bus in Galway and Gore-texed my way smartly into the foyer of the plush Eyre Square hotel just around the corner from the station. Shaking like a dog in the surf, I headed for the bar and dining area. The atmosphere was so convivial that I thought I'd stay for lunch and beyond. The tv above the bar was, oddly enough, showing parliamentary question time in England. Tony Blair and the then leader of the opposition William Hague were going toe-to-toe over the future of the Millennium Dome. Both sides of the argument were conducted eloquently with great intelligence and humour, and delivered so swiftly that it left me quite in awe of both men's debating skills. It made the droning of our own empty suits appear so pedestrian by comparison.

At the end of the telecast I went out to the foyer and called Donal's office. Not only was he there, he was actually the one who answered the phone. Surprised to find me in town without having called first, he immediately agreed to meet me over a pint at the hotel.

My luck was in and I was really looking forward to seeing him. During my stay in the mid-eighties, when Donal had been in his final year at UCD, we'd spent many happy hours in the pubs of Dalkey talking idealistic leftist shite and consuming far more Guinness than our inexperienced young bodies were capable of processing. Then after a bag of chips or some pie-like thing, we would stagger back home, prop each other up, sing heartfelt odes about wild colonial boys and low-lying fields, before suddenly and vigorously forgetting what gravity was for, and toppling headfirst into somebody's prize rosebushes.

Since those halcyon days, however, I'd heard that Donal had found middle class respectability and taken up hunting. My cousin, my dear idealistic cousin, who had once threatened—before toppling into the rosebushes, admittedly—to bring down the government (any government) with a heavily wielded right boot, was now striding about the fields with a gun and a dog, sneering at the *hoi polloi* and discussing the East India Company. It didn't bear thinking about.

When he arrived a little while later I realised that it was all just a scurrilous rumour. He may have taken up hunting and abandoned some of his Trotskyist ideals, but he was still the same Donal. I suppose at some point in our late twenties, early thirties, we had both come to the conclusion that we weren't going to change the world in any significant way, so we were content just to look after our own place in it.

'Ah, you're a great one for the phone,' said Donal, as we clinked glasses.

I told him that I'd been trying to get in touch but a combination of Irish telecommunications and his continual absence from the office had thwarted me thus far. I actually said "thus far". It was then I realised that I'd been in the bar for over three hours since arriving in town.

'It's amazing that you came in today. I'm hardly in the office at all.'

I decided to spare him my views on serendipity with a dash of Buddhism, largely because I felt that, given the number of pints I'd consumed over lunch and the Blair/Hague debate, I wouldn't be able to pronounce "serendipity" with any accuracy. So instead I told him of my failed attempts to get to Tullamore and how I'd been teased by the brief stop in Kilbeggan.

'Ah, that's a shame. You could have hitchhiked from there.'

I then, to my lasting regret, told him that I wasn't allowed to hitchhike because Jacqui had forbidden it.

Donal put down his pint and stared at me in disbelief. 'What sort of fuckin writer are you? *On the Road* by Jack Kerouac, with permission from my wife.'

'Yes, and look what happened to him,' I countered. 'Forty-six years old and dead of an abdominal haemorrhage, brought about by chronic alcoholism.'

We stared at our empty glasses.

'Another?' I offered after a while.

'Go on, then,' said Donal.

I trundled over to the bar.

'Just a second!' he called after me. 'We'd better phone Jacqui first to make sure it's okay.'

On the walk to the car park, he said that we'd go surfing the day after next, the Saturday, and afterwards spend the night in his caravan down at Spanish Point, and that it would be a gas. It was lucky that I'd come this particular week because he had to drive over to Dublin on the Sunday and he could drop me off at Tullamore on the way back.

I wouldn't be needing a B&B that night or the next because I would be staying at Ben's, apparently. Donal's girlfriend Amanda was in Galway for the week and she was staying at Ben's too. There was room for everyone at Ben's, except, ironically enough, Ben—who was elsewhere in the country. I didn't know if Ben was real or possibly some sort of curious Irish euphemism. But I decided not to push it and was determined to let the issue resolve itself if and when it saw fit, or Ben turned up.

We'd no sooner found Donal's enormous four-wheel drive than I was in for a bit of a culture shock. It was brand spanking new, but the back seat had been ripped out and the windows blackened in. When I asked him why this had been done, he told me. And I immediately assumed he was taking the piss.

•

'Why do Irish dogs have flat noses?'

'I don't know, Dad.'

'Because they chase parked cars.'

'Did you hear about the Irish dog that was chewing a bone? He got up and only had three legs.'

'When Paddy found out that his wife was pregnant with twins, he went out with a shotgun looking for the other man.'

'Paddy and Mick saw a job advertisement in the paper for tree fellers. "Ah, we can't apply for that", says Mick, "There's only two of us."'

'Paddy and Mick get jobs as airline pilots. On their first trip they are flying a fully laden 747 into Gatwick airport. Spotting the runway, Mick says, "Ah, Paddy, we'll never land on that ting." Paddy agrees, but despite their apprehension, they give it a go. Tyres screaming and engines on full reverse, they bring the plane down. Unable to stop before the end of the runway, however, they are forced to take off again. Two similar attempts later, and running desperately short on fuel, they realise that they're in serious trouble. So they dump all the baggage at sea and with what little fuel remains resolve to give it one last try. Again with tyres screaming, they screech along the runway and fishtail the entire length. Flames leap into the air from the white-hot brakes, but they manage to stop their tortured aircraft moments before it shoots off the end of the runway. "Bajaysus!" says Paddy. "That was the shortest runway I've ever seen." "Yeah," agrees Mick, looking out his side window, "but it's the widest."'

I grew up on jokes like these. My father was always bringing them home from work. I suppose he knew that he came from one of the most highly educated and best read countries in the world, so he didn't have a problem with them. And anyway, the Irish, like the English and the Scots, are great ones for self-deprecating wit.

The Irish themselves tell Kerry jokes, presumably because people from County Kerry are a little slower on the uptake than those from other counties.

'What do you call a sheep tied to a post in County Kerry?' Donal was to say as we drove towards the Cliffs of Moher the following Saturday morning. 'A leisure centre.'

Except for perhaps those who hold the politically correct moral high ground, and possibly a few lonely graziers in County Kerry, it's all meant as nothing more than a bit of harmless fun.

Occasionally, though, the Irish do something that is, well, Irish.

I should perhaps preface this next story by saying that unlike the Sydney and Dublin rail networks, which have overhead wires, the trains on the London Underground are powered by what appears to be a third rail.

Returning from a drinking session in Dublin during my stay in the mid-eighties, Donal, several of his friends and I were eager to make it back to Dalkey for last drinks at Flanagan's. Once the train had deposited us at Dalkey station we elected to take a short cut by jumping down onto the tracks, bolting across the road and down to the pub. As we were running across the tracks I couldn't help but notice that Donal's best friend Ronan was leaping over the rails like a demented frog with haemorrhoids. I feel it only fair to point out that Ronan is one of the most intelligent and best read people I have ever met, and at the end of this trip I had the pleasure of staying with him at his house in London where he now lives and is the headmaster of an exclusive boys' school. On the night in question, however, Mr Sanity was clearly taking a much-needed break. With the last round safely in, I asked him what on earth he'd been playing at on the tracks. Several of the other lads had noticed Ronan's crazy leaps too and were keen to find out what he'd been up to.

He just looked at us as if we'd taken leave of our senses. 'Well I didn't want to get electrocuted now, did I?'

I've often wondered if in fact Ronan wasn't having a gigantic lend of us all that night in order to prop up the stereotype, like a shy and considerate Australian twenty-something man turning into an enormous yobbo as soon as he arrives in Earls Court.

When Donal explained the reason the 4x4 had been modified I just gawped at him until I realised he was deadly serious. By ripping out the back seat and blackening the windows prior to the vehicle's arrival in the country, you turn a car into a van and apparently save yourself a bundle on import duty.

There is a scene in the old television series *The Young Ones* where, shortly after the boys' arrival at their new house, Vyvyan hurls the toilet out of one of the upstairs windows. When Rick asks him why, Vyvyan explains that they can now go to the rent tribunal and get a reduction in their rent because a house is cheaper with an outside lavvy.

As we drove through the streets of Galway that afternoon, this scene was very much on my mind. And although I can't say that I expected it to start raining porcelain bowls at any moment, I wouldn't have been the least bit surprised had it done so.

Sixteen

May You Be in Heaven an Hour Before the Devil Knows You're Dead

I slumped into my seat for the bus tour to Connemara, feeling quite green. I tried, but I just couldn't shake the image of raw oysters drowning in enormous barrels of Guinness and an extremely large gentleman, shooting up through the stratosphere under his own steam.

It transpired that Donal (and Ben) didn't actually live in Galway but out in Athenry, which was about twenty kilometres away.

Athenry was famous for its fields because of a song that not only extols their many virtues, but is at pains to tell you where they are. The fields of Athenry are not up in the hills, behind the mountains, across the road from the pub, down on the seabed, in front of the butcher's, or spending the day shopping in Dublin. They are in fact "low-lying". It's not unlike living in a country that's "girt by sea".

Because they had traditionally sung that soul-stirring chorus, "Low lie the fields of Athenry", on the Parkhead terraces, supporters of the Glasgow Celtic Football Club had adopted Athenry as a sort of spiritual home. So now at the end of the season the more *committed* followers engage in a pilgrimage to the fields themselves. Having made the laborious trek from Scotland and pitched their tents, and with few diversions on offer, the faithful immediately repair to the pubs of Athenry. After which they spend most of the night consuming the curries of Athenry, lying hunched over the walls of Athenry, before finally being violently and copiously ill onto the fields of Athenry. Much to the consternation of the farmers of Athenry.

Donal's (and Ben's) house wasn't actually in Athenry itself but, God forbid, out in the fields. After dropping off my bag we nipped along to one of the pubs for a quick pint before meeting up with Donal's girlfriend Amanda. With a PhD in something frighteningly intellectual, Amanda, like Donal, spent her workdays traipsing about the countryside in her gumboots and writing environmental impact reports on Scottish vomit.

About an hour or so later the three of us were sitting down to dinner in Moran's Oyster Cottage by the Weir at Kilcolgan, which is just around the bay and a bit to the south of Galway. Moran's Oyster Cottage is so quaint and unreservedly Irish, and the food so mouth-wateringly delicious, that you'll just have to go there. It isn't cheap, but it's certainly cheerful.

There is a famous Guinness and oyster festival that takes place in Galway once a year and (probably at the insistence of those who operate the sewers) once a year only. The main aim of the festival is to swill kegs of Guinness and slurp down whole buckets of oysters until your bowels liquefy.

Fortunately by the time Donal and Amanda had told me about it we'd finished our meals and were onto hot ports.

Feeling slightly squeamish, I hurried along to the men's room. As I was splashing my face with cold water, a rather rotund man, who was having a bit of trouble with a few drunken molluscs of his own, wedged himself into one of the cubicles. Given the tight fit of the cubicle, I couldn't see how he managed it without a couple of enormous shoehorns and a run-up. Once in, however, he immediately peeled off a fart of such awesome magnitude that, had it been conducted anywhere within ten kilometres of a burning taper, would have despatched either him or his soul to the heavens. It reverberated around the walls with such resonance that Moran's Oyster Cottage probably suffered serious structural damage. I didn't wait around for the oxygen masks to drop down from the ceiling. We're not talking about a canary down the mineshaft here; this thing would have polished off a flock of healthy pterodactyls.

These thoughts were still with me the following morning as I slumped onto the back seat of the tour bus to Connemara. Don't get me wrong. I love oysters. I adore Guinness. And, given time and the right breathing apparatus, I could probably grow to enjoy Rotunda-man's company. But all three together and in quick succession led to a conflict in my stomach for which I was still trying to negotiate a peace settlement.

With a day free before we were to go surfing, rather than loaf around the low-lying fields, I bummed a lift into Galway with Amanda and thought I might take in a tour. Although Galway is quite stunning and, with its twisting, turning streets, more reminiscent of a chocolate covered Swiss village than an Irish one, I was eager to experience the wilds of Connemara beyond.

After a quick cup of dried mud in one of the cafés, I moseyed on down to where the tour buses are known to graze, just off Eyre Square near the tourist information office. There were two tour groups preparing to depart when I arrived. One was off to Connemara, and the other to the Cliffs of Moher. Although signs in the buses' windows clearly indicated which tour was which, our guide, Mairtin (pronunciation close to "Mortein") obviously thought we needed him to wander up the aisle and announce that this was in fact the Connemara tour and not the one to the Cliffs of Moher. Clearly, he was right about the degree of neuro-dormancy in the place, because at least twenty people stood up, muttered that they thought that this was the Cliffs of Moher tour and why hadn't anybody told them, then bolted for the other bus, leaving our own half empty. Parity was shortly restored, however, following what must have been a similar announcement on the other bus. And people tell jokes about Irish stupidity.

I was joined at the back of the bus by an affectionate young Spanish couple. No sooner had they sat down than their hands were all over each other as if they were a pair of quarrelling octopuses. There was only one free double seat left by this time and it was towards the middle of the bus. I didn't feel like having my eye gouged out by a wayward elbow or foot when the couple reached page sixty-nine of the Spanish *Kama Sutra*, so I picked up my daypack and relocated.

Mairtin started the bus and announced that we would just have to make a short detour to the railway station. Evidently there were five American tourists waiting to be collected. They had managed to catch the morning train over from Dublin by themselves but now, having arrived in Galway, their orienteering skills were not up to the arduous trek around the corner to the tourist information office and the tour buses: a journey of about a hundred metres. I briefly and uncharitably wondered if they would be wearing name tags. 'Hi. My name is

Randy. I'm a 35-year-old systems analyst. If I'm lost, please call 555-MORON."

On joining us three of them immediately made for the back seat, much to the consternation of the throbbing Spanish couple, which had been lying across its entire length, engaged in a bout of tonsil hockey.

'Hi there, buddy. I'm Tom,' said the young man whose name was apparently Tom, plonking himself down next to me. 'This is going to be great.'

It sure is, Tom. In fact I would hazard a guess that it's going to be swell. 'Hello, Tom. I'm John.'

Tom's girlfriend, or wife or whoever she was—he didn't introduce her—sat across the aisle from him in what was now the only other unoccupied seat. The right thing to do would have been to offer them my seat so they could sit together. But as this meant giving up the window, I decided not to. And I thought I was a better person than that.

Tom was full of that puppy dog *bonhomie* that so often overcomes American travellers. The rest of us are usually a bit more cynical and hardnosed, partly because we're irritated by their belief that they come from the centre of the world. The fact that they're probably right only increases the irritation.

As we made our way out of Galway and into Connemara itself, I must admit that I found it hard not to share some of Tom's enthusiasm. When I told him what I did for a living he almost exploded with excitement. Then, after an impromptu rendition of my Irish accent, copied from my father, I had to practically wrestle him to the floor of the bus and perform CPR.

Politely I returned some of his questions, anticipating that Tom worked in the money markets, pulled down six big ones per annum, owned a Porsche, a weekender in the Hamptons, and although he'd puffed the magic dragon at college, it didn't really count because he didn't inhale and could therefore still run for president.

To my shame, Tom did no such thing. He was a habitat restoration specialist for the US National Oceanic and Atmospheric Department. In short, when oil tankers drop their guts off the coast (as they do), threatening thousands of kilometres of marine habitat and wildlife, Tom is the guy you call in to restore the environment. He's a guy you should hug. Having mentally kicked myself up the arse for being such a cynical prat, I finally did the right thing and offered him my seat to share with his girlfriend, wife, or whoever she was.

'That's very nice of you,' he said as he photographed something through the window. 'But we're fine.'

'Really?' I was a bit confused. If I was travelling with my girlfriend, wife, or whoever, I'd certainly want to sit next to her; maybe, glancing at the Spanish couple, even beneath her. Tom must have been reading my thoughts. He said that she wasn't his girlfriend, wife, or whoever; she was his cousin. Then, because these things no doubt need clarifying in the States, he added that they weren't from the Deep South.

Coming to the picturesque little town of Oughterard, Mairtin stopped the bus in the middle of the main street to chat to one of the locals about the health of a mutual friend. Their little chat lasted two or three minutes and led to a steady build-up of traffic in both directions. Either Mairtin had forgotten that he had a bus load of tourists with him, or it was all part of a cunning ruse to introduce us to the slower pace of life in Connemara.

'Only in Ireland,' suggested Tom with a smile, though he said it out of approval for Mairtin's actions rather than in criticism. In fact the whole bus embraced the moment in the right spirit. And although there were a couple of moans emanating from the direction of the back seat, I had a sense that these were pre-orgasmic rather than anything else.

Leaving Oughterard behind, we entered the wilds of Connemara. Now this *was* Ireland. I was almost overcome by its staggering, unkempt beauty. Tom spontaneously combusted.

The countryside of Connemara is at once heart-thumpingly beautiful but at the same time rugged and windswept, befitting a landscape that has been carved and torn out of the earth by a passing glacier. The Maumturk Mountains, which simply ached to be climbed, were flecked with the distant specks of scattered sheep like a completely bald man who has the added misfortune of being afflicted by dandruff. It'd have to be hard work for a sheep dog out there.

'Get 'em in, Rex!'

'What, are you fucking kidding me?'

As well as being an expert on the west of Ireland, Mairtin was a keen film buff. Did we know, for instance, that the Irish army, rather than sit around painting rocks or abseil off mountains, frequently appeared as extras in the movies? Pretty much all of them had been in *Highlander*, apparently. I supposed that a neutral country had to find something for their military personnel to do. And, unlike their Swiss counterparts, who were either off guarding the Pope or sat around fiddling with the attachments on their penknives, it was good to see that the Irish armed forces were being usefully employed.

Pulling up by the side of the road, Mairtin pointed out a little stone bridge that was just across the way. This was the bridge where John Wayne and Barry Fitzgerald stopped to gaze across the fields at the fictional town of Inisfree in John Ford's classic film *The Quiet Man*. This meant absolutely nothing to anyone on the bus except me and there I was, leaping about and snapping photos, just as Tom had earlier.

I asked Mairtin if we were far from Cong, which was where the film had been shot. He said that we weren't far at all but unfortunately the tour didn't go there. This was the only time that things didn't work out for me on this trip. To come to Connemara and not make it to Cong was tantamount to sacrilege.

"Classic" is a fairly arbitrary term that we apply to a film just because it's old or because its lead actors are long dead. You see some chinless English wonder toffing around in a baggy suit and an oversized hat, saying things like, 'Do you know something, Beddington-Smythe? I've a good mind to give you a bunch of fives', and because it's in black and white and it's a six-pack of Kleenex number, you sit there thinking, *Classic*. So forty years from now, we'll probably be sitting there watching Samuel L. Jackson, in his shiny hair phase, firing off lines like, 'I just thought it was some cold-blooded shit to say to a mother-fucker before I popped a cap in his ass', and we'll be thinking, *Classic* about that too.

For me a contemporary classic would be something like the *Alien* series. The cold, clammy, psychological hide-and-seek thriller of Ridley Scott's *Alien*, and James Cameron's GI-Joe-shoot-em-up-go-get-em-girlfriend sequel, *Aliens*. Brilliant. The only shortcoming in the *Aliens* movies is that we never really see the development of the aliens themselves. They seem to go straight from being those little screamy things that burst out of the unfortunate gestator's stomach to being fully fledged adults.

I for one would like to have seen teenage aliens interacting with their parents. (You're going to have to work with me on this one, bearing in mind that we're about to call a teenage alien Gavin.)

'C'mon, Gavin. We're going over to the compound to frighten some colonists.'

'Bor-ing!'

'C'mon, Gav. Get into it, mate. It'll be fun.'

'Quit bossing me around!'

'How was school today?'

'As if *you* care! It sucked, like it always does.'

'Do you think—?'

'Just leave me alone!'

'I was only wondering what you'd like for tea.'

'God, it's like living in Nazi Germany round here!'

'I've just about had it with you and this attitude, young alien.'

'Yeah? Well, I didn't ask to burst out of a colonist's gut!'

I think Mairtin was pleasantly surprised to find someone who shared his passion for *The Quiet Man*, especially with its fiftieth anniversary coming up. Though he couldn't have begun to imagine just what the film meant to me. With such an enormous gap between my first and second visits, *The Quiet Man*, together with a few fleeting and frankly bizarre images of Tullamore, had become my portrait of rural Ireland.

And it's my father's all-time favourite film. Not long after we had arrived in Australia *The Quiet Man* was shown on tv late one evening. He actually had us sit up and watch it with him while he merrily pointed out landmarks and towns of a homeland that we had only visited together once.

In it John Wayne plays Sean Thornton, a retired Irish-American boxer returning home to Ireland to forget his troubles—those troubles being that he has recently and fatally beaten nineteen types of shite out of a fellow boxer. In Inisfree he meets Maureen O'Hara, a fiery redhead with a cute butt and a vicious right cross whom he is not allowed to marry until, due to some bizarre rural custom, he beats the tripe out of her brother.

From what I knew of American cinema when I first saw it, John Wayne was more at home under a hat, on top of a horse and behind the barrel of a smoking gun; or leading the Allies ashore after a rowdy voyage through swollen and angry seas with the GIs singing about how they'd really rather be back home with a gal called Mary-Lou.

He looks so out of place in Ireland, or, to be more accurate, Ireland looks so out of place around him. He is obviously taking a break from the shores of Normandy where he can shoot, more or less at random, a lavish selection of German storm-troopers whose basic decency will see them confess the error of their ways before succumbing to their wounds in the kind of performances not often seen outside a high-school production of *Hamlet*.

All through *The Quiet Man* John Wayne looks like

he desperately wants to shoot someone—anyone. And he seems so much more comfortable when he's dragged Maureen O'Hara off the train and all the way back to Inisfree and can finally get involved in the long promised fight with her brother—a man whose jaw is so large it appears to exert a gravitational pull all its own. The fight proceeds from town to town and comes with its own entourage. Up hill and down dale it goes for no other reason than the fact that the cinematographer obviously likes the look of the landscape. Occasionally the fight *BIFFs* its way into a pub where it's served pints of Guinness, presumably because half the cast is staying there. Then it starts anew and winds its way on to the next town and pub, which is obviously housing the other half.

Despite the wonderful scenery, though, which was the real Ireland to me, when I first saw *The Quiet Man* it left me somewhat confused because its way of organising courtships and settling dowries seemed so odd. I said earlier that my father is the quietest man I know; no wonder he left the street-fights of Tullamore for the relative sanctuary of South Yorkshire in the late fifties.

After *The Quiet Man* The Duke went back to shooting cowboys, Indians and the Japanese, all of whom seemed to annoy him to varying degrees. I used to think that if he ever came across a cowboy in a black hat of mixed Indian and Japanese ancestry he would probably try to obliterate him.

For months afterwards, every time Dad came in from work he would say, 'God bless all here', which was a line from the film. Then he'd have a grand laugh all to himself.

He was like that, our quiet man. He would happily make a joke and then keep it to himself. His dreams, the ones he chose to share with us, were like visions painted by Dali. They were mostly centred on livestock: about sheep playing chess with donkeys and how, if you happened to have crossed a horse with a goat, you would end up with a *hogo*. If he hadn't been such a good, church-going Catholic boy, I would swear that he'd dropped a couple of tabs of acid back in the sixties and was in permanent flashback. Perhaps that's why he was so quiet. Maybe he was looking out on a different, more abstract and brightly coloured world than the rest of us.

Prior to leaving for this trip I bought a video of *The Quiet Man* and watched it endlessly. It is, in every respect, a beautiful piece of filmmaking, and captures perfectly a sense of innocence in rural Ireland that perhaps never existed.

•

Our next stop was Leenane which, Mairtin assured us, was famous(ish) for the fact that the Tom Berenger, Richard Harris film, *The Field*, was set there. I'd never even heard of *The Field*, let alone seen it. But Mairtin insisted that it was excellent and what's more somehow managed to avoid featuring those compulsory elements of Irish cinema, a horse race on the beach and Colm Meany—though I've yet to verify this. Certainly Leenane, like Cong, has tried to make the most of its brief Hollywood connection. There's *The Field* Bar, *The Field* Restaurant, *The Field* Bar and Restaurant, *The Field* field, and *The Field* Inlet—though this was called, for reasons no one could explain, Killary Harbour.

As we got off the bus, most of the passengers followed Mairtin into *The Field* Bar. I decided instead to have a bit of a poke round the town, which was nothing more than a couple of shops. *The Field* notwithstanding, Leenane had very little to recommend it. I was keen to be back out in the wilds of Connemara, hanging off one of the mountains called the Twelve Bins (or Pins, depending on who you talk to), not stuck in some pokey little pub discussing the history of Irish-American cinema with Mairtin, interesting though he was.

I bought a chocolate bar at *The Field* Newsagent and Corner Shop, and, with nothing better to do, wandered up the road to check out *The Field* Visitors' Centre. As soon as I unwrapped the chocolate this huge gormless looking dog thing came bounding up out of the mist. I couldn't tell if it wanted to be friends or rip out my jugular, so I picked up a rock and mimed hurling it. The stupid thing ran off yelping, with its tail wedged so far between its legs that it practically gave itself an enema. I felt awful. So, rather than have a pleasant stroll around the tourist centre with a view to buying my daughter something in the chunky knitwear line, I ended up chasing this useless four-legged lump over rough terrain and across *The Field* field for about half a kilometre. All in a rather pathetic effort to restore primate–canine relations by sharing my chocolate bar with it. I've done stranger things in my time, but perhaps none quite as silly.

'What was the deal with that dog?' asked Tom back on the bus a short while later. 'Did it try to bite you?'

And I thought everyone else had been in *The Field* Bar. 'Er, not exactly.'

'What happened, then?'

'It was trying to be friendly.'

'And you weren't interested in pursuing the relationship?'

'Not initially.'

Tom paused, deep in thought. 'A word of advice, John. If the canine wing of the Garda turn up, plead the fifth.'

From Leenane it was a short drive down the road to Kylemore Abbey.

I hadn't noticed, until we stepped from the bus and into the car park some time later, that there were a couple of mid-twenties Australian guys on the tour. One of them had one of those slicked-back ponytails that you're just busting to wander up to and give a good, solid yank. While the other was so utterly forgettable that I've forgotten about him.

From the car park the abbey itself was eight hundred metres or so along a pleasant tree-lined path that curved around the small lake out front. On seeing this, Ponytail immediately announced that it was too far to walk, climbed back onto the bus and fell asleep. His mate followed him.

'A couple of yours?' suggested Tom.

'Can we pretend they're Canadian?' I said.

'Okay,' he said. 'We'll let this one go.'

In 1869, about a decade before the good people of Knock began experimenting with a rudimentary form of LCD, prominent surgeon and MP Mitchell Henry built Kylemore Castle as a present for his young wife Margaret. In doing so, the good doctor brought prosperity to the area, which in such harsh times was something of a miracle. It was not uncommon for people to walk thirty or forty miles to work for Mitchell Henry. He not only paid well, he looked after his workers too.

I immediately warmed to him. He was totally besotted with his wife, and he had a social conscience that was far ahead of its time, as an extract from his letter to the editor of the *Connaught Tribune* of 1880 shows:

> We may theorise and reform as we like but the commonsense of mankind teaches us that loyalty and starvation are not compatible and in my humble judgement the only hope that remains of producing permanent tranquillity in Ireland is to make a strong and well directed effort permanently to increase the prosperity of the people.

Like me, the good doctor was evidently one for long sentences.

But despite his obvious benevolence to the people and devotion to his family, the gods, whatever form they take, were not looking out for Mitchell Henry. In 1874, his much-loved wife died of Nile Fever, a rarity in Ireland, and one of his daughters was killed in a riding accident. I have no idea how, where or when the doctor died himself, though I suspect it must have been of a broken heart.

In 1922 the castle was bought by the Irish order of Benedictine nuns returning from Belgium, and it became an abbey.

I wandered around it and, enhanced by its picture postcard setting, as abbeys go it was rather lovely. But all the while I was struck by a feeling of sadness for kind-hearted Mitchell Henry, and I hoped that in death he found the happiness that was denied him in life.

Every corner I turned, though, I seemed to bump into our pulsating Spanish couple who were always at that advanced stage of foreplay that stops just this side of ecstasy. This further coloured my mood. So, with time fast running out, I left the abbey, took a stroll around the lake and returned to the bus.

I didn't know where the day had got to but by the time we made our final stop in Clifden for lunch, it was after three o'clock. The Irish have a pretty relaxed attitude when it comes to timekeeping, so the lunch zone stretches from about ten-thirty in the morning to four in the afternoon.

Clifden's claim to fame stems from the fact that it was the landing point (or, more accurately, crashing point) for the first direct non-stop transatlantic flight. Although their place in history has generally been usurped by Charles Lindbergh, who made the first solo transatlantic flight (and secured himself a prize of $25,000) two British Biggles had actually beaten him to it by eight years. On 14th June, 1919, Captain John Alcock, with Lieutenant Arthur Whitten-Brown as navigator, took off from St Johns, Newfoundland, and about seventeen hours later crash-landed in a bog near Clifden. Although undoubtedly a skilled aviator, Captain Alcock was clearly better at takeoffs than landings. He crashed his planes no fewer than three times in his flying career. First, over the Dardanelles during the First World War, then into the Clifden bog, and then finally and fatally near Rouen in France, only months after his and Whitten-Brown's successful Atlantic crossing.

I had lunch at the Station House Hotel bar, which was a great place to eat. The Station House Hotel has everything that a modern rail commuter could possibly desire, with the possible exception of trains. The last one pulled out in 1935, which suggests that either the line immediately fell into disuse, or the next train is running a bit behind schedule.

I had an excellent seafood chowder, a dish I was fast

becoming addicted to, and then went for a wander around the town. The shops in the square off the Station House Hotel were mostly of the upmarket wool-knit variety, while the museum that looked promising and was said to contain details of Alcock and Whitten-Brown's famous flight was frustratingly closed.

Making my way back through the square and towards the bus, I met an elderly man who seemed to be the only resident of Clifden out and about that day. No sooner had we nodded hello than he immediately forgot about the laws of gravity and went crashing to the ground quite spectacularly. I hurried back, got him to his feet and then helped him pick up the few bits of belongings that were now scattered about him: his newspaper, reading glasses, a copy of Sir Isaac Newton's *Mathematical Principles of Natural Philosophy*, and a tin of cat food.

He thanked me profusely for the help and then, vigorously shaking my hand, offered me a blessing of sorts. 'May you be in heaven an hour before the devil knows you're dead.' So I suppose that no matter what happens with the rest of my life, at least I've got that going for me.

While the other passengers piled back onto the bus for the return journey to Galway, I stood out in the dreary drizzle and made a few notes. Looking up at the bus I noticed that Ponytail and his forgettable mate were staring out the window at me, pointing, and obviously cracking jokes at my expense, presumably about how I was standing out there making notes in Gore-tex while they were on the bus.

I remembered their type from school. The cool kids who sat down the back of the bus on the way to the swimming carnival and got the girls because of the jokes they made about my trousers, the waistband of which was generally up around my neck. So I mouthed at them through the window that they should go and fuck themselves. They were so shocked that they immediately pretended I hadn't said a thing, as if to save face with each other.

On the drive back to Galway we came across a sign on the side of the road that said, NO SHOUTING, which was odd, perched out there in the middle of nowhere. I'd come across a sign in a pub earlier on the trip that said NO SINGING OR DANCING, which was so miserable I could hardly stand it. And so unIrish. What was next: NO DRINKING OR TALKING? But NO SHOUTING: why? And surely anyone who'd come all the way out here for a good, solid yell, was not going to be put off by a sign. Tom and I looked at each other and shook our heads.

When he wasn't pointing out things of interest, Mairtin played one of those *Di-Dicky-Do-Dum-Di-Dum-Doe* tapes that initially make you want to dance a merry jig, but then, several hours later unaccountably evoke this strong urge to ram an accordion over someone's head.

'What's crack?' asked Tom, who'd been listening to the song about a group of young Irishmen who went out for the evening looking for some.

'It just means fun. A good time.' I then suggested that going into town for some *craic* in Dublin as opposed to, say, Miami had vastly different connotations. It was just one of those linguistic curiosities that existed between America and the rest of the English-speaking world, or in this case Ireland and the rest of the English-speaking world. Like the curious American relocation of the 'fanny'.

With the tour finally over and having shaken hands and exchanged email addresses with Tom, I made my way through the glistening streets of Galway to meet up with Donal—and came to an abrupt halt outside a bookshop when I saw that Ronan Keating, the lead singer of Boyzone, had just released his autobiography, *Life is a Roller Coaster*. How old was he: thirteen?

I stood at the shop window, shaking my head and mumbling incoherently, 'Life is a roller coaster, my arse.' What sort of complex metaphorical image are you trying to draw for us, Ronan? That in life you have to queue up a lot and occasionally it makes you dizzy and causes you to vomit? Like at a Boyzone concert?

There's a radio program in Sydney that I enjoy listening to if I'm driving home at night. Called *Love Song*

Dedications, it's hosted by Richard "The Love God" Mercer. I've never met The Love God, though judging by the depth and texture of his voice, his testicles must weigh about twenty kilos apiece. There are times when it simply drops below the threshold of the human audio range and you literally feel it through the pit of your stomach like a sub-woofer as it distorts your speakers.

Whoever these people are who phone in their requests, the object of their affection is usually elsewhere in the country or being held in a secure location at the governor's pleasure. And "life is a roller coaster" is generally the philosophy.

'Hi, Richard it's Beryl here. I'd like you to play *Tie a Yellow Ribbon Round the Old Oak Tree* for Warwick for me, will ya?'

'*AND HOW LONG HAVE YOU AND WARWICK BEEN TOGETHER, BERYL?*'

'Fifteen years on and off, Richard. Mostly off.'

'*AND WHERE'S WARWICK THIS EVENING, BERYL?*'

'He's out on parole shortly, Richard.'

'*DO YOU MISS HIM?*'

'K'noaf I do.'

'*DO YOU THINK HE'S LEARNED HIS LESSON, BERYL?*'

'Yeah. He's real sorry he got caught. But he knows now that you just can't stick live budgerigars up your bottom within a four-hundred-metre radius of a schoolyard.'

'YOU SOUND LIKE YOU'VE BEEN DOING IT PRETTY TOUGH, BERYL.'

'Yeah, Richard, I have. But you know, life's like a roller coaster. It's got its ups. And it's got its downs.'

Ronan Keating may have been young, rich and handsome, but would he be in heaven an hour before the devil knew he was dead? I didn't think so. And with that in my favour, I turned up the collar of my coat and sloshed off through the streets of Galway to look for Donal.

Seventeen

Who Hung the Monkey?

I did try surfing once. Sort of. I was twelve years old and still at that stage when I was trying to determine whether I was the rugged outdoorsy type, or an indoors bookworm. My general feeling was that the outdoors would be so much better if it had a roof over its head and was carpeted. But this notion wasn't, at that stage, set in concrete. There was still a chance that I could go the other way, slim though it was.

I was on holiday with my family on the north coast of New South Wales when we came upon a picturesque and sheltered little beach somewhere past Newcastle. The shade from the thick canopy of gum trees practically ran down to the water's edge, which, given the fluorescent glow of my skin in those pre–factor 30 days, was an absolute godsend.

While Mum and Dad set about laboriously

transferring the entire contents of the car onto the sand, I bounded into the swell with my Kentucky Fried Chicken genuine imitation foam surfboard tucked under my arm. The board had been given to me as a Christmas present from some friends of ours who didn't care very much for surfing or its subculture but had got it free with their twenty-four-piece bucket of chicken.

While Trish relaxed on an air mattress reading a book, and Paul bobbed in the shallows buoyed in enough plastic floaties to raise the *Titanic*, I sat out just beyond the break, waiting for a set. I could certainly talk the talk. I wasn't sure how you actually went about catching a wave, but at least I sounded the part. I thought I looked the part too, until I realised that my board was shedding flecks of white and red styrofoam and I was leaving a little trail in my wake.

Trish and Paul had returned to our picnic blanket so they could get stuck into the hard-boiled egg and mayonnaise sandwiches, so Colonel Sanders and I were the only ones out in the water.

Then I remembered a recent news item. This surfer had claimed that while he was waiting for a wave, a shark had stuck its head out of the water and checked him out like a diner surveying the dessert trolley. Having made its selection, the shark removed a good chunk of the surfboard and a significant portion of his leg. I glanced down into the water just as an enormous shadow slid under my rapidly decomposing surfboard.

My skin was crawling off my body while my sphincter snapped shut like a Venus flytrap. To say that I came out of the ocean in a hurry doesn't do the moment justice. My arms spun like the Roadrunner's legs as I thrashed the surf to a lather. I cleared the picnic blanket on the full.

Several hours later, having finally been coaxed down from the tree, I sat in the back of the car for the long drive home and vowed that I would never set foot in the ocean again. And I pretty much kept that promise.

•

This was all very much on my mind as Donal and I made our way out through the low-lying fields of Athenry the following morning.

With the surfboards strapped to the roof of Donal's ~~car~~ van, and the sky a startling shade of puce, we must have made an incongruous sight as we swept along the mud-spattered lanes of County Galway.

'Me bollocks he has!'

'I'm telling you he has.'

'What's it called, then?'

I told him.

'Life is a roller coaster, my arse.'

'That's exactly what *I* said.'

'Life is a crock of shite.'

Clearly Donal was as big a fan of boy bands as I was.

'What's it written in, crayon?'

I gazed out at the murky low-lying fields, delighted to have changed the subject.

But Donal's tirade was far from finished. 'They're a feckin embarrassment to this country!'

'Which one? Boyzone? Westlife?'

'The whole miserable shower of shites. Four dozy bollocks in baggy jumpers up there, wiggling their arses at the camera and making millions. There's no feckin justice in the world. Just wait until your gig gets taken over by them.'

'What, writing? It'll never happen.'

'Don't be too sure. "Here, sonny. You look great in those trousers and with that haircut. How about writing us the sequel to *Ulysses*?".'

We stopped for breakfast at Mother Hubbard's in Kilcolgan. Although the town was nothing more than a depressing series of petrol stations, truck-stop diners, nondescript houses and a couple of shops, I mention it because the service in the restaurant was the best I've ever had—anywhere. Mother Hubbard's was run by a couple of gorgeous elderly women who fussed over every customer in a wonderful grandmotherly way. Nothing was too much trouble.

'Now, can I get you boys some more coffee? Are you okay for tomato sauce? If you'd like some hot toast I've got a fresh batch coming up in a minute and I'll bring it out to you if you like, so I will.'

'Ah, no thanks,' replied Donal. 'We're grand.'

'What about a hug? Can I give you a hug? Your friend there looks like he's a long way from home. I'm sure he'd be liking a hug, so he would.'

She didn't actually say this, but I'm positive that all we had to do was ask and she would have gathered both of us up in her arms and smothered us into her deep cleavage.

With our stomachs and hearts full we staggered out of Mother Hubbard's, ready to hang the necessary number of digits. We still had a fair drive ahead of us, though, because we were off to Lahinch in County Clare, a good hour or so to the south.

Turning off the N18 we detoured back out along the coast road so we could take in Kinvarra—the head of the sea. A pleasant fishing village with easy access to Galway and the Dublin road, Kinvarra is now one of the most sought-after addresses in County Galway, if not the whole of Ireland. Unlike the dour greys of Frank McCourt's Limerick, the jaunty cottages of gentrified Kinvarra have been painted to match the personality of their occupants, most of whom seemed to work in advertising. Even in winter, with the sky practically dripping blood, there was a vitality about Kinvarra that I hadn't found anywhere else in Ireland. In summer the place must literally chime.

Leaving Kinvarra in the ~~car's~~ van's side mirrors, we made our way over The Burren, which has to be one of the most desolate landscapes in the whole of Europe.

Oliver Cromwell is reported to have said of The Burren that there wasn't enough wood there to hang a man, nor enough water to drown him, nor enough dirt to bury him. I don't believe that Cromwell ever said such a thing, it's just too neat. Though it does rather capture his attitude to the Irish, which was something like Hitler's towards the Jews.

I was going to say it's difficult for us, in these relatively enlightened times, to come to terms with the appalling deeds of Cromwell and his men; tragically, though, perhaps it's not. And remember that Cromwell committed his genocide against the Irish in the name of God, claiming that his murderous rampage and the skewering of women and babies on spikes was "a righteous judgment of God upon these barbarous wretches...".

Although the landscape of The Burren now looks more like the surface of the moon than the earth, Donal said that it had—until recently, in geological terms—once been fertile agricultural land. The limestone beneath The Burren is so porous, though, that the soil simply eroded away. You could still make out the stone walls left by farmers who once worked this hostile terrain. It was rather handy having an environmental scientist for a cousin.

On the way out of Ballyvaughan we came across a series of signs that read, in the following order: MAJOR ROAD WORKS AHEAD, DO NOT PASS, FLAGMAN

AHEAD, PREPARE TO STOP, MEN AT WORK, EXPECT DELAYS, and END. A bit further down the road we saw an old guy resting on a shovel, chatting to another bloke who was leaning out of his truck.

'Ah, ba*jay*sus!' said Donal. 'Major road works, my arse.'

I snorted back a laugh while I made a couple of notes.

'You write about that, you bollocks,' said Donal, 'and I'll disown you.'

I already had enough material on rural road signs, so I assured him that I wouldn't.

'That's just embarrassing,' he continued, because he did enjoy a good rant. 'Imagine any tourists coming along this stretch. We'll look like a bunch of hicks. And those two fellas were the head and deputy head of national roads infrastructure.

'Still,' he said, glancing at me out of the corner of his eye, 'only a fuckin eejit would come to Ireland in December.'

A gale was whipping in off the Atlantic as we made our way along the coast road towards Doolin. And a thin sheet of arctic slush was building up on the hood of the car as Donal took me on a more "scenic" route over the hills to Lisdoonvara.

'Bajaysus. What a feckin climate!'

On a clear day you could see for miles, he assured me. We could barely see for feet.

We passed a couple of damp-looking donkeys in a field. They seemed so miserable out there and to keep out the cold they were standing *toinlegaoithe*, which is Irish for 'arse to the wind'.

Back on the coast road it wasn't long before we arrived in Doolin. Though not as yuppified as Kinvarra, Doolin had much to recommend it, particularly the shop on Doolin pier, which was the one in "Father Ted". The one owned by the married couple who were constantly threatening to murder each other.

We had a bit of a walk along the pier and then wandered down to the water's edge to check out the waves. The sea was boiling as if it was on fire and I assured Donal that I was about as likely to pull on a wetsuit and wade out into it as I was to attend a monster truck rally.

Donal gazed out at the sea and then up at a sky that bulged like a waterlogged sponge. Then he hunched his shoulders against the rain. 'Another dim, dark, miserable fuck of a day in paradise!'

It was the cold and the cold alone that drove us into O'Connor's pub about ten seconds later.

We ordered a couple of mugs of hot mud and engaged in a bit of light banter with the young barman who seemed to derive a disproportionate amount of pleasure from the fact that he wasn't a member of Boyzone.

He picked my accent and immediately asked whether we had boy bands in Australia. I told him that although we did I wasn't prepared to admit to the fact publicly and anything further I had to say on the matter was completely off the record.

'It's the English isn't it?' said Donal. 'It's all part of a master plot to destabilise the country. You wait and see. Ronan Keating and the rest of those baggy-jumpered bollocks will be up there wiggling their arses and then all of a sudden we'll be invaded.'

When Virgin Megastores started stocking condoms, the joke doing the rounds in Ireland was that young men would go into the shop and emerge with a packet because they were too embarrassed to ask for a Boyzone CD.

As I drank my coffee I was pleasantly surprised to discover that the appeal of Irish culture had reached the "Far East". Sitting along the bar from us was an attractive young Japanese woman of about nineteen or thirty-seven. She was tucking into a steaming plate of Irish stew and draining the dregs of a pint of Guinness. She looked briefly up from the postcard that she had been writing to share a smile with me and Donal and to order another pint of the black velvet. But she had obviously miscalculated the alcoholic content of Guinness. About twenty minutes later, her party was summoned back to their tour bus, and this stylish woman settled her account, placed the postcard carefully into her daypack, levered herself off the stool, and collapsed to the ground in a screaming heap. She was eventually helped from the premises, still singing a racy version of "Molly Malone".

I wondered what was scrawled on her postcard. "Having a grand time in Ireland. Pissed you were rear."

Donal said there were a couple of talented Japanese violinists who were in hot demand around the pubs of Galway. The nuances of Irish humour had also arrived in the east because the couple had decided that their names were too difficult for the Irish to pronounce, so they'd adopted the stage names Seamus and Mary.

Further down the coast road we arrived at the awe-inspiring Cliffs of Moher, a mind-numbingly impressive formation eight kilometres long and over two hundred metres high. Anywhere else in the world you would have a throng of hang-gliding enthusiasts queuing up to leap off the cliff and ride the updrafts. But not here. With nothing but the boiling Atlantic far below and no gentle beaches to land on nobody was in a hurry to leap off anything.

The sheer drop of the cliffs steals your breath away. With the wind hurtling about you like a banshee, people approach the edge lying on their stomachs. Some of them, having abased themselves before the abyss, return to their cars the same way.

Unfortunately, though, Mother Nature (the bitch) had closed the cliffs the day we were there. We leaned against the safety rail only metres from instant death and peered into the sodden gloom.

'Well they're out there somewhere,' said Donal, yelling to make himself heard above the roar of the gale.

Back on the road, we passed a field with a bull that was so enormous it was more like a hairy tank. We were so blown away by its sheer size that Donal slammed on the brakes and reversed back up the road for a closer look, much to the chagrin of the coach load of Japanese tourists coming around the bend, one of whom was leaning out the window and singing "Sweet Vale of Avoca".

'Bajaysus, will you look at the size of that fucker,' said Donal. He was referring to the bull.

I was equally impressed. 'I'd like to see a strutting Spanish matador get in the ring with *that*,' I said.

'It'd only need to fart in his direction and he'd be leapfrogging the nearest wall.'

I pulled my camera out of my daypack and took a few shots. 'Could you do me a favour, Donal? Climb over the fence and stand next to the bull. I need something in there for scale.'

'Yeah sure,' he said, and wiped his glasses for a better look. 'Just as soon as you kiss my arse.'

We drove on into Liscannor and parked in front of McHugh's pub. Donal fiddled with the radio, trying to find the latest news on a threatened DART drivers strike scheduled for the Monday. This was going to cause him severe problems if it went ahead. He only went into his Dublin office once a year, and he had been planning to stay at his parents' house in Killiney and catch the DART into town from there. On Monday.

'Couldn't you just drive in?' I suggested.

'I haven't got a week.'

Since I'd arrived in Ireland just about everyone had either been on strike or was planning to be. Train drivers, teachers, airline catering staff (though that wasn't necessarily a bad thing) and taxi drivers, just to name a few, had all been at it. Donal was threatening to go on strike himself, but he was worried that no one would notice.

'Before we go in,' he said, as he turned off the radio, 'I ought to warn you that this place is probably a little more hardcore than you're used to.'

'Hardcore?'

'A real spit-on-the-floor swill pit.'

I tried to hold back a gulp and failed. 'How do you mean?'

'It's not exactly one of your Irish theme bars. You won't find any leprechaun coasters or rusty old bicycles nailed to the wall in here. Or at least if you do it will have been ridden in by one of the patrons.'

'You're winding me up.'

'Me bollocks I am,' he went on. 'We're talking about the sort of pub that gets hosed out at the end of every session. If we come away with only one black eye apiece, we'll be doing well.'

He told me a story about the pub's legendary former

owner, Joe McHugh. Apparently Joe was cooking breakfast on the pub's grill one morning when the enormous blowfly that had been bothering him for the past hour landed on one of the sausages. In one vicious, calculated blow, Joe managed to bring down his spatula on top of this maggot bag, squelching it to kingdom come and beyond and smearing its innards across the grill. Then he turned to the early morning regulars and said, 'I does like a bit of hygiene.'

Needless to say, I approached the front door of McHugh's with some trepidation.

'If anyone offers to fix you a fry-up,' said Donal, 'refuse.'

I bravely followed him in.

The pub was so small that you would have been forced to go outside to change your mind. Lining the bar were about half a dozen weather-beaten old farmers and fishermen, all of whom immediately turned and looked at us in a manner that invited some acknowledgement.

'How are yahs?' said Donal with a wink.

'Dubliners,' muttered one of the barflies under his breath and turned back to his pint.

Nearest the door was a stocky man who was so short that I'd almost tripped over him on the way in.

'Hguht gregght antorgthree oughhtt thergghhh,' said the stocky little man and I noted with alarm that he had a hunchback of sorts that drew him even closer to the ground. Here was a guy who could map his family tree back to the apes, some of whom were probably still alive.

I nodded hello.

'Hguht gregght antorgthree oughhtt thergghhh,' he repeated when it was clear that I hadn't picked up his meaning.

I looked at Donal, who leaned in and whispered, 'Don't ask me. You're on your fuckin own with this one.'

I covered my mouth with my hand. 'Is he speaking Irish?'

'I think it's a language he's just invented himself and he's trying out on you.'

'Hguht gregght antorgthree oughhtt thergghhh.'

I decided that honesty was the best policy. 'I'm terribly sorry,' I said, 'but I can't understand a word you're saying.'

'He wants to know where you're from,' said the big guy who was standing closest to Monkey-man and doubtless used to acting as interpreter.

'Oh, sorry. I'm from Australia.'

'Whergghghtr?'

'Australia. Oz. Tray. Lee. Ahh.'

'Well, then, you're very welcome,' said the big guy and held out his hand. I shook it before it wrapped itself round my neck.

I shook Monkey-man's hand as well. 'Thghgghh iggh spghoren in the mogrhren.'

'Thank you,' I said, hoping that was the right answer.

And that was that. We were both folded into the microcosm of the pub as if we were locals. Unlike the English when they meet Australians, the Irish don't feel the need to make hilarious references to kangaroos, koalas, corked hats, didgeridoos and that side-splitter about the dangers of having the blood rush to our heads as a result of being down under.

After a pint or two, the diction in McHugh's became markedly clearer. It was as if someone had stuck a Babel fish in my ear. I even found myself being able to follow Monkey-man's strange tangential conversation, as he grew more and more animated about something on the floor at the darkened end of the bar, which was where we were now sitting.

The thing at the end of the bar turned out to be a Liverpudlian fisherman who had lived in Liscannor most of his life but had been unable to lose his Scouse accent.

'Get the fookin thing out!' demanded Monkey-man.

'He's not doing you any harm,' said the Scouser.

'He's stinking the place out.'

'He smells a damn sight better than you,' the Scouser shot back. 'What year did you last have a bath?'

Biting my lip I whispered to Donal. 'What are they arguing about?'

'The dog.'

'What dog?'

Donal pointed to the Scouser's stool, and under it, curled up in a snoozing ball, was a small black dog.

Monkey-man made a lunge at the Scouser but had his bluff called when the Scouser stared impassively into his Guinness.

'I'll kick its fookin arse outside.'

'Touch him,' scowled the Scouser, 'and it'll be the last fookin thing you ever do.'

I turned to Donal. 'This is a theme bar, isn't it? And this is the floorshow.'

Donal smiled and gave me one of his winks. 'They'll be the best of mates again in a minute. You watch.'

'Useless fookin thing,' argued Monkey-man. He swayed slightly and seemed to lose confidence in his argument.

'Useless?' spat the Scouser. 'That dog's been at sea more than you have.'

For some reason this struck a note with the patrons of McHugh's. Strange sounds snorted out of noses and fists pounded against the bar.

The Scouser had won the audience over and moved in for the kill. 'If you were at sea with me, and you and him fell overboard, I'd throw him the lifebelt.'

That finished me off. Convulsing like a hyena on nitrous oxide I staggered out the back to the toilets.

When I returned Monkey-man and the Scouser were

engaged in a private conversation. Monkey-man had an arm around the Scouser's shoulder.

Donal looked at me and winked. 'What did I tell you?'

'Who hung the monkey?' said Monkey-man to me.

'I'm sorry.'

'Who hung the monkey?' the Scouser said, though he directed this to the rest of the bar rather than solely at me.

The rest of the bar made it clear that they didn't have a clue what the two of them were talking about, and that things had been much more interesting when they were at each other's throats.

'Come on,' said Monkey-man. 'You two look educated. Who hung the monkey?'

'I haven't a clue what you're talking about,' said Donal.

'Don't they teach you owt at university?' snapped the Scouser.

We freely admitted that tertiary institutions were lagging on the subject of hanged simians.

'Go on,' said the Scouser to Monkey-man. 'Tell 'em.'

'It was the English,' said Monkey-man. 'The bastards!'

'The English "hung" the monkey?' I said.

'That's right,' agreed the Scouser. 'They bloody well did 'n'all.'

'At Durham jail,' interjected Monkey-man.

'So let me get this straight,' I said. 'Are you telling us that the English actually *hanged* a perfectly good monkey?'

'Aye,' said the Scouser. 'It were a chimpanzee.'

'Right,' said Donal out of the corner of his mouth. 'That settles that.'

'Why?' I asked.

'They thought it was a spy?' said Monkey-man.

Of course.

'A French spy,' exclaimed the Scouser.

Naturellement.

'It was on a ship,' said Monkey-man, 'that was coming back from Africa.'

'The ship was hit by a storm and was sunk off the English coast,' said the Scouser, picking up the torch. 'The monkey managed to swim ashore.'

I turned to Donal. 'I didn't know monkeys could swim.'

'Yeah,' he said. 'And pigs can fly.'

Monkey-man continued. 'There were a few other things washed up with the monkey. A French flag and er...' he trailed off.

'A little plastic dome containing the Eiffel Tower that snows when you shake it?' I suggested, trying to be helpful.

'No it was long before the Eiffel Tower was built,' replied the Scouser. 'The English had never been to Africa, you see. Never seen a monkey before.'

'They thought it was a Frenchman,' interrupted Monkey-man. 'Took it to Durham jail and interrogated it. When it refused to speak, they hung it as a spy.'

And that is a story far too good to debunk with research.

'Lucky you weren't around at the time,' said the Scouser to Monkey-man, their moment of camaraderie suddenly over, 'or they would have fookin hung you.'

•

When we could speak again, we sadly farewelled McHugh's pub and made the short trip around Liscannor Bay and into Lahinch, or "LA Hinch" as Donal preferred to call it. It lent the surfing capital of Ireland an exotic southern Californian ring.

We stood at the end of the road next to the surf shop and stared out at the hissing Atlantic. Arctic winds whipped off the sea, blinding us with salt spray and forcing us quickly back into the van. Donal said there'd be no surfing today and I was relieved. You could hardly be expected to catch a wave you couldn't see.

We had dinner in O'Looney's bar, which was an appropriate name given that the pub's only other patron—a woman of indeterminate age, origin, and gender—had a laugh like a donkey on steroids. After our experience in McHugh's, however, it all seemed a bit sedate by comparison.

Night was fast drawing in by the time we'd finished

our meal, so we settled the bill and carried on down the road to Donal's caravan at Spanish Point.

Despite the size of the park, Donal and I were the only ones "eejit" enough to spend the night in a flimsy caravan this close to the pounding Atlantic and at the start of December.

Donal had promised me a big night out in Milltown Malby, which apparently had some great pubs and the added attraction of being further inland than Spanish Point and out of the wind. I must admit that my heart wasn't in it. I was all for crawling into Donal's spare sleeping bag and getting my head down for a good fourteen, fifteen hours' kip. We'd had a big one in Galway the night before, and my head was still recovering. I just didn't feel up for another.

•

The mysterious Ben whose house I'd been staying at had finally turned up, proving that he wasn't a euphemism after all. So, following my return from Connemara the previous night, the three of us had gone to a wonderful pub in Athenry and had a couple of pints by a roaring fire. There was only a handful of us in the pub and it was lovely—sitting by the fire on the comfortable chairs, talking shite and drinking Guinness. But in the strange way of lads out on the tiles, we decided to ditch Athenry and catch a train into Galway. And in next to no time we were jammed shoulder to shoulder with hundreds of others in the packed pubs in town.

We met up with another of Donal's friends, Seamus Hartigan (a lovely man who was a dead ringer for the dancing priest in *Father Ted*), and together the four of us got seriously wasted.

For some reason (possibly to do with the fact that I was a guest in his country and his house) Ben had put himself in charge of my alcohol consumption. When I steadfastly refused to take on any more Guinness (six pints is my absolute limit), Ben moved me over to Bailey's Irish Cream. Several glasses later, after I'd given an impromptu stand-up set to the wall, he shifted me on to Lucozade, which was available behind the bar— and I'm still not sure why.

This morning when I woke up complaining of a mild brain tumour, Ben said that it was because I was mixing my drinks.

•

With the gale buffeting the caravan I zipped myself into the spare sleeping bag and was adamant that I would not be doing the same again. At least not so soon.

'Ah come on, you soft bollocks!' said Donal from his corner of the caravan. 'It'll be a gas. You only live once.'

Not me. I was a Buddhist.

We had a refreshing three- or four-hour nap, then we got ourselves ready and stepped out into one of the bleakest nights I've ever seen. The wind literally howled in off the ocean and swept the rain horizontal.

People say that Spanish Point is haunted by the spectres of lost sailors from part of the Spanish Armada that was wrecked there. And I believe it. I felt several shivers run down my spine as we pushed against the wind along the pitch black road towards the Spanish Armada hotel, our way lit only slightly by Donal's torch.

Donal looked out to the blackened ocean and said that there was nothing between us and America except cold, wet and utter misery. If Joyce had said that, it would have been on a calendar.

We entered the foyer of the stylish Spanish Armada hotel, hoping to get a taxi to take us to Milltown Malby. With no taxis on offer, the hotel's owner, the wonderful Mr Johnny Burke, got up from his armchair and his pipe and drove us there himself in his brand new Mercedes. Only in Ireland.

We made for the back room of Friel's pub (also known as "the kitchen") and sat on a couple of upturned kegs by the fire. Three old farmers, their hair growing out through their caps, welcomed us into their conversation but we couldn't understand a word. Along with the barman, that made just six of us in the place.

'Great pub,' I mumbled to Donal. 'It's really swinging. Can we go yet?'

'Give it a while, you bollocks,' he said. 'You'll see.'

Less than an hour later we were packed in shoulder to shoulder. An hour after that the band turned up for a trad session and the place really took off. One of the musicians, the flautist, a thick-set woman with thighs like a prop forward, tapped her foot in time with the fiddler and the walls literally shook.

To buy a round you had to shout your order over the top of all the heads and then have your drinks and change relayed back to you by those in front. It all somehow worked as people passed drinks and money over their heads without a break in their own conversations. It was as if their arms were acting independently of their brains.

Around midnight, just as I was starting to sway like Monkey-man, I asked Donal what the front bar was like.

'Have a look,' he said.

I popped my head around from "the kitchen" and could hardly believe what I was seeing. About forty to fifty elderly people were sitting in the front bar, sipping their drinks, with faces as long and wet as the night outside.

'What I miserable shower of shites,' I said, slipping into the vernacular, which was noticeably easier after several pints.

'They're down for a wake,' replied Donal with just a mild hint of reproach in his tone. 'Go easy on them. They're not long for this world themselves.'

Ireland is an old country with an ageing population. And sometimes it seems that there is so much death about the place that there is hardly any room left for the living.

I slurred something to Donal along these lines, but he was convinced that I was talking complete shite.

We left Friel's pub around three-thirty, and were the last ones out. I can say "left" just like that, but it wasn't as easy as it sounds. First I had to place a steadying hand on the bar and then launch myself in the general direction of the door.

I still don't know if I was part of a genuine lock-in. For a start I know nothing about a pub's licensing hours on a Saturday night, Sunday morning in rural Ireland; and secondly, I didn't go anywhere near the door until we passed through it on our way out so I was unable to tell whether or not it was locked.

Despite being thirty kilograms lighter and three pints ahead of me, Donal still managed to help me into the cab, direct the driver to the caravan park, and finally pour me into the sleeping bag.

The glow from the galaxy stars stuck on the ceiling of the caravan kept me awake for a while. So did the wind pounding against the caravan and Donal's occasional 'Ba*jay*sus!'. But when I slept, I slept like the dead.

Meanwhile, out in the night, the dead roamed the land.

Eighteen
The Little Fisherman

We finished a pleasant late breakfast in LA Hinch, abandoned a futile search for *Father Ted's* parochial house which was supposedly just to the north of Lisdoonvarna, and started out on the long, slow trek to Tullamore. Donal had kindly agreed to drop me there before he went on to Dublin.

'Well I can't have you hitchhiking, now can I? Your *wife* might find out.'

Halfway between LA Hinch and Ennistymon we stopped at a simple yet touching shrine to the victims of the famine, with a bronze statue of an orphaned boy, painfully thin and trying to gain access to a workhouse. The inscription included these poignant words:
"Survivors of the horror could rarely bring themselves to speak of it to their children, and when they did were never able to speak of it as other than *An Drochshaol*—The Bad Times."

Despite the fact that Donal and I trod a secular path, I believe at that moment we both uttered a silent prayer for the two million or more souls who had either perished in the potato blight famine of 1845–1847, or were forced to flee Ireland forever.

We walked back to the car in a sombre and reflective mood.

Driving along the R460, we came across the turn-off to Thoor Ballylee, an old square stone castle that W.B. Yeats had bought in 1916 for the princely sum of thirty-five pounds. He lived here happily for many years with his English wife, Georgie Hyde-Lees, once he'd finally acknowledged that his enduring love for the beautiful and fiery revolutionary Maud Gonne would not be reciprocated.

I was surprised to find Thoor Ballylee out this far because I'd always assumed it would be in Sligo, where Yeats had spent much of his childhood and was now taking his final rest in the shadow of Ben Bulben.

Under bare Ben Bulben's head
In Drumcliff churchyard Yeats is
laid...
Cast a cold eye
On life, on death
Horseman, pass by!

I would love to have stopped at Thoor Ballylee to pay my respects to the great man. Unfortunately, however, time was against us. Donal still had a long drive to Dublin ahead of him and if we didn't get a move on he would be forced to fight his way through the snarling gridlock of the returning Sunday hordes.

My own time in Ireland was fast drawing to a close as well and I still had to get to Shannon Harbour and then back down to Killarney to meet up with Richard for our planned cycling odyssey around the Ring of Kerry. I had asked Donal if he would be interested in joining us, but he suggested that I could cycle around his arse.

'This isn't Hawaii, you know,' he said. 'I mean, you are aware of that? It'll be freezing out there on the *Ring*.'

'I know,' I said. 'But the salt spray from the Atlantic will surely melt any ice on the road.'

'Ba*jay*sus!'

Fiddling with the radio, we found a news update confirming that the proposed DART drivers strike scheduled for the following day would definitely go ahead.

'Can you believe it?' snarled Donal. 'The one shagging day a year I go into Dublin to work and they go and pull a stunt like this. What a fuckin shower of shites.'

Still recovering from the previous night I uttered what I hoped was a sympathetic grunt.

'The whole arsing country is coming to a standstill because of everyone's shiteing greed.'

I pointed out, somewhat charitably in retrospect, that Ireland was, for the first time in its history, awash with money and that the people just wanted what they considered was their fair share.

'I tell you this country can't handle being rich. We were better off when we were poor. At least then we were all *miserable* together.

'"I haven't got any money."

'"Neither have I."

'"Will you have another pint?"

'Now we're all swanning in and buying each other glasses of chardonnay.

'"Will you be having another pina-colada, Seamus?"

'"Ah, go on then, Paddy, I will."

'I tell you, this country is going to the dogs. And the greed? It'll catch up with us. You wait and see.'

In my second grade class at Toongabbie Public School, we had a firm but kind teacher called Mrs Thrower—aptly named, since she wasn't above hurling a potentially wayward child against the wall.

Like most children I simply loved it when Mrs Thrower told us stories. Whether they were lifted from a book or her own experiences as a child in London during the Blitz, I would sit there with the rest of my classmates, totally enthralled. I remember one cold, rainy day Mrs Thrower telling us the story about a little fisherman and his wife. I think it was one of the folktales collected by the Brothers Grimm on their travels around

JOHN LARKIN

Germany. Although I didn't completely understand its message at the time, the story did, nonetheless, make a big impression on me.

The Little Fisherman

Long, long ago, there lived a little fisherman who, with times being as they were, was forced to live in a pigsty with his somewhat demanding wife.

You could hardly say that the little fisherman was a commercial success in the fishing industry. Toiling hour after hour, day after day by the cruel sea, he barely caught enough fish with his little rod to keep body and soul together.

One day, however, he hooked an enormous fish, which took him by surprise, because he hadn't been able to afford any bait for his hook. After a mammoth *Old Man and the Sea*-type struggle lasting the best part of the day and most of the night, he finally managed to drag the thrashing fish ashore.

'Oh,' said the little fisherman to himself, as he marvelled at the size of the fish. 'We'll eat well tonight.' And, with that, he prepared to beat the fish's brains out with a stick.

'Wait!' said the fish, covering its head with a hastily raised fin. 'Please don't kill me. I'm not a fish, you see. I'm an enchanted prince.'

'Oh!' exclaimed the little fisherman. 'Is that a fact?'

'Indeed it is,' said the fish. 'You don't want to eat me. Please let me go.'

Well the little fisherman didn't fancy eating anything that he'd had a conversation with, except perhaps his wife on occasion, but that's another story.

So he unhooked the fish and returned it to the sea.

'Thank you,' called the fish and disappeared into the depths.

Later that night when the little fisherman had finished work, his wife greeted him at the entrance to the pigsty. She was wearing a pair of scummy old checked slippers, her hair was in rollers. She had a wet fag-end wedged in the corner of her mouth, and several hairs sprouted from an enormous mole on her chin. In short, all the stereotypes.

'Well, husband,' said the wife. 'Did you catch anything?'

'Ah, no,' replied the little fisherman contritely. 'I didn't. Sorry about that.'

'You useless, shagging arse [these may not have been Mrs Thrower's words exactly]!' snapped the wife, and she hit the little fisherman repeatedly over the head with a rolling pin.

'I did catch *one* fish,' cried the little fisherman, dodging her blows and narrowly avoiding a coma.

'Well, where is it then?'

'I, er, I let it go.'

When the little fisherman had regained consciousness

he told his wife that he had been obliged to let it go because it wasn't a fish at all, but an enchanted prince.

'You let it go without making a wish?' she screamed.

'Er, yes,' replied the little fisherman. 'Never occurred to me actually.'

'Well, then, get your arse back down to the sea and demand your wish!'

'I couldn't.'

'Get down to the sea,' the wife tapped her rolling pin against the wall, 'and tell your enchanted prince that your wife is sick and tired of living in a pigsty. She wants a little house!'

Still airborne when he left the pigsty, the little fisherman went back down to the sea.

'Hello, fish,' called the little fisherman.

The enchanted prince fish-thing poked its head out of the water. 'Hello there,' cried the fish. 'Good to see you again.'

'Ah, the thing is,' the little fisherman began. 'The thing is, I, I did let you go after all, and my wife said that you should have granted me a wish.'

'A wish is it you're after?' said the fish.

'Er, not me,' corrected the little fisherman. 'It's my wife. She's sick of living in a pigsty and fancies a little house of her own.'

'Well go to her,' said the fish. 'And you will find her, in her house.'

The little fisherman returned home to find his wife

on the doorstep of her gorgeous little cottage and with a rare glint in her eye.

In the morning the little fisherman awoke quite sated, but he ventured out to the kitchen for breakfast anyway.

'It's a bit pokey!' snapped the wife. 'Your enchanted prince might have given us one a bit bigger.'

'Oh I don't know,' said the little fisherman. 'It's big enough for the two of us. And it's a far sight better than the pigsty.'

'Now listen to me!' she shouted. 'I want you to go back down to the sea and ask for a bigger house. No. I want a castle. An enormous grey stone castle, with turrets and ramparts and a drawbridge.'

'I can't,' protested the little fisherman. But he realised that there was no alternative.

'Back again?' cried the fish.

'She thinks the house is too small,' said the fisherman. 'She wants a castle.'

'Well go to her,' said the fish. 'And you will find her, in her castle.'

Back home, there was the fisherman's wife on the drawbridge of her enormous stone castle.

'Isn't it magnificent!' she said.

'It is,' he replied. 'So you'll be happy now?' he added hopefully.

'Well we'll just have to see about that,' she said and folded her arms.

The castle was everything a medieval fantasist could desire.

'There's just one problem,' said the wife, digging the little fisherman in the ribs as he drew languidly on his cigarette later that night.

'And what's that, baby?' murmured the little fisherman.

'What's the point of living in a castle if you can't be the queen?' asked the wife.

'Oh no!' he groaned.

'Tomorrow,' she said.

'What is it now?' cried the fish the following day.

'She doesn't think it's right her living in a castle if she isn't queen.'

'Well go to her,' said the fish. 'And you will find her, the queen.'

The little fisherman returned home to find his wife sitting atop an enormous pure gold throne with a diamond-encrusted crown resting her head. Servants, toadies and sycophants hovered about her, complying with her every whim.

'Now how good is this?' said the wife. 'Check it out.'

That night the little fisherman got to baste himself with caramel fudge and [**Publisher's note: Due to the graphic and frankly tasteless nature of the remainder of this paragraph, we have been left with very little choice other than to remove it in its entirety** and refer Mr Larkin to the appropriate counselling body.]

The following morning the wife slept late but was eventually woken by the sun streaming in through the curtains. Such was the intensity of the glare that she was forced to squint in a rather unattractive fashion as she made her way across her enormous bedroom to draw the curtains.

'If only I could tell the sun when to shine,' said the wife to herself, because the little fisherman, still wearing his Spiderman outfit, slumbered on. 'Hold the phone, Reg. That's *it*!'

'Wake up!' the wife yelled into the little fisherman's ear. 'I've got it.'

'And we're fresh out of penicillin,' he said sleepily.

'No, not that,' said the wife. 'There's no point being queen if I can't tell the sun when to rise or the stars when to shine. Go back and tell your poncey little prince that what I really want is to be the ruler of the entire universe.'

'I think you're pushing your luck on this one, sugar buns,' replied the little fisherman, stepping out of his lycra bodysuit.

'Just do it!' she said.

Outside there was an enormous storm raging. A hurricane was ripping huge oak trees out of the ground by their roots, and twisters picked up entire fields of cows and deposited them elsewhere in the kingdom. The hail hammered like bullets into the ground and weathermen made hilarious "in" jokes with newsreaders about how it wasn't really their fault.

'What is it *this* time?' cried the fish.

'She wants to be ruler of the entire universe,' replied the little fisherman.

'What?' yelled the fish above the roar of the raging storm.

'I said, **SHE WANTS TO BE RULER OF THE ENTIRE UNIVERSE.**'

Just then the storm abated, the wind ceased, calm returned to the land, and cows started in on the long mooch homeward.

'Well go to her,' said the fish. 'And you will find her, back in the pigsty.'

And she's still there today.

•

I can't say that this is exactly what's happening to Ireland, but it's in the region.

Nineteen
The Flash Wears Tweed?

If this journey was a spiritual homecoming, then the address for that homecoming was Shannon Harbour, where my father was born and where he spent much of his childhood.

Before being transferred to Tullamore, my grandfather had been the harbourmaster in Shannon Harbour, a prestigious position that came with its own house which he and my grandmother immediately set about filling like good Catholics.

Now don't go searching for Shannon Harbour on any maps. For one thing it isn't actually on the coast—and no, this isn't an Irish joke—but slap bang in the middle of the country. For another, it is so small and nondescript as to be almost insignificant. Since arriving in Ireland I had been navigating my way around with a fairly detailed map and Shannon Harbour simply wasn't on it. I'd been given the coordinates by Donal, so I carefully marked its position with a cross—my tongue poking out the corner of my mouth in a slightly unappealing fashion.

Shannon Harbour is a forgotten little town at the intersection of the Shannon River and the Grand Canal, and it's where old pleasure craft now go to die.

Yet just a bit further downstream sits the rich and stylish Banagher. Tied up at the marina were dozens of hair-gel slick cruisers, patiently waiting for the arrival of summer and the cases of chardonnay and crates of canapés to be brought on board. Banagher had clearly embraced both the twenty-first century and the spirit of the Celtic Tiger generation. Upstream in Shannon Harbour, though, it was still 1927.

I knew none of this when Donal dropped me at my Uncle Seamus and Aunt Veronica's house and when I told them of my desire to go to Shannon Harbour, they exchanged a couple of furtive glances as if to say "eejit".

It was soon clear that without my own transport, I wasn't going to Shannon Harbour at all.

'There's a bus goes to Banagher,' said Veronica, 'but then you would need to make your own way back to Shannon Harbour from there. But it's too far to walk.'

'And he's not allowed to hitchhike without special dispensation from Jacqui,' said Donal, winking at me over his coffee.

I cast him a look indicating that he could go and bollocks.

'Ah, but there's no Banagher bus tomorrow,' said Seamus, inspecting a timetable that had materialised out of nowhere. 'It only runs once a day on public holidays, and twice on Ascension Sunday.' That's not exactly what Seamus said, but pretty much the gist of it.

'Is there a bike?'

Veronica shook her head. 'Well there is, but it hasn't got any wheels.'

Well, this was just ducky. I'd been bragging all along that things had worked out for me so spectacularly well, and that every decision that I had taken so far had turned out to be right. Now this. If you're going to let serendipity be your light, make sure that you at least have a contingency plan.

So it seemed that, short of walking the seventy kilometres or so round trip in the three hours of daylight on offer during the Irish winter, I wouldn't be able to complete my spiritual journey.

'Arsing, shiteing, shagging Buddhism!' I mumbled quietly into my coffee. Donal's influence was definitely starting to rub off.

At that moment my cousins Fiona and Mary returned from their shopping trip to Athlone. Told about my dilemma, Fiona said that she'd taken a week's leave from her job in the bank and, with nothing planned for the following day, would be delighted to run me down to Shannon Harbour.

So how good *was* this Buddha bloke?

The next day, motoring along through the fields around Tullamore (which are every bit as low-lying as those of Athenry) I can't say that Fiona's driving gave me a great sense of confidence. She was sitting so close to the steering wheel that she was almost on the other side of it.

'That can't be comfortable,' I said.

'It is,' replied Fiona. 'I'm grand.'

She was literally hugging the wheel.

'I mean you wouldn't want to take a thousand kilometre road trip like that. You'd end up with a serious bout of cramp.'

'This is Ireland, John. Not Australia. If we drive for a thousand kilometres we'll be halfway to America.'

Good point.

If I had any memories of Shannon Harbour at all from my visit as a three-year-old, then they were rolled in with those of Tullamore.

Coming from a dour South Yorkshire mining town as I did, Tullamore/Shannon Harbour was just so exotic by comparison. Exciting, picturesque, and full of friendly folk who sang warbling, whiney old songs about how much they missed the place just before falling off their barstools. It was jumping with life.

As we crossed over the small bridge into Shannon Harbour now, though, it appeared anything but. This place was dead. A long time dead. It was as if the Irish had put on a show for us all way back then, and had since gone about their business, retired, or died, clearly not expecting anyone to turn up thirty years later for an encore.

Fiona turned off the road and onto the dirt track that ran along the canal.

'Is this it?'

'This is it,' she said. 'Don't blink or you'll miss it.'

She pulled up alongside the old harbourmaster's house, which glistened with a recent coat of paint. It was the only house that remained fully standing in what I was reluctant to call a street. The other buildings—large storage sheds, factories, or whatever they were—had long since been abandoned and were slowly crumbling back into the earth. There was an open air "dry dock" a bit further along the lane. Which in Ireland is just about as oxymoronic as these things get.

The harbourmaster's house had been lovingly done up and was now an extremely stylish and modern B&B. The owners must have sunk close to half a million pounds into its refurbishment. But I couldn't for the life of me understand what they were thinking? Who on earth would volunteer to stay in this godforsaken dump of a place?

Perhaps I was being grossly unfair. Maybe once winter had been put to bed Shannon Harbour sprang to glorious life and colour. Maybe the rotting carcasses of the old abandoned pleasure craft in the canal shucked off their cocoons and the cruisers were reborn, shining and ready to be loaded up with cases of chardonnay and crates of canapés—their owners sashaying down from Dublin in BMWs and Audis to take a well-earned break from moving and shaking, cutting deals, and talking bollocks on mobile phones.

Now, hunkering down for its winter hibernation, Shannon Harbour was every bit as cold, dank, dark, and utterly miserable as, say, Sydney Harbour wasn't.

Squinting down the lane at the decomposing buildings and then back at the shining harbourmaster's house, it looked to me like the god of insane dentistry had painstakingly inserted a solid gold tooth into an old wino's mouth, alongside all his gungy old incisors and molars.

'Are you planning to go in and say hello?' asked Fiona, interrupting my thoughts.

'Do you think I should?'

'Yeah, I do. Your woman is really nice.'

My woman? 'What should I say?'

'Just tell her that your granddaddy and grandmammy used to live there and you'd like to have a look around. It is a hotel, after all. They're used to visitors.'

Had Fiona just said "grandmammy"?

'Are you coming?'

'No,' she said and turned up the heater. 'I've been in. I think you should go alone.'

Whether she said this because she was aware of the

poignancy of the moment for me, or because she wanted to stay where it was warm, I couldn't say.

I climbed out of the car into the penetrating cold and drizzle and walked up the front steps.

A sign on the door read "Back in Twenty Minutes". What? Twenty minutes from now, or twenty minutes from twenty minutes ago?

'No luck?' asked Fiona.

'Twenty minutes.'

'Shall we get a drink?'

I couldn't imagine there being anywhere to get a drink around here, but Fiona was fairly certain that the Harbour Bar would be open, so we left the car outside our granddaddy and grandmammy's old house and made the short walk down the main street.

Just before we got to the pub we passed a chained-off compound containing rusty and abandoned old fairground rides. It was a wretched sight. Peering through the chain-link fence I could hear the laughter and excited screams of children echoing down at me from the past.

The site was being guarded by one of those dogs with three legs, one eye and a tattoo. The second it spotted us it erupted into a snarling and salivating paroxysm. We got out of there and hurried down to the pub.

From the outside the Harbour Bar looked about as warm and inviting as the rest of Shannon Harbour. This was an old-style rural pub where chardonnay and pina-coladas would be thin on the ground. Donal would have loved it.

I told Fiona that I thought it was closed because places that were open for business didn't generally board their windows up from the inside.

'That'll be from last night,' she insisted. 'Try the door.'

I did, and to my surprise it wasn't locked. No sooner had I opened it just wide enough to allow my ninety-kilogram frame through, than the alarm started screeching.

'Let's get out of here,' Fiona said.

'We might get shot,' I replied. 'I think we'd better go in and tell the owners that we've just set their alarm off.'

Fiona looked at me as if I'd lost it completely. 'I think they'll know by now.'

Regardless, I groped my way into the gloom. 'Hello!' I yelled above the screeching. 'Is there anyone...' I tailed off. What was the word: "home"? 'Is there anyone here?'

'Oh hello,' shouted an elderly woman emerging from an even darker recess.

'I seem to have set your alarm off,' which was possibly one of the stupidest things I've said in a long history.

She reached behind the bar and switched it off.

'There now.' Then she looked at me as if to say, "Now what the fuck do *you* want?". 'Can I help you?'

'Are you, er, open?' Idiot, Larkin! Not only had all the chairs been hoicked on top of the tables; it was so dark in here I would have needed a miner's helmet just to feel my way to the bar. And then, of course, there'd been the slight matter of the alarm.

'Indeed we are,' she said and it threw me so badly I think I actually dribbled.

'Now what can I get you?'

'Just a second,' I said, holding up my finger and pointing towards the door. 'Let me get my cousin. She's outside in the getaway car.'

I was back moments later with Fiona in tow.

After basic apologies and introductions, Mary, the publican, poured us both lemonades. It might have been an Irish pub, but it was only about eleven in the morning after all and I still needed time to dry out after my night with Donal.

Mary's husband John joined her behind the bar. He was wearing one of those musty old tweed coats that get handed down from generation to generation of Irishmen having been bought, centuries before, from the local Farmers "R" Us outlet. Certainly every time John coughed, which was frequently, surprising amounts of dust leapt from his coat and settled in an ever-growing pile on the bar.

He picked my accent and said that he was looking

forward to the upcoming test series between Ireland and Australia. With the Irish not playing cricket I didn't have a clue what he was talking about at first. Then I realised that he was referring to that strange hybrid of Gaelic Football and Aussie Rules: a game that requires the players to beat each other up until such time as a goal is scored.

'So what brings you to Shannon Harbour?' asked Mary. 'Are you lost?'

Luckily I managed to turn my snort into a cough.

'No,' I said. 'Our parents grew up in the harbourmaster's house along by the canal. Just came down for a look.'

John's eyes widened. 'Your parents? What were their names?'

'Brendan and Veronica.'

'So you're *Larkins*?' he said brightly.

'Indeed we are.' I smiled. 'Well *I* am. Fiona's a Lambe, technically. But, yeah, we're Larkins.'

'Well there you go,' said Mary, holding up her glass. 'Cheers to you both.'

'Ah your father,' said John, his eyes starting to mist over. 'A brilliant hurler if ever there was one.'

'That he was,' I said, giving him one of Donal's winks.

'Is he dead?' he asked, with more enthusiasm than I thought appropriate.

'Er. No. No. He isn't. He's bought himself a

Hawaiian shirt and he's living in the Western Australian equivalent of Florida.'

'He had two brothers, didn't he?' asked John.

'Three. Aiden died of tuberculosis when he was young.'

John nodded. 'And what about the others? Colm, was it?'

I nodded back.

'Now is *he* dead?'

The lemonade went up my nose. 'Sorry,' I said, dabbing at it with a sleeve. 'I've had a bit of a cold.'

And then it dawned on me that old John, having reached this late stage of life, had been forced to accept that he would never compose a symphony or write the next great Irish novel—and now went on vigorously trying to outlive everyone. It wasn't much of a goal, but it gave him something to be getting on with.

'Colm?' I said, trying to bite down a smile. 'I caught up with him just recently. He's in grand form.'

'Who was the eldest?' asked Mary.

'That'd be Dom,' said Fiona. Although she was as quiet as a mouse, I got the sense that she was enjoying herself immensely.

'He must be eighty if he's a day,' said Mary.

'I guess so.'

'*He's* dead surely!' It was more a demand than a question.

'Never better,' I smiled, and winked again.

'The girls,' said Mary. 'There was a lot of them, I recall.'

'Six,' said Fiona.

'Imelda was the eldest, was she not?' asked Mary.

We both nodded.

I quickly looked up at John. 'Alive, well and living in England.'

'And the others?' said Mary. 'What were their names?'

'Annette, Margaret, Veronica, Dympna, and Jody,' I said, dropping into a growl like Donal because it seemed better suited to the occasion. 'And I tell you what, John, I've never seen them in such great form.'

'I had a brother myself,' he mumbled in the background. 'Peter his name was. Dead now.' This seemed to cheer him up a bit.

Looking about the pub I was reminded of an old Norman church. I was about to compliment them both on their decision to leave it as they'd found it when Fiona, perhaps divining that I was about to wedge my foot in my mouth, said, 'When were the refurbishments completed?'

While Mary chatted to her about their extensive redecoration program, I noticed that behind the bar, next to John, was a bottle of Malibu. I tried to imagine an old tweed coat wearing farmer coming in off his fields at the end of a day's toil and asking for a Malibu on ice with a Pimms chaser, but it just didn't sit right.

I checked the old church-style windows again more

carefully and saw how mistaken I'd been. I mean I might not have known very much about the invading Normans, but I was reasonably certain that they hadn't gone in for double-glazing.

Skulling down the dregs of my lemonade, I was suddenly aware that John was no longer with us. No evidence of a door behind the bar, so it was as if he'd just vanished into thin air. Without vibrating his molecules at such a velocity that he could dissolve into and through walls, I couldn't see how he'd done it.

As a ten-year-old I could move across the surface of the earth like a whippet with a bum full of dynamite. My athletics coach predicted that one day I'd represent Australia at the Olympics over one hundred and two hundred metres. Speed was everything to me. So while all the other kids at school were getting into Superman, Batman, Batfink and Karate, Wonder Woman, the Incredible Hulk and so on, I aligned myself with the Flash, the fastest man in the universe. Forget Speedy Gonzales: you couldn't even see the Flash when he decided to get a move on. One moment he would be standing next to a tree, and a picosecond later there he was, up on a distant hill, and he'd roped a couple of baddies. Apart from a blink there was no apparent time delay between his leaving one location and arriving at another. I used to try doing the same thing in our backyard with my younger brother Paul. I had to get from the barbecue to the shed without him seeing me move.

But I was usually forced to beat him up when he caught me running behind the pool, because he hadn't held his blinks long enough to be impressed by my breathtaking speed.

Apart from his blinding pace, the Flash's other talent was to stand next to a solid object, a wall, say, or the bank-robbers' getaway tank, and vibrate his molecules so fast that he would pass right through it. I tried to master this particular technique but with only moderate success. I did once claim that I'd vibrated myself from the pool deck, through the outside wall and into the kitchen, but I was forced to give Paul another sound thrashing when he said that he'd seen me sneaking through the laundry.

•

Considering the trail of old John's leftover molecules and dust on the bar, though, I suddenly thought that it was possible after all. And, without the Flash's skintight green lycra kit, John had managed to do it in tweed.

Mary wouldn't hear of us paying for our drinks (I think she secretly enjoyed the idea of our relatives outliving the hell out of her husband). She showed us to the door and asked us to remember her to our parents.

We headed back up the road and along the lane to the harbourmaster's house. Unfortunately, though, the "Back in Twenty Minutes" sign had been replaced by one that read "Back at Five O'Clock". I checked my watch. It was just after eleven-thirty. Clearly the task at hand was going to take longer than "your woman" had envisaged.

Was it possible to kill five and a half hours in Shannon Harbour? We could, we supposed, go back to the Harbour Bar and let old John in on some other people we knew who weren't dead yet. But that idea had a strictly limited appeal—good for about three or four hours at most. There was also the possibility that we mightn't have been able to find him at all, and that he'd vibrated all the way to the earth's core in sheer frustration.

It looked as if I'd have to be content with ending my spiritual homecoming on the front doorstep.

'You don't want to stay, do you?' pleaded Fiona.

I shook my head. 'No,' I said sadly. 'Let's go home.'

A word of advice: if you're planning to make a spiritual homecoming, make sure that someone's actually in.

Twenty

Pounded Round the Ring

I rested for a day at Richard and Paula's house, then I was off again to the terminal and a bus to Killarney. Richard had sent me on a "reccy" to arrange accommodation, bike hire, and to find the best way out of town for our proposed anticlockwise jaunt around of the Ring of Kerry. Several people had told me, or had told other people to tell me, that the scenery (no kidding) was far superior out on the ring if you travelled anticlockwise.

Richard was under immense pressure at work to implement this and reconfigure that, but still, God love him, planned to drive down to join me sometime the next evening, provided that I'd organised everything at my end first.

The bus ride to Killarney via Limerick and every other godforsaken, one-horse, sheep shit of a town along the way, was five hours of utter tedium that we can skip here. In fact the only note of marginal interest stemmed from the fact that the man sitting beside me for most of the journey smelled like a horse float. This wouldn't have bothered me had it not been for a story Donal had told me on the drive down to LA Hinch the Saturday before.

Apparently a young entrepreneur had bought a horse-float and furnished it with a mattress, shag pile carpet, and a mini bar. Then, having secured the services of a couple of prostitutes, he took his "mobile leisure centre" on an extended tour around the farmsteads and remote hamlets of rural Ireland.

Having finally been jemmied out of my seat once we'd arrived in Killarney, I stepped off the bus to find that the rain was not horizontal: the wind was actually driving it upwards.

Zipping up my coat, I hurried towards the beckoning light of what turned out to be an extremely plush hotel. I stood in the foyer making *brrrrrrrrrrrrr*-type noises and shaking off the excess water.

'Is it still wet out?' offered a young woman behind the reception desk.

'No,' I said with merely a hint of sarcasm. 'I've just walked across the Atlantic using nothing more than a thousand foot snorkel and a robust set of ankle weights.'

'Ah, go on with you,' she said. 'You're pulling my leg, so you are.'

The porch light was on. The doorbell worked. But Ms Brain had gone on holiday.

She told me the rate for a night's single, but fifty pounds was more than I was prepared to pay for bed and breakfast. So I dripped a bit more water onto the foyer floor, said farewell, and flapped out into the night. On my way I met an American mother and daughter coming down the hotel's stairs.

'Excuse me,' said the mother. 'But is it still raining?'

'Let me put it this way,' I said, zipping up my jacket. 'If it gets any worse, I'm going to start building an ark.' Boy was *I* on fire tonight.

'Who was that mysterious Gore-texed man?' the daughter seemed to say as I made for the door.

'I don't know,' mumbled the mother. 'But don't you think he smelled strangely of horse float?'

Ten minutes later I was safely ensconced in a pleasant and affordable B&B. My room may have been small, but it was warm, clean, dry and airy. From the front the B&B looked like an ordinary house. Once you were inside, though, it seemed to stretch back forever. There must have been thirty or forty rooms to it.

I'm not sure how well regulated the B&B industry is in Ireland, if at all. Once Jacqui and I had stayed in a room that contained a bed and a cupboard but nothing else. On closer inspection, the cupboard turned out to be the en suite. I couldn't see how they'd actually manoeuvred the bed into the room. Perhaps they'd simply put it in position and then built the room around it. To get into the room, guests had to climb up onto the bed. A trip to the bathroom meant bounding across the bed, but controlling the bounce in your step and remembering to keep your head low enough to avoid the blades of the ceiling fan. The en suite itself was so tiny that when you were having a shower, most of you was still back out in the bedroom.

•

After a long soapy bath and a change of clothes, I was off into the glistening streets to look for a bite to eat. The rain had abated but it was bitterly cold out and I could see my breath in front of me like the speech balloons of a cartoon character.

On my last trip to Killarney I'd managed to attract the attention of several startled passers-by when I'd given an impromptu Basil Fawlty impersonation. Jacqui and I had arrived tired, fractious and hungry after a long cross-country drive from the Waterford Crystal factory. We checked in, then drove to town to find somewhere to eat. It was so late that by the time we'd parked the car, there was very little open. After being turned away at a couple of doors, Jacqui refused to get out of the car again until I'd found somewhere that was open, warm and inviting. Just then a gust of wind sprang up out of nowhere and turned my umbrella inside out, rendering it completely useless. Needless to say I spent a few rewarding minutes beating what was left of the umbrella against the hire car's windscreen.

This time, without Jacqui, I shuffled into one of the pubs on the main street, had a miserable plate of lukewarm fettuccine carbonara with a couple of granite rolls. The chef must have heated the main course in his armpits. Anyone else would have sent it back to be nuked. Not me. I have a friend who used to work as a kitchen hand for an extremely volatile French chef—and is there any other sort? Once, when a steak had been sent back for being too rare, Le Chef, in a moment of Gallic pique, hurled the troublesome piece of meat against a wall. He then jumped up and down on it several times as if it were GI Joe, wiped his backside with it and baked it down the front of his underpants for a good couple of minutes. Then he had the waiter return, what by now would be loosely called, the steak to the diner. And the diner continued with his meal, blissfully ignorant and in fact sent a note to the chef complimenting him on his culinary expertise.

It was only about seven o'clock when I forced down the last of my cold, but at least coloform-free, carbonara. Without Donal to lead the way I was pretty much at a loss what to do with myself for the rest of the evening. There didn't seem to be a cinema in town, and the place was probably too small for a comedy club, which I would have checked out in the hope of getting on the bill with my "Australians overseas" routine.

Above the bar, drawing everyone's attention was a tv monitor, and I could only wish that St Patrick had held out his staff and belted television from pubs, bars and taverns the world over. And, while we're on the subject, poker machines too. That awful psychedelic carpet that makes it impossible to detect vomit and other spills: history! Mobile phones and men who lean against the bar at a forty-five degree angle to check out the action: finished!

Now I enjoy a little tv as much as anyone, but not in pubs. And that goes double if what's on the box at the time is *EastEnders*—that miserable English soap opera that has made the dropping of aitches chic. "Allo Arry love. Ave you eard from Orace? I ear e's gorn ang-gliding with Illary and then onto the Enry the Eighth for an alf pint of Arp. I ope no arm comes to im."

The only reason you'd watch *EastEnders* would be to convince yourself that your own life isn't so dreary after all.

As I watched Barbara Windsor playing someone's grandmother in the distance I wondered what it would be like to write something under the influence of alcohol. And not just slightly under its influence either: I mean seriously rat-arsed.

Before I go on, though, I want to say that I've never done illegal drugs and apart from a couple of pints here and there and the occasional glass of wine, my substance abuse is minimal—though I must admit that I'd let myself go a bit on this trip.

Artists and writers have held to a long tradition of altering their state of consciousness, however, and it seems quite natural that those who make a living through the use of their minds would want to test its boundaries occasionally or attempt to discover just how deep the rabbit hole goes.

Some acid-heads say Lewis Carroll wrote *Alice's Adventures in Wonderland* under the influence of LSD. Let's not worry that LSD didn't make its first appearance until 1943, some forty-five years after Carroll's death: it's just too good a story to sully with facts.

Brendan Behan was, to put it mildly, a notorious boozehound. Jackson Pollock is said to have ingested and imbibed anything he could get his hands on. Our own Brett Whiteley, heroin. Welsh poet Dylan Thomas consumed a world record number of glasses of whisky before dropping dead in a New York hotel—and his ashes would have been scattered about Westminster Abbey only they couldn't put out the fire. And if ABBA's Benny and Bjørn weren't whacked out of their skulls on something when they conceived the lyrics for *Bang a Boomerang*, then they really should have been.

So in the name of artistic experimentation, I bought a bottle of wine and a six-pack of lager and retreated to the safety of my room. With the neck of my wine bottle sticking out of my daypack like a ninja warrior's sword, I tiptoed through the reception area and up the stairs to my room in order to avoid attracting attention. Then I had to tiptoe back down the stairs and ask the hotelier for a bottle opener.

Back in my room with my bottle opener and glass, I poured the wine, opened a couple of cans of the lager and the packet of roast beef chips, and switched on the television. I did this for no reason other than to help pass the time while the alcohol went to work on altering my state of consciousness. Television has its uses. I didn't just want to skull the stuff down and collapse into some sort of stupor, but rather allow the feeling to creep up on me like my daughter trying to scare the bajaysus out of me when I come back from putting out the garbage.

Fortunately as I tipped my second can of lager I flicked the channel and an old episode of *Father Ted* had just started. It was the one where the travelling show comes to Craggy Island and Father Dougal is desperate to go and see the spider baby and climb the ladder of death.

'How do you know it's a spider baby, Dougal?'

'Ah, they keep it in a pram.'

By the end of the show I was roaring and rolling about on the bed. And this was only partly due to the empty bottle and four cans lying round me.

I was desperate for a curry, but I flicked on my

bedside lights, using several of my new thumbs, picked up my notepads from the floors and set to work.

So here, copied verbatim from my notebook and totally unedited, is what a lonely mind altered by alcohol comes up with in the early hours on a dark and miserable Killarney winter night...

Larkin about in IRELAND

The next day I slept late—and I can't remember why. The hotelier served me my breakfast with as much good grace as she could muster at two in the afternoon.

'Is it the full Irish you'll be having?'

'Oh yes please, if it's not too late.'

'Not at all,' she said, glancing at her watch and wondering if it was time to start thinking about dinner. 'Bacon, sausage, egg?'

If it had been on a farm, I wanted it. 'Yes please.'

'Black or white pudding?'

'What's the difference?'

'Why don't you try both and you can decide which you like best for tomorrow *morning*.' She did seem to emphasise "morning". 'Tea or coffee?'

'Coffee, please. And a large glass of water if you could.'

'It'll be a pleasure,' she said with genuine warmth. 'Oh, and while you're having breakfast I'll have your tings moved out of the single and into one of the twins in preparation for when your friend arrives tonight.'

About half an hour later I emerged blinking into the sun. The rain had gone and Killarney looked splendid. I still had a lot of organising to get on with, so I didn't linger. But with bikes available for hire at the hostel next door and the road leading out to the Ring of Kerry just around the corner, I'd completed my "reccy" in under a minute.

So I went for a walk round the town. Killarney was

smaller than I'd remembered it, but it was pretty and prosperous. If Ireland was awash with money then clearly a lot of it had been filtered through Killarney. Economics tells us that there must have been some scummy bits to it, but I couldn't locate them. Not that I tried all that hard.

I walked out of town along Ross Road and down towards Ross Castle on Ross Bay, which is part of the stunning Lough Leane. I didn't know who this Ross bloke was, but he was paranoid enough about something to warrant building himself a fortified castle. I had a bit of a poke around the outside of the Ross Castle but it was "Closed for the Season". I had a bit of a rant about how would you go about closing a castle, and then realised that of course that was the very idea.

There are some beautiful walks around Killarney. I took one now by deliberately choosing the long route back into town around the lovely Lough Leane, followed a path next to a bubbling canal straight out of *Tales of the Riverbank*, and then finally took a short cut back through a field of cows. It was as I stared at the cows in that half-arsed way of mine when the rhythm of the walking starts to throw up random sentences and comedy routines that I realised that these cows didn't have any udders. And then it dawned on me that a cow without an udder is a bull. There were six of them and they were about a hundred metres away to my left. Even though they didn't seem at all bothered by my being there, I did walk across the rest of the field sideways, a gormless-looking, six-foot-tall bipedal crab.

I came out of the parklands just across the road from St Joseph's cathedral. It looked as though it had only recently been refurbished. It had a high bell tower and the bells must have been operated by a timing sequencer. I remembered being woken at some point during the early hours in my mind-altered haze when the cathedral suddenly got the idea that it was sixty-one o'clock. Having used up all its dings in one fell swoop, though, the bell tower had since lapsed into a protracted silence.

I legged it back to my room to start on a record-breaking nap and wait for Richard.

•

After a hearty breakfast (there's a phrase that cholesterol has consigned to the past! I had the white pudding) Richard and I dropped in to the hostel next door to hire a bike for me. Richard had carted his down from Dublin in the back of the car. He'd finally arrived at about one-thirty in the morning and had lapsed into a troubled sleep. Now and then he shouted out instructions about installing the new LAN to someone on the other side of his office. Richard clearly needed to get away for a while.

The rain was back with a vengeance but it couldn't dampen our spirits. We were definitely going.

We knocked on the door of the hostel, and this ageing hippie told us that "Pa" was out but would be back shortly. We were welcome to sit by the fire if we liked, just as long as we filled the world with peace, love and harmony while we were at it.

It was actually quite pleasant in the hostel, provided you could stand the earthy smell of legumes, hemp or whatever the hell it was. While I sat by the fire, Richard took down a communal guitar from its rack on the wall and began to strum a few bars of something that was a bit too laid back for my liking.

'If you as much as look like you're thinking about "Stairway to Heaven", Richard,' I said, 'I'll be forced to break that guitar over your head.'

I looked about the gathering of hippies and ferals by the fire for their reaction, and one by one they nodded their agreement.

After a short while Pa returned from taking his daughter down the street for a hamburger and he smartly fixed me up with a bike, a helmet and so on. He even gave us a map of Killarney and drew directions out of town for our anticlockwise route round the Ring.

'Excuse me, Pa,' said Richard, 'but that's clockwise.'

Pa considered the map and then cocked his head at an angle. 'Ah, so it is. Well then, do exactly the opposite of what I've just told you.'

No problem.

The Irish did seem to have a bit of a problem with the direction of their clocks. Just prior to popping next door to hire my bike, we'd asked our lovely hotelier to confirm our route.

As Pa had done, she drew a fairly detailed map for getting out of Killarney. But again, despite our stipulation, she'd pointed us in a clockwise direction. When we told her of this she too cocked her head, then said that it was only clockwise from her side.

Grabbing my helmet, I asked Pa if what we were about to undertake was hard.

'There are some difficult bits,' he said, opening up his map. 'This section here, for instance, is a bit hilly.'

We nodded our thanks.

'You are aware that this is December now, aren't you, lads?' said Pa. 'It gets a bit wild out there at this time of year.'

We told him that we were rugged mountain men who had kicked Croagh Patrick's arse and weren't overly bothered by a bit of wind.

Once outside we got things organised, and were keen to be away. Richard took something out of the back of his car and unfurled it on the ground next to his bike. Whatever it was it was a startling fluorescent shade of blue and appeared to me, on closer inspection, to be a tarpaulin with sleeves.

'What the hell is *it*?' I said.

'It's a bike poncho,' he said, trying to work out a way to climb into it.

'You can't wear *that*.'

'Why not, John?'

'It looks ridiculous. People will laugh at you.'

'Which people?'

'Well, me for a start.'

Now clad in the poncho, Richard considered himself in the reflection of the hostel window. He knew what he looked like. He didn't need me to remind him. 'I *have* to use it.'

'Why?'

'Because it's Paula's. And she wanted me to wear it.'

'Well can't you just chuck it back in the car and tell her that you *did*?'

'I can't tell her a lie.' They hadn't been married all that long.

'Why not? She won't know.'

'Yes,' replied Richard. 'But *I* will.'

I suddenly realised that it was just as well that Donal hadn't decided to come with us after all. What with my no-hitchhiking edict and Richard's bike poncho, he would have laughed us out of town.

We cycled cautiously out through the rain-soaked streets of Killarney and onto the Ring of Kerry, which takes its name from the road that loops around the edge of the Iveragh Peninsula. From where I was sitting (behind him) it looked as though Richard was gliding along the road with his head poking out the top of a tent.

Let me just say right now that cycling the Ring of Kerry was the hardest thing I've ever done in my life. And we didn't make it halfway. Or even a quarter of the way.

Since higher forces seemed to be saying that we shouldn't go anticlockwise, we saw no reason to tempt fate, and promptly set off clockwise.

Following a gentle rise out of Killarney we began a steady climb up through Pa's "bit hilly" section. In no time the lactic acid was at my thighs and they were on fire.

After an hour's solid pedalling we arrived at a small old stone bridge that spanned a stunning but unnamed cascade. There was a little stone church beside the road, the windows of which weren't so much boarded up as concreted.

We had a short rest break and then carried on up to Ladies' View. Named for Queen Victoria who on alighting from her carriage here apparently said of the view, "Fuck that's nice", or something to that effect. I knew there were shops at Ladies' View where we might buy refreshments and supplies for our climb up to the charmingly named Moll's Gap. When we arrived panting and sweating at Ladies' View a while later, though, the shops had been closed for (you guessed it) the season.

Following another short break we left Ladies' View only to discover that the climb had become alarmingly steep. Half an hour later we lost the power of speech.

And half an hour after that, I lost Richard. He was considerably fitter than me and had forged on ahead. Occasionally I caught faint images from the glow of his poncho as he made his way around distant bends. But all the while he was getting smaller and smaller until he'd almost vanished.

Coming round a sharp bend, I was startled to find him lying spreadeagled across a large boulder. I figured that he'd crashed and I panted up to him, but then realised that people who'd crashed their bikes didn't usually park them next to the road with the stand on.

'How fucking hard is this?' he gasped, looking up out of his oxygen tent.

This climb was a "bit hilly" in the sense that the Nazis were a bit naughty. These weren't hills, they were arsing, shiteing, shagging mountains, and big ones at that.

'How far away is this Scrubber's Gap or whatever it's called anyway?'

I looked at my map. On a mountain, one bend looks suspiciously like any other. With only half a Mars Bar and a caramel Space Food stick in my bag when we'd set off—both long since eaten—my energy resources were pretty low. If Moll's Gap wasn't around the next corner, I honestly didn't think I would be able to carry on. And edict or no, I would be forced to stick out my thumb and beg for a ride.

'It shouldn't be too much further,' I said.

'That's what you said an hour ago, John.'

'I know. And I was even less delirious then.'

Richard stood up and dusted down his poncho. 'Come on, then. Let's see if we can find this Whore's Hole. And may I warn you, John,' Richard clambered back onto his bike and tangled his poncho in the spokes, 'if it isn't open, I'm going to kick its fucking door in.'

I hadn't even thought of that. If the restaurant at Moll's Gap wasn't open, I was in serious trouble.

Round the next bend I almost went insane when I saw that Mother-Fucker's Gap wasn't there. With my tank empty I climbed down off my bike and trudged along beside it. I just wanted to go home.

I was literally in tears when I rounded the next bend and saw to my utter relief that it was there.

Richard shot on ahead and reserved a table for two by the window in the restaurant.

'What can I get you?' said the lady behind the counter when I finally arrived about twenty minutes' hard slog later.

'Food. Food. Gimme food.'

We heaved our trays across to our table and tore into them like sharks on honeymoon.

I now know why they recommend you go in an anti-clockwise direction around the Ring of Kerry. It's simple. The bit at the end, the bit we had just completed, is part of the Killarney National Park and is at once quite breathtaking and possibly the most stunning scenery on the entire Iveragh Peninsula. A perfect end to a perfect journey.

With our stomachs bloated we debated our next step. To carry on to the town of Sneem had been the original plan, but as soon as we'd arrived in Moll's Gap the weather, which had been threatening all day, had turned quite violent and caused a blackout in the restaurant.

With Richard on limited time and with me not relishing another day like the one we'd just been through, we made the wise decision to ride back to Killarney.

We jumped on our bikes and hurtled down the hilly mountains and into Killarney. We hadn't realised just how steep the climb had been until we plunged back down it. What had been a four-hour ascent turned into a half-hour descent, even with an enforced five-minute break to lift a large tree off the road.

I returned my bike to Pa and, proving that he was definitely a contender for the loveliest man in Ireland award, not only did he refuse to gloat at our abject failure, he gave me a full refund for the bike.

With Richard driving like Michael Schumacher, we tore around the Ring (anticlockwise) just so that we could say that we'd seen it. And our decision to abandon the cycle was vindicated by the gale now howling so strongly that Richard had trouble keeping four wheels on the road—never mind two.

Back at Moll's Gap we made a right turn and wound our way down into the town of Kenmare where we stopped for a drink at one of its pubs. Australia was playing New Zealand in the rugby league World Cup final but no one seemed to care except for one troubled young man who was sitting at the bar, surrounded by coins and watching television.

Figuring that he was Australian, Richard asked him who was winning, mate.

'I don't think I like this game too much,' he said, only half turning to greet us. His tone was harsh and his voice sounded as though he'd been eating gravel.

'C'mon, the Ozzies,' yelled Richard, but no one was interested—not even me.

We introduced ourselves to the gravel eater, who turned out to be from Latvia. He tried to tell us his name but either because it was made up entirely of consonants or because he'd been at the bar since sunrise we weren't quite able to get our tongues round it. So rather shamelessly we decided to call him Seamus.

'This game is rugby union I think,' said Seamus the Latvian. 'It's very popular in Ireland now.' His voice was the sort that makes you acutely aware just how feminine your own is.

'**ACTUALLY THIS GAME HERE IS RUG**by league,' I replied, attempting to slip into love-god mode but damaging my vocal cords irreparably in the process.

'What is the *difference*?' he asked.

While Richard watched the game, I launched into a lecture on the subtle differences between the two codes, but it was a bit like trying to initiate your mother into the inner workings of the offside trap or LBW rule. After a couple of minutes it suddenly dawned on me that neither of us gave the remotest shit, so I shut up.

It transpired that Seamus was a motor mechanic who'd come to Ireland seeking work, hadn't found any and now all he wanted was a single cigarette. And although he desperately wanted to kill some Russian guy over the misplaced affections of a certain girl, the cigarette was the immediate problem.

'Why can't I buy just *one* cigarette?' snapped Seamus the Latvian, fiddling with the slew of coins scattered about him on the bar.

'Because,' said the barman with a world-weary sigh, 'they only come in packets. You want a packet, I'll sell you as many as you like.'

'Can't I buy one from you?'

'I told you before, I don't smoke.'

'What sort of barman doesn't smoke?'

The barman ignored him.

'Why can't I buy just *one* cigarette!'

So we were back here again.

'If you ask me for just *one* cigarette again,' said the barman, 'I'll have to ask you to leave.'

'The pub or the country?'

Having been forced to accept that he couldn't buy just *one* cigarette, Seamus the Latvian turned back to his conversation with us. After a brief but informative description of what would happen to a certain Russian windpipe, he went on to tell us about his brother who had apparently become a religious fanatic and gone insane—though not necessarily in that order. Then he ran his fingers around his ears in ever decreasing circles and started doing strange things with his eyes. Meanwhile his tongue lolled out of his mouth as if he was a dog in the desert. Whether this display was to prove his brother's insanity, or clear evidence of his own, I really couldn't say.

We were glad to get back on the road and head round part of the desolate Beara Peninsula and on into the town of Bantry. The flow of the streets in and around Bantry didn't as much entice visitors into the town as fling them out. And after a futile search for a hotel or B&B to hole up in for the night, we flung ourselves out and back to Killarney.

Between the towns of Glengarriff and Kenmare we entered a fairly long tunnel and what we encountered in there made both of us let out a high-pitched scream.

'What the fuck is *that*!' yelled Richard as he slammed on the brakes.

About a hundred metres along the tunnel were about twenty to thirty pairs of glassy eyes peering back at us through the gloom.

'Back up, Richard!'

'What *is* it?'

'I don't care!' I yelled. 'Just back up!'

'But I want to know what it is first.'

'It's Aliens with curling wands for all I know. Let's get the flock out of here!'

Richard flicked on his high beam, which immediately lit the far end of the tunnel.

We looked at each other and sighed. 'Cows.'

By gently honking the horn to hurry them along, we coaxed the cows to turn on their hooves and high-tail it out of there and off into the miserable night.

'I didn't know cows did that sort of thing,' said Richard.

'What. Seek shelter in caves?'

'Yeah,' agreed Richard. 'Weird.'

'Well how *would* you?' I replied. 'You don't get a lot of exposure to livestock in the IT industry. Caves a bit thin on the ground too, I suspect.'

We arrived back in Killarney relieved and our favourite hotelier was only too happy to receive us.

After a quick shower and change of clothes we wandered down into the main street. We had a great meal in an Italian restaurant, where the owner and kitchen staff joined us at our table because they were fascinated by all Richard's electronic gadgetry—digital camera, palm-pilot, satellite tracking shoe-phone.

On the way in we'd met the same American mother and daughter that I had come across when I'd first arrived in Killarney a couple of days earlier.

'Excuse me,' said the mother. 'But is it still raining?'

'Let me put it this way,' I said, unzipping my jacket. 'If it gets any worse, I'm going to start building...' I trailed off. 'Hang on a second. I've done that one already, haven't I?'

Twenty-one
An Irish Wake

I'd entered Ireland from the sea, and felt that I had a duty to leave the way I'd come. Or at least visit the town where so much Irish transportation—forced and voluntary—had begun. I was going to Cobh.

Cobh (pronounced "Cove") sits around the harbour from Cork in not quite the way that Manly does "seven miles from Sydney and a thousand miles from care".

I knew very little about Cobh before I started this trip, except that it was once called Queenstown and that it was the last port that the *Titanic* called at. (More precisely, the ship anchored at the mouth of the harbour and passengers were ferried out to it.) Cobh was also allegedly home to a man who had recently won the lottery and who had used his winnings to open a *Titanic* theme bar and grill, proving that money can buy you practically everything but taste.

Formerly known as Cove of Cork its name was changed to Queenstown in a monumental bit of toadying after Queen Victoria's visit in 1849. When Ireland won its independence from Britain, Queenstown reverted back to Cove, only this time it adopted the Irish word for Cove (Cobh), though it's still pronounced "Cove". Confused? Good. So was I.

I'd said goodbye to Richard and caught the bus from Killarney to Cork.

As Irish cities go, Cork seemed quite agreeable on the surface. While I waited at the station for the short train ride around the harbour to Cobh, however, I noticed that every single postcard I picked up at the tourist booth proclaimed just how "Picturesque" Cork was. True beauty requires no adjectives.

My destination in Cobh was its Heritage Centre, which is part of Cobh railway station. Tom, my American friend from Connemara, said that it was brilliant and had insisted that I go there.

When I finally arrived in Cobh I had only a couple of hours before it closed for the day. My original plan had been to visit the Centre, then catch a train on to Dublin, thence London, Cambridge, and all stations to Sydney. Figuring that I would need more than two hours to take in all the attractions at the Heritage Centre, I decided to spend the night in Cobh and return to Dublin the following day.

I left the station and wandered down through the pleasant harbour-front village until I came upon a memorial anchor dedicated to those who had been lost at sea and those who'd risked their lives to save them.

The plaque's inscription read:

We commemorate all Irish seafarers who have served this island nation, particularly those who perished at sea. We express our gratitude to the life-saving services, merchant marine & naval service R.N.L. British & Irish Helicopter crews for their heroic deeds saving lives off our coasts. To give and not count the cost.

Coming from a nation whose newsreaders become morally outraged on the taxpayers' behalf each time the *Adelaide* is despatched to rescue a solo-yachtsman or some downed American balloonist, I felt that we could use a few similar plaques about our own harbours, not to mention television studios.

"Let the fuckers drown," seems to be the general attitude these days. "And if they happen to be French or British, so much the better."

I looked out across the harbour and the sea beyond and thought of all the lost souls who had departed here in search of a better life. Some of course found it, while others found nothing except more misery and a watery grave.

About two and a half million people emigrated from Ireland through Cobh. Sailing across the stormy Atlantic first on coffin ships, old-fashioned steamers, and then finally the vast ocean liners.

The night before they departed there would be an Irish wake held in their honour. For although they were heading off to a new life across the world, they would, nonetheless, be dead to those they left behind.

With this cheery thought I turned up my collar and trudged off through the murky streets in search of a B&B. But wherever I went, I had the feeling that someone was following me. Lurking over my shoulder. Watching my every move. Finally I realised what it was. High on the hill dominating Cobh is the awesome St Colman's cathedral. Built in the French Gothic style, its enormous three-hundred-foot spire thrusts up into the sky and makes for an imposing sight.

The notion of The Church watching over your every move was probably quite apt about fifty years or so ago. Now, with Ireland becoming a more secular society, St Colman's domineering presence above Cobh seems disproportionate to its place in society.

I climbed up the hill towards the cathedral and rang the doorbell of a friendly looking B&B. I thought I could hear hastily gathered-up clothes just before the door was opened by a forty-something Maureen O'Hara look-alike. She was rather flustered at first, but then when she saw that it was me she relaxed a bit.

She adjusted her jeans into a more comfortable position. 'Can I help you?'

'Have you got a room for the night?'

'Ah no. We're closed for decorating.' Right on cue the tradesman appeared in shot and returned to his painting in the front room.

'You might want to try up the hill,' she said, pointing further up.

'Thanks.' I picked up my daypack to leave. I thought perhaps I should warn her that her t-shirt was on back to front, but I figured that it would only embarrass her.

'Did you know that your t-shirt's on back to front?'

She closed the door a bit harder than was necessary.

The B&B up the hill was open but full, so I threaded my way back down the hill and through this "picturesque" little town.

On my walk along the front earlier, I'd passed the stylish and expensive-looking Waters Edge hotel. It was obviously in the five-star league, right out of my daily budget, so pausing only to mentally lock it away as a contingency, I'd carried on into the centre of town.

Maybe it was the thought of all those poor souls who had emigrated from here, but I felt that a sadness hung over Cobh like a dark cloud. Or perhaps it was just my own shroud grown bigger.

Ten minutes later while walking down the street with the multi-coloured houses known as "the pack of cards", I came across an enormous rat lying dead in the gutter.

Well that did it. With nobody else apparently willing to receive me, I bolted for the Waters Edge hotel as fast as my damaged knees could convey me.

There's nothing like a good dose of five-star room service and in-house movies to cheer you up. Admittedly it's even nicer when somebody else is paying, but I was prepared to overlook that on this occasion. It was my last night in Ireland, after all, and I felt that for this reason alone I deserved a bit of a treat.

When they told me that the rate for a night's single bed and breakfast was fifty pounds, I just waved my hand.

Once in my room I helped myself to everything that wasn't nailed down. While the bath water was busy building up a good head of steam, I flossed my teeth with the complimentary flosser, smeared myself in that gel that you never know exactly what to do with, and polished my shoes despite the fact that they were suede. I even found myself wearing the shower-cap and the plush William Holden-style bathrobe. Then I lowered myself into the sort of immense bubble bath that for some perverse reason called to mind Doris Day, and immediately set about using up every last drop of shampoo and conditioner.

I booked in to the Jacob's Ladder restaurant, which was part of the hotel and absolutely first rate. Then, having decided to hold a bit of an Irish wake of my own, I had seafood chowder, a creamy mushroom risotto, and a rather expensive bottle of wine. I was going out in style.

The next morning I woke early and got out of bed a couple of hours later. I'd been offered a late check-out and with it being miserable out again I intended to milk the luxury for all I was worth. I think I may have even watched a movie, though my memory on this point is a bit hazy, possibly due to the wine.

I presented myself at the reception desk at exactly eleven o'clock. As I was settling my account I got talking to the genial owners of the hotel. When I told them what I'd been up to wandering about their country they immediately phoned a friend of theirs, a local historian and author named Michael Martin who agreed to come down and meet me. Like the owners, Michael Martin was something of an entrepreneur. He'd created the extremely popular "Titanic Trail" walking tour and had recently branched out into the macabre with his "Ghost Walk tour of Cobh".

Although he was used to leading large groups around the town, Michael took me on my own personal tour. And believe me, what Michael Martin doesn't know about Cobh hasn't happened there yet.

With my time again running short, Michael kindly dropped me at the Heritage Centre and I hurried to the ticket booth and eagerly parted with my £3.50.

Well, it was fantastic. Everything that Michael and Tom said it would be and more. Interesting and informative, it even had a wow-can-we-see-it-again-mom factor as the floor seemed to shudder beneath your feet as you watched footage of an old sailboat crashing through the swell. All of which was designed to bring about a slight queasiness if not rampant seasickness and give you a brief taste of what it must have been like for the immigrants who were thrown on the mercy of the Atlantic.

I spent three thoroughly riveting and enjoyable hours wandering through the displays and absorbing the information.

Afterwards I sat in the Heritage Centre café, drank a cup of the Irish equivalent and made a few notes.

My journey was over and I suddenly found myself filled with a great sense of loss.

Perhaps the umbilical chord had been severed too long ago or else stretched too far, but I knew then that Ireland would never be my home.

If I was any sort of geographical Don Juan, Australia would be my wife, England my mistress, while Ireland would be a girl from school who I'd fantasised over for years and still possessed strange yearnings for, despite the fact that she'd married a chiropodist named Trevor and had relocated to Dapto.

I'd had a long, healthy relationship with Australia, even if the marriage had been an arranged one. While the feelings of displacement I'd carried with me since leaving England as a six-year-old, and for which I have always blamed the dark shroud, would need to be dealt with at some point in the future before insanity set in permanently. Perhaps I would go Larkin about there next and try and discover just what it is I missed. Ireland, though, was lost to me, and I knew that I had finally to let it go.

Larkin about in IRELAND

I came looking for the Ireland of *The Quiet Man*, the one my father had left behind, but it had gone. And I don't mind admitting that I shed a few tears as I made these notes in the Heritage Centre that cold, bleak day last December, just as I'm shedding them now as I type these words.

Ireland's greatest export has always been its people, followed by its Irishness. There *are* pockets of retro-Irishness still to be found in the country if you're prepared to look. The excellent Johnnie Fox's pub on the outskirts of Dublin for instance will serve you up both an excellent meal and as much *Di-Dicky-Do-Dum-Di-Dum-Doe* music as your stomach can handle. But as the last line of the old tweed-coated farmers begin to drop off their tractors, and Ireland continues its transition from the old to the new, the poor to the rich, the rural to the urban, the religious to the secular, you may shortly be forced to go looking for your Irishness elsewhere. Consider this piece of inspired graffiti that supposedly lines the toilet wall of one of the pubs in Sydney's Rocks area: "Why do English backpackers come halfway around the world to spend their time in Irish theme bars when there are literally thousands of them in New York?"

Everyone who left Ireland has a story. I've got one myself and I suppose this has been it. I'd come twenty thousand kilometres looking for my spiritual home, only to discover that my spiritual home was twenty thousand kilometres back the other way.

One of the many stories detailed in the Cobh Heritage Centre tells of parents who were forced to send their four little children off to America in the hope of finding them a better life. They never saw or heard from them again.

This was a timely reminder that halfway across the world a little girl and my heavily pregnant wife were patiently waiting on my return so that we could put up the Christmas tree together.

So with a heavy heart and a lump in my throat I picked up my backpack and turned for home.

Epilogue
Aussie Rules!

To borrow from Jean-Paul Sartre's view on Nazis, if Ireland didn't exist we'd find it necessary to invent it. Only we'd probably choose to keep it well away from England and murderous pricks such as Oliver Cromwell. We'd probably put it somewhere a lot warmer. Give it a chance to dry out. It'd have to be bigger too. A lot bigger. We'd definitely elect to keep much of its culture—its music, its yarn spinning, its booze—and we'd probably invent a unique version of football that nobody else in the world would play or understand. And although the inhabitants of this new land would be all for putting in a hard day's toil, the general view would be that we worked to live and not the other way round. We'd live in a pluralistic and harmonious society. And although there'd be the odd redneck about the place, we would generally welcome those seeking a better life and a fair go.

And we'd probably call such a place Australia.

Acknowledgments

This book would simply not have been possible without the priceless support of my wonderful wife Jacqui and my children Chantelle and Damian.

But I would like to thank the following people, who have, in large ways or small, made this journey a reality:

Donal Keegan, Richard and Paula, Fiona Lambe, Vivienne and Karen Soo, Alice Lee, Jon Appleton, the Comers, Ronan O'Brien, Amanda Browne, Ben Gunne, Seamus Hartigan, Tom Moore, Michael Martin, Uncle Vladimir, the Scouser, Monkey-man, Seamus the Latvian, Ronan Keating and Boyzone, Westlife and of course the Larkin, Lambe and Keegan families, but particularly Mum, Dad, Trish and Paul and Annette and Tony Keegan.

I am deeply indebted to Mark Macleod whose support, encouragement and Gandhi-like patience with the deadlines as they continued to hurtle by was nothing short of phenomenal.

Also to Lisa Highton, Mary Drum and the wonderful staff at Hodder Headline for allowing me to live the dream.

John Larkin's soccer career seemed destined to take him all the way to the top until a series of knee injuries forced him to retire at twenty-one. Disillusioned and heartbroken, he backpacked around Europe for a year and was bitten by the writing bug while sitting in a cafe in Paris, reading *The Hitchhiker's Guide to the Galaxy*, as you do. Many years later, he is well-known as a standup comic and novelist.

John lives in Sydney with his wife Jacqui, his children Chantelle and Damian, and a robust case of arachnophobia. He hates gardening, yapping dogs and is the worst handyman on the face of the planet. So he had to be a writer. His ambition is to retire to a cottage in the Yorkshire Dales and join the professional Morris-dancing circuit.